MW00784887

MAGIC
AND
HEALING

THE HISTORY AND FOLKLORE OF MAGICAL HEALING PRACTICES FROM HERB-LORE AND INCANTATIONS TO RINGS AND PRECIOUS STONES

C. J. S. THOMPSON

BELL PUBLISHING COMPANY
NEW YORK

This 1989 edition is published by Bell Publishing Company,
distributed by Crown Publishers, Inc.,
225 Park Avenue South, New York, New York 10003.

Printed and Bound in the United States of America

Library of Congress Cataloging-in-Publication Data

Thompson, C. J. S. (Charles John Samuel), 1862-1943.
    Magic and healing / by C.J.S. Thompson.
       p.   cm.
    Reprint.
    ISBN 0-517-68833-6
    1. Medicine, Magic, mystic, and spagiric. 2. Medicine,
Magic, mystic, and spagiric—Great Britain.   3. Healing.
4. Healing—Great Britain   5. Medicine—History.
6. Medicine—Great Britain—History.   I. Title.
R133.T39   1989
615.8'52—dc20   89-33855
                                                    CIP

h g f e d c b a

Contents

Publisher's Note:

The modern reader may be surprised
to discover certain old-fashioned
and British styles of punctuation and
spelling, but these have been retained
in order to convey the flavor
of the original edition.

PREFACE

Magic and Healing is a fascinating history of the magical powers, practices, and folklore associated with cures both physical and mental, practical and miraculous.

One can compare the transition of magical healing into modern medicine with the changing meaning of the word "power" in the ancient world. The early Western meaning of "power" was that of an elementary force such as heat or cold, might, or bodily strength —always linked with and leading to authority. In the middle stages of definition, "power" came to mean a quantity, faculty or capacity. Physically, it stood for a medicine or a magically potent substance or object; spiritually, "power" meant bona fide magical powers, miracles, or other divine manifestations. The fully developed abstract Aristotelian definition represented the capability of existing or acting—what we now call potentiality. Practical interpretations of "power" subsequently opened the way for theories of mathematical "powers" and other non-visible investigations. Like "magic," the word "power" had a force that leapt cultural and temporal boundaries.

The transition from magic to science mirrors this great cultural transformation—the shift from an oral to a literate culture in ancient Greece, and the subsequent development of language capable of expressing the abstract and the invisible. The magical transition is inexorably joined with the more modern but just as critical shift of Western culture from scribe to printing press in the fifteenth century, a shift from which stems all modern technology and Western culture.

The medieval, or scribal, mentality seems very primitive today. A fusion of internal and external universes combined ideas on nature and man, the moral world and the material universe, the wind and the humours, birth and death, the soul, resurrection, and the nature of God. There was no distinction between physical occurrence, moral truth, and spiritual experience. The relationship between magic and science parallels that of medieval and modern natural philosophies.

The intellectual and curative functions of magic matured into true science by means of the knowledge explosion brought about by the development of moveable type and release from the restraints of scribal tradition. Yet magic remains a potent alternative force today. The role of magic in the science of healing is of significant interest to historians, scientists, and practitioners of magic alike. In this excellent book, C.J.S. Thompson has provided an engrossing account of the history of magic and healing.

Lois Hill

New York
1989

Foreword

IN a letter to his publishers dated May 17, 1942, Dr. C. J. S. Thompson wrote: "I hope to live to see the day of victory and the publication of the book into which I have put so much labour." Unhappily, my father's hope was not fulfilled, as he died in the following year at the age of eighty. Thus *Magic and Healing*—its publication postponed owing to the exigencies of war—may well be the last in a long series of literary excursions into the byways of medicine, chemistry and pharmacy to the history of which Dr. Thompson devoted a lifetime's study.

Other manuscripts, partially finished, he left in my care, and it is my ambition in the fullness of time to give certain of them to the public. Among these are his notes for a Life of Paracelsus in whose strange career my father was so greatly interested that we spent some weeks in Switzerland together tracing the early footsteps of this medieval "Prince of Philosophy and Medicine." It was during this journey that the photograph which forms the frontispiece to the present volume was taken.

My sister, Miss Caireen Fawcett Thompson, who was closely associated with my father in much of his work, has borne the larger share in preparing *Magic and Healing* for the press; and she has taken such care to verify my father's references as the difficulties of the time have permitted. My grateful thanks are due to her for so readily undertaking a task that should rightly have been mine.

J. R. FAWCETT THOMPSON

Chapter I

MAGIC AND HEALING—EARLY BELIEFS IN THE ORIGIN OF DISEASE

MAGIC is generally believed to have been the earliest known system of natural philosophy, the origin of which goes back to a period of unknown antiquity and is lost in the mists of time.

From primitive man in virgin woods and the astrologers and magicians of Chaldea and Babylonia, to the priest physicians of Egypt and Greece, all who practised the art of healing were influenced by magic. Healing, indeed, without the aid of the occult was practically unknown. Although magic lay outside religion in all the civilized states of antiquity it was never regarded as a mere imposition, and while religion was the worship for the good of the community, magic was the supernatural relation for the individual.

So far as we know, the earliest general belief as to the cause of disease incidental to man was that it was due to the effect of unseen demons or evil-spirits that entered his body and were so able to affect it for ill. Thus, when a person fell sick from the attack of a resentful spirit the first step towards cure was to get rid of the intruder. In most cases the method adopted was used in the hope that the evil-spirit might transfer his baleful influence from the body of the sick person into some other object.

In magic, three things were regarded as necessary for the perfect exorcism of such an evil-spirit. First, the Word of Power; second, the name of the person or demon working ill against the afflicted person; third, some drug or charm to aid the healer.

The magicians believed that everything belonging to the person or touched by him, such as his hair, teeth and nails, were all organic portions of the real man himself and that if injury was directed towards them, ill could also be inflicted on the person.

In Serang today, if a native wishes to work ill on an enemy, he obtains a little of his hair and burns it, together with some of his food, which he believes will give his victim a severe headache. In the Islands of Luang and Sumatra, burning the hair or nail-parings of an enemy will, it is believed, cause him to have a swelling of the hands.

Several methods were employed to drive away the demons that caused disease, and some light is thrown on them and the connection between magic and healing in the early ages, from the clay tablets found in Assyria inscribed in cuneiform over 3000 years ago. Among the methods employed was the clay or wax figure, which was afterwards consumed in fire; and another was the slaughtering of a kid into which the demon

9

was inveigled to enter, when the magician was then able to destroy it.

As civilization advanced, it is probable that the idea of the slaughtered kid became merged into an ordinary sacrifice, and the animal played the part of a sin-offering. The magical use of the clay figure or effigy was also common in Babylonia, Assyria and Egypt.

Fever could be induced by exposing the effigy to fire and the prick from a knife caused the victim to feel a sharp pain. This belief is expressed in the following text:

Those who have made images of me, reproducing my features,
Who have taken away my breath and torn my hairs,
Who have rent my clothes and hindered my feet from treading the dust,
May the Fire-god, the strong one, break their charm.

The underlying idea of the use of the effigy is to be found in the belief that whatever may have been in contact with an individual embodied something of his personality, and the effigy being an image, HIS IMAGE, so a lock of his hair, his teeth or nails, remained part of the man. Another method of expelling the demons or evil-spirits was by incantations, or prayers, entreaties and threats, or sometimes fumigations or the burning of evil-smelling substances was resorted to in order to drive out the intruders. Among barbaric peoples today, the medicine-man, or witch-doctor, makes himself as terrifying as possible by wearing hideous masks and robes, to frighten away the spirits of evil.

From ancient Mesopotamian lore we learn that there were three classes of men who performed the ceremonies by means of which the disease-demons were exorcized. The first may be called the seers, the second the wizards and the third the chanters. The first-named consulted the gods or the future, by the inspection of the liver and entrails of animals or by the flight of birds. The second was the incantation priest, or exorcist, who chanted the rites prescribed in the magical ceremony, while the third chanted or sang the parts allotted to him. Sometimes the incantations were accompanied by offerings of honey, dates, butter, garlic or other food, and these were generally destroyed by fire afterwards, thus indicating the sympathetic connection between the destruction of the ban and that of the object.

The incantations which accompanied the ritual of magic were the vocal expression of what was in the mind of the magician. They may generally be considered as being prayers or invocations to an over-ruling power such as a traditionary deity of the race. It might be the utterance of a wish, a blessing or a curse. It had to be spoken in the presence of the person concerned, and it may be noted that healing incantations were also used in the preparation as well as in the administration of medicine. Some incantations were specific and others of a general nature, as instanced in the following from an Assyrian tablet dating from about 2500 B.C.

Sickness of the head, of the teeth, of the heart, heartache.
Sickness of the eye, fever, poison.
Evil-spirits, evil-demons, evil-ghost, evil-devil, evil-god, evil-fiend.
Hag, demon, ghoul, robber sprite,
Phantom of night, night wraith, hand-maid of the phantoms,
Evil pestilence, noisome fever, baneful sickness,
Pain sorcery or any evil,
Headache, Shivering.

.   .   .   .   .

Evil spell, witchcraft, sorcery,
Enchantment and all evil,
Drive from the house, go forth, Unto the man, the son of his god, come
     not into,
Get thee hence !

The demons or evil-spirits to which disease was attributed showed their power in several ways. Sometimes they contorted the body in fits or convulsions, as in epileptic attacks, or with violent shivering and fever, symptomatic of ague.

The aid of certain powerful deities was invoked in some incantations, as instanced in the following from an Assyrian tablet:

(To be said over a sick man—)
He that stilleth all to rest, that pacifieth all,
By whose incantation everything is at peace,
He is the great Lord Ea.
By whose incantation everything is at peace.
When I draw nigh unto the sick man
All shall be assuaged.
I am the magician born of Eridu
Begotten in Eridu and Subari
When I draw nigh unto the sick man
May Ea, King of the Deep, safeguard me.

Then the magician is thus to address the deity sought:

O Ea, King of the Deep, see
I am the magician, am thy slave.
March thou on my right hand,
Assist (me) on my left,
Add thy pure spell to mine;
Vouchsafe (to me) pure words
Make fortunate the utterances of my mouth,
Ordain that my decisions may be happy,
Let me be blest where'er I tread,
Let the man whom I now touch be blessed.

Ea, or Oannes, was the powerful Babylonian deity known as "Lord of the Deep", for he was supposed to have come out of the sea, and was represented as part-man and part-fish. He was worshipped throughout Babylonia and Assyria.

It is evident from some of the cuneiform texts that the magician healer sometimes employed drugs or herbs in the form of fumigation in conjunction with the incantation as instanced in the following:

> For sickness of the head, of the teeth or the heart,
> Sickness of the eye, fever, poison—
> Come my sorceress or enchantress
> Over a nulukhkha-plant shalt thou recite.
> Upon the fumigation bowl which is at the head of the bed
> Shalt thou place it with an upper garment
> Shalt thou envelop the bed.

Whether it be an evil spirit or an evil demon
Or an evil ghost or an evil devil or an evil god or an evil fiend,
Or a hag-demon, or a ghoul or a Robber-sprite,
Or an evil spirit that holdeth the man in its grip,
Or an evil ghost that hath seized the man,
Or an evil man or one whose face is evil, whose mouth is evil, whose tongue
    is evil,
That incantation at his head, may they be removed.

This text indicates that belief in the Evil-Eye was prevalent in Assyria over 2000 years ago.

Although certain of the magical rites associated with healing may have been based on conscious fraud, some of the early beliefs as to the causation of disease seem to have resulted from rational reasoning. Thus, when a person was suddenly seized with an epileptic fit, was violently convulsed and foamed at the mouth, it was but natural for primitive man to have concluded that the cause was an evil-spirit or demon that had suddenly entered his body.

Among some primitive tribes in New Zealand it was indeed believed that a separate demon existed for each distinct disease. There was one that caused epilepsy, another fever and ague and so on; therefore some amulet, talisman or charm was sought that would placate it or frighten it away.

The ancient Egyptians appealed to Thoth, who was specially skilled in the art of healing, while later, the Greeks besought Asklepios, with the aid of the sacred serpents kept at the temple at Epidaurus, to cure their ills. His personification, Æsculapius, was regarded as the deity of medicine by the Romans, and his help was invoked to heal the diseased.

In Teutonic healing, Woden was often invoked, as shown in the following charm from a tenth-century manuscript at Merseburg Cathedral in Saxony:

> Then charmed Woden
> As well he knew how
> For bone sprain
> For blood sprain
> Bone to bone
> Blood to blood
> Limb to limbs
> As though they were glued.

A similar charm was employed for sprains in the Highlands of Scotland, but in the Gaelic the name of Christ is substituted for Woden. The Romans identified Woden with Mercury, whom he resembled in that from him proceed both the diseases and their cure.

     •   •   •   •   •

The pathology of the New Testament is largely demoniac and many of the miracles of healing are exorcisms to banish the devils of blindness, dumbness, madness and epilepsy. St. Luke, the physician, appears to have regarded the "great fever" of Simon's wife's mother as being due to a demon, for "Jesus," he says, "stood over her and rebuked the fever and it left her."

The Apostles frequently cast out the evil-spirits that were believed to cause disease, as mentioned in Acts viii, 7. When Philip went down to Samaria we read that "unclean spirits crying with loud voice came out of many that were possessed *with them*; and many taken with palsies, and that were lame, were healed".

St. Paul, when in Ephesus, performed similar miracles on the people, and "the diseases departed from them and the evil-spirits went out of them".

There is also mention of travelling or vagabond Jews, or exorcists, who took upon them "to call" over those who had evil-spirits. These exorcists, who evidently travelled about the country like the quack-doctors of a later period, were the pseudo-magicians who professed to cast out evil-spirits by conjuration and incantations. They must have continued their work for centuries, for Justin Martyr tells us of Jews who exorcized demons in the second century. "Now assuredly," he says, "your exorcists make use of craft when they exorcize even as the Gentiles do and employ fumigations and incantations."

Throughout their history the Jews have studied and practised magic as an aid to healing and, as recorded in the Book of Enoch, their daughters and young women were instructed in incantations, exorcisms and the cutting of roots by the Sons of God, who came to earth and taught them. The Talmud is full of magical formulae and the Jewish belief in the occult persisted for centuries. In the Near East, especially in Turkey and Syria, prayers and invocations as well as many curious substances are still used in healing, as instanced in live grasshoppers, pieces of mummy, human bones and wolves' livers which are still regarded as cures for biliousness, sore eyes and fits; but in all these cases the administration of the remedy must be accompanied by the appropriate incantation.

Among the Anglo-Saxons the same idea as to the cause of disease prevailed, and intermixed with their leechdoms many incantations and invocations are to be found.   The following are some instances from the *Leech Book* of Bald:

Against fever : Let a man sing many masses over the worts (herbs), wet them with ale, put holy water on them, boil very thoroughly; let the sick man drink a large cupful as hot as he may before the disorder be upon him; name the four gospellers and a charm and a prayer—Matheus . . . Marcus . . . Lucas . . . Johannes . . . intercedite pro me.   Tiecon Leleloth patron adiurovos.

(Leleloth was the name of an Arabian deity.)

Against fever disease, a man shall write this upon the sacramental paten and wash it off in the drink with holy water and sing over it: "In principio erat verbum; In the beginning was the Word and the Word was with God and the Word was God."   Then wash the writing off the dish into the drink; then sing the Credo and the Pater Noster and this lay; Beati Immaculati, the Psalm cxix with the twelve prayer Psalms, I adjure thee, and let each of the two men (the leech and the sick) then sip thrice of the water so prepared.

For flying venom and every venomous swelling (probably for epidemic disease and for the bubonic plague), churn butter on a Friday which has been milked from a neat or hind all of one colour and let it not be mingled with water.   Sing over it nine times a litany, nine times the Pater Noster and nine times the incantation—"Acrae, aercrae, aernem, nadre, aercuna, hel, aernem, aeradspice."

The fathers of the Christian Church in the early centuries preached a mixture of demonism and magic.   Paganism gave way to Christianity and for healing, the Virgin Mary or some tutelary saint was invoked.

The custom of making votive offerings for recovery from sickness was revived from Roman times, and many of these can be seen in churches in various parts of Europe today.   The cure of disease by prayer, paternosters and exorcisms was sanctioned, while Holy water, Holy oil and reliquaries embellished with magnificence were paraded and were believed to possess curative powers.

In this way the advance of the true art of healing was stifled until the twelfth century, when the School of Salerno was founded.

Chapter II

HEALING BY INCANTATION

INCANTATIONS or invocations to an unseen power are the earliest methods of healing known and are recorded on cuneiform tablets dating back at least 5000 years.

Among the Sumerian and Babylonian peoples disease was generally believed to be caused by the entrance of demons or evil-spirits into the body of man. To heal his sufferings the sick person had recourse to the magician who, by his knowledge of magical words, incantations and offerings, could invoke the aid of the all powerful gods to gain control of the demon and expel him. The treatment naturally resorted to was that which would be most likely to get rid of the noxious intruder and to this end the magician, as auxiliaries to the spells which he chanted over the patient, would use those animal, vegetable or mineral substances which had a ceremonial importance and were supposed to be endowed with magical power. Of these the simplest was pure water, which was sprinkled over the possessed person at the conclusion of an incantation. This had a double meaning, symbolizing, as it did, the cleansing of the man from the spell and the presence of one of the great gods such as Ea, whose emanation always remained in water and whose aid was always invoked by those means.

Meteoric iron was sometimes employed as a charm, and this is quite as intelligible as the use of water, since from the nature of them both they are obtained from the habitations of the gods. The magician often held a branch of tamarisk or the date-palm aloft in his hand during the exorcism, to repel the attacks of the demons and lay them under a ban. This shows that they were also possessed of magical power. The idea is similar to the use of water in magic, for just as water contained the power of the god, so will the piece of tamarisk contain the emanation of the tree-spirit which lives in the sacred tamarisk shrub. This use of branches in magic shows that the early inhabitants of Babylonia held the belief common to many other peoples that trees were inhabited by spirits or gods.

Incantations were often accompanied by fumigations and offerings, the latter usually consisting of honey, butter, dates, garlic, wool and fragments of gold or precious stones. These were generally destroyed by fire, indicating the sympathetic connection between the destruction of the ban and that of the object.

The magical ceremonial of the Babylonians was usually accompanied by the burning of incense during the recital of the incantation. The

15

formula afterwards employed generally began with the name of the person, as for example in the following prayer to Tasmitu:

I —— the son of —— whose god is —— whose goddess is ——
In the evil of an eclipse of the moon ——
May the sickness of my body be torn away; may groaning of my flesh be consumed!
May the consumption of my muscles be removed!
May the poisons that are upon me be loosened!*

Among the many interesting incantations used by the Babylonians is one embodying the "Legend of the Worm" that was written to relieve toothache, believed to be due to the gnawing of small worms. The translation reads:

> After Anu (had created the Heavens)
> The Heavens created (the earth)
> The Earth created the Rivers,
> The Rivers created the Canals,
> The Canals created the Marshes,
> The Marshes created the Worm.
> Came the Worm and wept before Shamash,
> Before Ea came her tears :—
> What wilt thou give me for my food?
> What wilt thou give me to devour?
> I will give thee dried bones,
> And thy scented —— wood?
> Let me drink among the teeth,
> And set me on the gums;
> That I may devour the blood of the teeth,
> And of their gums destroy their strength.

By repeating the story of the Creation and the subsequent action of the original Worm, the magician shows clearly that he has knowledge of the name of his enemy and his methods, a fundamental principle in magic. He then proceeds:

> So must thou say this; O Worm!
> May Ea smite thee with the might of his fist!

After chanting the incantation three times he would then proceed to rub a mixture of beer, a certain plant probably of a pungent nature, and a little oil on the aching tooth.

This legend as to the cause of toothache is especially interesting as it has survived for centuries and is still believed in some parts of the country today, where the decayed tooth is filled with henbane seeds to relieve pain. The warmth of the mouth causes the seeds to burst and the

*The Devils and Evil Spirits of Babylonia. R. Campbell Thompson.

cotyledons which emerge are declared to be the worm which has caused the pain.

Another example of a Babylonian incantation has been translated from a text over 2000 years old, as follows:

> It is I who (recite) the incantation for the sick man
> Whether thou be an Evil Spirit or an Evil Demon
> Or an Evil Ghost or an Evil Devil
> Or an Evil God or an Evil Fiend
> Or sickness or death or Phantom of Night
> Or wraith of Night, or disease or evil pestilence,
> Be thou removed from before me!
> By Heaven be thou exorcized!

Another, which illustrates the use of water, reads:

> A sorcerer of Eridu whose mouth is purified (am I)
> The sick man upon whom sickness hath seized,
> Fever hath taken up its seat upon him.
> When I draw near unto the sick man,
> When I examine the muscles of the sick man,
> When I compose his limbs,
> When I sprinkle the water of Ea on the sick man,
> When I subdue the sick man,
> When I bring low the strength of the sick man
> Nor evil god or evil Fiend
> Draw nigh unto the King
> By Heaven be ye exorcized!   By Earth be ye exorcized!

Another tablet records an incantation of a more comprehensive nature suitable for people suffering from many diseases affecting various parts of the body.   It reads:

> Sickness of the head, of the teeth, of the heart, heartache,
> Sickness of the eye, fever, poison,
> Evil Spirit, evil Demon, evil Ghost, evil Devil, evil God, evil Fiend,
>   Hag-demon, Ghoul, Robber-sprite,
> Phantom of night, Night wraith, Handmaiden of the Phantom,
> Evil pestilence, noisome fever, baneful sickness,
> Pain, sorcery or any evil,
> Headache, shivering;
> Roaming the streets, dispersed through dwellings, penetrating bolts,
> Evil man, he whose face is evil, he whose mouth is evil, he whose
>   tongue is evil,
> Evil spell, witchcraft, sorcery,
> Enchantment and all evil,
> From the house go forth!
> Unto the man, the son of his god come not nigh,
> Get thee hence !

In his seat sit thou not,
On his couch lie thou not,
Over his fence rise thou not,
Into his chamber enter thou not,
By Heaven and Earth I exorcize thee,
When I recited an incantation over the sick man,
When I perform the incantation of Eridu,
May a kindly Spirit be present at my side,
Whether thou art an evil Spirit or an evil Demon
Or an evil Ghost or an evil Devil

                .   .   .

Or an evil pestilence or noisome fever,
Or pain or sorcery or any evil,
Or headache or shivering or
An evil man or evil face,
Or evil spell or evil tongue, or evil mouth, or sorcery
Or any evil,
Be thou removed from before me !
By heaven be thou exorcized !   By earth be thou exorcized.

The idea is probable that as the magician here reduces the strength of the sick man and thereby that of the devil in him, so will he frighten into subjection the evil power which has possessed the body of the patient.

To prevent an evil-spirit or demon entering a house bitumen was placed beneath the door by the magician, as described in the text:

I am the messenger of Marduk
As I perform the pure incantation
I put bitumen on the door beneath,
That Ea may rest within the house
May a kindly spirit, a kindly Guardian
Enter the house,
May no evil Spirit or evil Demon
Or evil Ghost or evil Devil
That thou mayest depart.

The earliest records of magic among the ancient Egyptians indicate that it was practised as far back as the fourth dynasty and, as with the Babylonians, magic began with the gods.

Thoth was considered the most powerful magician and from him arose the fame of Hermes Trismegistus.

The early Egyptian medical papyri abound with incantations, but a difference is made between the incantation and the remedy to be employed, for even some of the drugs used were supposed to possess medical power. Like the Babylonians, the Egyptians believed that sickness and disease were caused by evil-spirits that entered the body of man and the sick came, or were brought to the Temples to be treated either by incantations, drugs or incubation.

The priest-physician had first to discover the nature of the disease and the name of the possessing demon, after which he was able to exercise his magic functions to rid the patient of the intruder. "He who treats the sick must be an expert in magic, learned in the proper incantations and how to make amulets to control disease," is stated in one papyrus.

Among the other deities, Isis was regarded as a great enchantress and healer, as shown in the following incantation:

> O Isis, great Enchantress, free me, release me from all
> evil red things, from the fever of the god and the
> fever of the goddess. From death and death from pain
> and the pain that comes over me; as thou hast freed,
> as thou hast released thy son Horus, whilst I enter
> into the fire and go forth from the water.

The early Egyptians had an all-prevailing faith in magic, and it was invoked in all questions of life, death, health and disease. It was closely interwoven with both religion and healing and so was practised by the priests in the temples.

Psychology also played a part in the healing by incantation, as there is little doubt that the solemn recitation of certain sentences and words of invocation over a sick person, tended to reassure and calm the patient and soothe his troubled mind and nerves, caused in most cases by the effect of fear of some unknown power, the origin of which we now call superstition.

Many of the early Greek philosophers sought the aid of magic in healing Pythagoras believed that the whole air was full of spirits which sent men dreams and symptoms of disease, but that they also influenced health. To these spirits lustrations and averting ceremonies, together with invocations, should be made. From these evolved incantations for such divers complaints as headache, dimness of sight, quartan fever, gout, spasms, toothache, lumbago, epilepsy, dysentery and poisoning. The magician of his time believed that if anyone swallowed the heart of a mole freshly extracted and palpitating, he would at once become an expert in divination. We are told that the heart of a hen placed upon a woman's left breast while she is asleep will make her reveal her secrets, while the gall of a sacrificed goat smeared on the eyes, or placed under the pillow at night, would certainly improve the sight.

Democritus tells us of a herb, the root of which wrought into pills and swallowed in wine, would make guilty men confess their crimes, after being tormented at night by strange visions of the spirit world.

Even some of the more enlightened of the Greek physicians believed in the magical effects of certain strange and curious substances. Thus,

40 years after the death of Alexander the Great, Serapion of Alexandria (278 B.C.), one of the principal exponents of the Empirical School, prescribed the warty excrescences found on the forelegs of animals, camel's brain and gall, rennet of seal, dung of crocodiles, heart of hare, the blood of the turtle, and stones found in the bodies of boars, rams and cocks.

Pliny, to whom we owe so much of the folk-lore of medicine in his time, tells us that pills of the squirting cucumber (*elaterium*) hung round the waist in ram's wool helped parturition if the patient was ignorant of the source. He declares that Sappho fell in love with Phaon because he found a masculine root of eryngium. According to tradition, men affected with tertian fever could be relieved if they tied on their bodies a root of autumnal nettle, provided that when the root was dug up the names of the sick man and his parents were duly pronounced aloud during the process. To prevent getting the legs chafed it was recommended to carry a wand of poplar in the hand when walking. Another cure for quartan fever was the dust in which a hawk had been rolling, tied up in a bag of cloth with a red thread, or the longest tooth of a black dog, the head of a viper cut off, or its living heart cut out, and put in a piece of cloth or the right eye of a living lizard tied up in a goatskin.

A holly bush planted in the courtyard or garden of a house was believed to avert witchcraft, and a herb picked from the head of a statue and tied up with a red thread was said to take away a headache.

Xenokrates, who flourished about sixty years before Galen, mentions the good effects he obtained following the eating of human brain, flesh or liver, and by swallowing with a drink, the burnt or unburnt bones of the head, fingers or shin of a man.

Even Galen himself (A.D. 200) was a believer in the efficacy of incantations and observes: "Some think they are like old wives' tales as I too did for a long time. But at last I was convinced that there is virtue in them by plain proofs before my eyes." He mentions their beneficial use after the bites of scorpions and choking from bones stuck in the throat being immediately thrown up, after repeating an incantation.

But of all the early physicians there was no firmer believer in the efficacy of amulets and charms in the healing of disease than Alexander of Tralles (A.D. 550). To relieve colic he recommended from experience, the dung of a wolf or the bits of bone in it shut up in a pipe and worn on the right arm, thigh or hip during the attacks. A lark's heart plucked out whole while it was alive and worn on the left thigh, was especially efficacious, or a piece of a child's navel enclosed in a box of silver or gold with salt would always give the patient ease. For the gout he recommends the sinews of a vulture's leg and toes, tied on the feet and the skin of a seal for soles in the shoes, but the sufferer must be careful that the right leg goes to the right and the left to the left. Henbane, gathered when the moon was in the signs of Aquarius or Pisces before sunset, and dug up with thumb and third finger of the left hand and an incantation was also regarded as a sure cure for gout.

For epilepsy, Alexander prescribed jasper and coral with the root of nux vomica, to be wrapped up in a linen cloth. Worms out of a goat's head, the occipital bone of an ass's head in skin, a rivet from a wrecked ship made into a brooch, or the bone from a stag's heart taken while living, he also regarded as powerful remedies.

The influence of magic in healing held sway between the years 500 and 1000 when the Anglo-Saxons and Gothic races came to occupy the west of Europe.

Marcellus, writing about A.D. 380, records numerous charms employed in his time for every imaginable ailment. Thus, he says: "As soon as ever a man gets pain in his eyes, he should tie in unwrought flax as many knots as there are letters in his name, pronouncing them as he does it and afterwards tying it round his neck. If a man has a white spot as catarack in his eye, he should catch a fox alive, cut his tongue out and then let him go. Dry the tongue and, after tying it up in a red rag, hang it round the man's neck." He observes that "if anything causes annoyance in a man's eye, let him shut the other eye, touch gently the vexed eye with the ring finger and thumb and say thrice, 'I buss the Gorgon's mouth'." His method of removing a foreign body from the eye survives today and often proves effective without the magical incantation which used to accompany it. For toothache, the sufferer is instructed to spit in a frog's mouth and request him to make off with the pain; and for a troublesome uvula it is recommended to catch a spider, place it in a nutshell and wear it round the throat, a charm which was practised down to the end of the seventeenth century. A charm to prevent stomach-ache was to put in the left shoe, after it had first been put on, a gold-leaf bearing the words "L Mpria" written three times.

From the coming of the Christian era the Church, unable to root out these superstitious traditions and practises, began to combine them with religious exercises, rites, exorcisms and masses. In place of the names of the pagan deities, hitherto employed, they invoked sacred names to drive out the evil-spirits or demons of disease by exorcism.

The Christian exorcists appointed were recognized as officials of the Church, and the name of the deity or certain saints were invoked. This is reflected in innumerable incantations such as the following, from a manuscript of the eighth century, in the library of the monastery of St. Gall, in Switzerland:

To remove a thorn. Say, "Nothing is higher than heaven.
Nothing is deeper than His sea.
By the Holy words that Christ spoke from His Cross, Remove from me the thorn."

A cure and incantation for toothache was as follows:

I adjure thee toothakes of blood, worm and rume, by the virtue of our Lord Jesus Christ and by the merits of Joseph His Foster Father and as he was betrothed to that Blessed Virgin Mary, not a husband and a witnesse of undefiled virginitie; soe by soe much the more suddenly depart thou toothake from this person, now, and annoy him no more nor trouble them nor vex them, now appear in their body by the virtue of the Father, Son and Holy Ghost, by the virtue of all the Holy names (of) God, obey to my bidding and avoid thou toothake from this person, now and without any more delay. Although this had been said three times, now repeat the Lord's Prayer three times and the Creed once.

Another remedy recommended is for the sufferer to "go to a young oak tree and cut off a slip off the tree, cut off a bit of his hair, then spin together with hair from a dog and hair from a lion and thread three cornelians thereon, then bind it on the sufferer and he shall recover".

In the later Eastern magic, love charms compounded of the brain of the hoopoe made into a cake, or the bones of a dog buried seven days, then dug up would, if placed in water, prove good for love or hatred. If they sank when put in the water it would be a charm for hate, but if they floated they would aid lovers.

Compression was a common form of treatment and binding a thread of wool round the painful part was a recognized method of ridding the body of the demon. Thus, to drive away a headache, the priest-physician was directed to

Take the hair of a virgin kid,
Let a wise woman spin it on the right side
And double it on the left,
Bind twice seven knots.
Then perform the incantation of Eridu;
Bind (therewith) the head of the sick man,
Bind therewith the neck of the sick man,
Bind therewith his life.
Cast the water of the incantation over him,
That the headache may ascend to heaven.

To drive away a fever, the magician was directed to take a thread of cotton, single and not plaited, three-fold, tie seven knots in it and bind it round the patient's wrist and say the following incantation:

Bind white wool doubled in spinning on his front and sides
Bind black wool doubled in spinning on his left hand,
That there may enter no evil spirit nor evil demon . . .

The connection of magical beliefs with herbs used in medicine is frequently illustrated in the early herbals. Thus, Albertus Magnus in his *Virtutibus Herbarum*, writing on heliotrope, says:

If one gathers it in August and wrap it up in a bay-leaf with a wolf's tooth, no one can speak an angry word to the wearer. Put under the pillow it will bring in a vision before the eyes of a man who has been robbed, the thief and all his belongings. If it be set up in a place of worship, none of the women present who have broken their marriage vows will be able to quit the place till it be removed.

A survival of the incantation in healing still remains in some parts of northern England where a sick child is commonly taught to repeat the words "Pray God bless it and make it do me good", before swallowing a dose of medicine.

Chapter III

HEALING AND ASTROLOGY

THE influence of astrology on the art of healing and the important part that was believed to be played by the planetary bodies and stars on human beings in health and disease, are shown from records that date at least from the fifth century before the Christian era. Throughout the Middle Ages down to the sixteenth century, the study of the heavenly bodies and their movements was considered a necessary part of the physician's practice. It was the chief method employed in diagnosing disease, and to the influence of planets and stars was attributed the potency of the herbs and plants used in the treatment of human ills.

The association of the Signs of the Zodiac with various organs and parts of the human body was also regarded as another important factor in the well-being of mankind. The belief that each of the twelve signs influenced a certain organ, or part of the body, is of great antiquity and formed a connecting link with methods of healing.

In the Middle Ages, diagrams were drawn showing the part affected accompanied by the corresponding planetary sign for the guidance of the physician. These astrological figures are frequently found in manuscripts, books and calendars, down to the end of the seventeenth century.

The origin of the belief is unknown, and as Babylonian and Assyrian records reveal no evidence of its existence among those early people, it is thought that it originated in Egypt and passed from there to Greece and Rome. Pettigrew says that the "ancient Egyptians apportioned certain parts of the body to the signs, and treated disease by invoking the Zodiacal regent of the part affected".

This doctrine spread to Greece, and about the fourth century B.C. we find Hippocrates alluding to the power of the heavenly bodies over the human frame and of some mysterious influences that emanated from them. In the time of Ptolemy (A.D. 130) the doctrine was recognized, for remarking on the theories on which it is based he observes: "Such parts of the signs as contain the affected part of the horizon will show in what part of the body the misfortune will exist, whether it be a hurt or disease or both."

Manetho, the Egyptian priest and early traveller, remarks that each degree of the heavens in late Egyptian astrology was assigned to some special activity and to some disease. By the time we come to the Alexandrian School of medicine, about 300 B.C., astrological prognosis and diagnosis were both recognized and practised. Diseases of the more important bodily organs were diagnosed according to the influence

24

of the Signs of the Zodiac at the time, and remedies were administered which either acted by suggestion, or were wholly inoperative.

It is thought by some that the origin of the idea of planetary influence

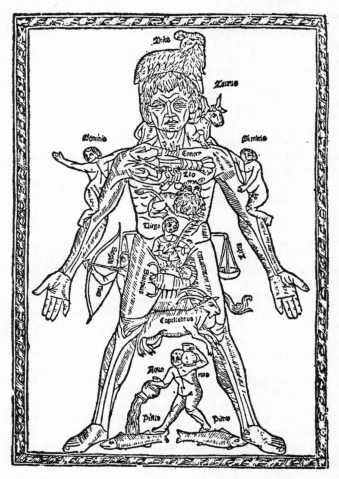

The Signs of the Zodiac and the parts of the body that they govern, as shown in an astrological figure from "*Epilogo en Medicina Y Cirurgia*" 1495.

on the body, in health and disease, lay in the supposition that the spirits of the heavenly bodies radiated their influence and that, as those radiations were of a similar or dissimilar character to that of the human frame, so they were beneficial or harmful. Thus, a cold planet might through its influence, which was generally evil, be made advantageous in fever, and the plants and minerals which partook of its nature, might be administered with good effect.

According to astrological rules, "plants and herbs for medicinal use should be gathered during the hours of the planets to which they were appropriated, for at that time they were believed to have increased power, whereas in the hour of supremacy of a contrary planet, they lost their virtues and became ineffectual".

The time of gathering had to be calculated from an almanack, and tables were compiled showing the planetary hours of rising and setting. Thus, all plants and herbs coming under the dominion of the Sun were to be gathered on Sunday, while those ruled by the Moon were to be collected on Monday and so on through the days of the week, according to the planet governing the day. Not only the plants and herbs came under the influence of the planets but also the vegetable and mineral substances that were employed in healing. Thus, according to the astrological doctrine, the Sun governed cedar, laurel, anise, St. John's-wort, almond, camomile, fennel, dill, juniper, lavender, marigold, mistletoe, pennyroyal, rosemary, rue, sage and saffron; and his metal was gold.

Then follows a list of herbs and plants that are most suitable for various diseases. These include apoplexies, carbuncles, coughs and colds, consumption, convulsions, digestion, dropsies, fevers, headaches, heart-fainting, jaundice, liver, quinsy, rheums, sciatica, throat and stomach complaints, and sleeplessness.

The value of astrology and the esteem in which it was held in the diagnosis of disease were recognized in the sixth century by Isidore the Jew, who ascribed to the Moon an influence over plant and animal life and control over the humours of man.

A later writer says:

The end of the physitian's employment in ye case of ye patient that he may accomplish this with more certainty and facility, astrology is very necessary as the handmaid to attend his and other physicall sciences. "First to ye knowledge of what part the disease is in and which cause it comes you are to remember what parts of man's body are signified by ye twelve houses and signs of heaven, by ye planetts and by ye position of ye planetts which use the significators in any of the houses and signs."

With the advent of Arab learning, astrology became of further interest, special attention being paid to the Zodiacal signs and the planets, each of which was believed to govern or have a special influence over some region or organ of the human body.

For this purpose, the quaint astrological figures representing the human body, male and female, with the Zodiacal signs placed over the regions of the body they were believed to govern, were employed. They were drawn for the instruction of those who could not read, and the earliest known dates from the tenth century. At a later period, they were often produced in the Books of Hours, many being beautifully delineated by masters in the art of miniature painting, as well as being reproduced from wood blocks in early printed books. The first sign, Aries (the Ram), is depicted as governing the head, face, ears, eyes and mouth. The second, Taurus (the Bull), rules the neck and throat. Third, Gemini (the Twins), the arms and shoulders, hands and fingers. Fourth, Cancer (the Crab), the breast, stomach, and lungs. Fifth, Leo (the Lion), the heart, ribs and back. Sixth, Virgo (the Virgin), the viscera, liver, spleen and intestines. Seventh, Libra (the Scales), the reins, bladder, kidneys, thighs, and the upper parts of the buttocks. Eighth, Scorpio (the Scorpion), the generative organs. Ninth, Sagittarius (the Archer), the hips and thighs. Tenth, Capricorn (the Goat), ruled the knees. Eleventh, Aquarius (the Water-Carrier), the legs and ankles. Twelfth, Pisces (the Fish), the feet and toes. Thus, the physician was able to know the parts of the body that were influenced and came under the rules of the Zodiacal signs. This being completed, he proceeded to his diagnosis, the first step being to take note of the sign the Moon was in when the patient took to bed and by what planets the Moon was afflicted at the time. Then, according to the set rules under the planets, he was able to name the disease.

The Moon was said to govern all plants full of sap, such as cucumber, palm, mushrooms, melon, moonwort and herbs that turned to the luminary; while her metal was silver. The Arabs, indeed, believed that it was the Moon that brought down the virtue of all the planets that influenced the herbs on earth, for Abraham Avenezra, the Arabian astrologer, says: "The Moon is assimilated to the body of man. She brings down the virtue of the other planets to the creatures and to man on earth."

Saturn was said to rule the pine, cypress, yew, black-alder, hemlock, nightshade and poppy, while Jupiter governed the oak, elm, birch, hazel, agrimony, betony, columbine, foxglove, hyssop, larkspur, mallow, periwinkle, parsnip and thyme.

Mars ruled the hawthorn, box, broom, buckthorn, dock, garlic, horehound, hemp, hops, mustard and wormwood. His minerals were iron, antimony, arsenic and sulphur.

Venus governed apple and cherry trees and their fruits, also coltsfoot, dandelion, elder flowers, myrtle, white poppy and violet leaves; while her metal was copper.

To Mercury were assigned the medlar, quince, willow, barberry, succory, tansy and vervain.

According to an index of diseases given in the *Sickman's Glass*, a book written for the guidance of the physician in the sixteenth century, "to cure all agues you must take notice under what planet the patient was most afflicted and so make choice of herbs accordingly".

If the Moon was in Capricorn and afflicted by Saturn, the chest and stomach would be affected; the lungs might be oppressed and the patient would have shortness of breath and cough. Another method was to observe the "sign of the twelve houses" and then give judgment if the Moon was in any of the twelve signs and by the infirmities affected. By rules also, the physician-astrologer was supposed to be able to prognosticate whether his patient would live or die. If the signs showed that he would live then he would recover. The signs of recovery were foretold by a "benevolent" planet being stronger in the ascendant than the "afflicting" one.

It will be seen, therefore, that the selection of suitable remedies was a very important step, and in doing this the physician had first to note one of the elemental qualities of each planet, *viz.* whether hot or dry, or hot and moist, cold and dry, or cold and moist. This having been ascertained, it was necessary for him to consult his Herbal and find the elemental qualities of the herb or plant. If both the plant and the planet were in accord in elemental qualities, then the plant was regarded as being under that planet. Thus, for instance, Saturn is a planet which is cold or dry in the third or fourth degree, and such plants or herbs as hemlock, henbane, and nightshade being also dry in the third or fourth degree, he would conclude they were properly attributed to Saturn. Having decided on the remedies to employ, the physician had then to discover the most suitable form in which to administer his medicines. A certain quantity three times a day was far too simple a proceeding, so he had to find out when the Moon was in a watery sign or whether a watery planet was in the ascendant. According to the rules he had to "let the moon be aspected by any planet which was direct if swift in motion and under the influence of the earth." "By no means let the Moon be aspected by any retrograde planet for then the patient will be apt to vomit." "When you attend to give a vomit," says the rule, "let, either the moon or the Lord of the ascendant be an earthly sign aspected by a planet retrograde."

It will be seen that the task of the physician, when called to diagnose a sick person, was neither an easy nor simple one, if carried out by astrological rules.

Bleeding was often carried out at regular intervals whether the patient was ill or not and was also subject to astrological rules. To avoid harmful results, an individual should only be bled when the planets were favourable and it was laid down:

Let not the Moon be in Gemini nor in that sign when you let blood in the feete and let not the Moon be in Capricorn if ye bleed in the legges. The best time to let bloode is when the Moon is aplyeth to Aries. Let not bloode when in the house of Jupiter or Venus and finally, let not bloode from the middle of Julie until the middle of September, nor when there is frost or snow and it is further not goode to let bloode in ye house of Jupiter.

Ptolemy warned surgeons never to operate when the Moon was in the sign governing a certain part of the body and says: "Pierce not with iron that part of the body which may be governed by the sign actually occupied by the Moon." He further observes that "the Moon indeed is the most important planet to be considered in connection with medical treatment" and this was acknowledged by most physicians throughout the Middle Ages.

In conclusion, a writer on medico-astrology of the period states:

Wise men have experiences of many virtues of the starres and physicians in old time have found out the changes and terminations of diseases by the course of the Moon, wherefore the 7th, 14th, 20th, 21st, 28th or 29th dayes of sicknesses are called critical dayes. Know then, that the crisis viz. upon the critical day, the Moon being well-aspected by good planets, it goes well with the sick; if to ill planets, it goes ill with the patient.

Chapter IV

TRANSPLANTATION OF DISEASE

AMONG the beliefs associated with healing long before the Christian era was the idea that certain diseases affecting humanity could be transferred from man's body to trees and plants.

This is supposed to have originated in the ancient theory that the demons giving rise to disease in trees and plants were those that caused similar maladies in human beings, and it was therefore necessary to confine them to the tree or plant which they normally inhabited.

Gilbert White records that at Selborne there stood, in his time, a row of pollard ashes which, when young and flexible, had been severed and held open by wedges. To these apertures fond mothers used to bring naked children suffering from ruptures and pass them through the holes, in the belief that their infirmity would then be cured.

A similar belief prevailed in Cornwall and other districts of Britain, where children suffering from rickets and the effects of the evil-Eye, were passed through the branches of a maple tree. Sick sheep were made to go through a cleft in a young oak tree, so that the disease might thus be transferred to the spirit of the tree.

In some parts of the country it was customary to tell persons suffering from ague to go in silence and without crossing a stream or water, to a tall willow; then make a cut in it, breathe three times into the place, close it quickly and haste away without looking back. They would in this way be healed of their ailment.

The plants chosen for the transfer of disease were usually those bearing the signatures of the particular disorder from which the person was suffering, so that it might attract the specific influence from the planets or stars that governed it. Some of these herbs and the planets to which they were sympathetically related have thus been tabulated:

Plants accorded to Saturn had a hairy, hard and dry appearance, with dull, greenish, dirty white, or pale red flowers, disagreeable smell and spreading roots. To Jupiter, smooth leaves, shaped or pointed, of greyish-blue-green colour, pleasing flowers of flesh colour, blue or yellow, small roots with short hairy filaments and a pleasing odour. To Mars, hard long leaves, hot to the tongue, flowers red, purple, yellow or blue-green; roots highly fibrous, creeping underground and with an oppressive or acrid odour. To Venus, large rich green leaves, flowers white, blue and pleasing to the eye, roots not deeply fixed and subtle odour. To Mercury, varied leaves pleasing to the eye, agreeable coloured flowers, roots deep in earth, spreading and with a penetrating, refreshing smell. To the Sun, succulent leaves with stout stalks, handsome yellow or golden flowers, roots deeply fixed in the earth and with a pungent and agreeable smell. To the Moon, leaves pale, succulent, bottle-green, with strongly marked veins, flowers pale yellow or greenish, roots easily decayed and of earthy odour, with no pungency.

The ancient belief in the transference of disease from the afflicted person to running water so that it might be carried away, is illustrated in the following charm: "Take a hazel or an elder stick; write thy name thereon, cut three scores and fill the name with thy blood. Throw it over thy shoulder or between thy thighs into running water and stand over the man. Cut the scores and do all this in silence."

The belief in the transference of disease was common among all races and is shown in various ways. Thus in Cheshire, the ailment commonly known as "Frog-in-the-throat" was treated by holding the head of a young frog in the mouth of the patient, in the belief that the ailment would pass into the reptile as it hopped away. It was also believed that disease could be transferred to trees, and in Hertfordshire there were certain oak trees used for curing ague. A lock of the sufferer's hair was pegged into the trunk, and then by a sudden wrench the patient left his hair behind him in the tree and with it the disease. The South Sea islanders used to make a model canoe or boat and man it with dolls, then send it adrift on the sea, in the belief that it would bear away the cause of the sickness.

Perhaps the best known example of the early belief in the transference of disease to running water is that of Elisha's direction to Naaman when he suffered from leprosy—"Go and wash in Jordan seven times," said the prophet, after which, we are told, he became whole. There are two points of interest in connection with the prophet's command: first, the number of times Naaman was told to dip. Seven was regarded as a divine and magical number and was often used in Jewish ceremonial and religious rites. It is called "the number of an oath" by the Hebrews and was so used by Abraham. Elijah, on the top of Carmel, sent his servant seven times to look for rain, and when Jericho was taken the city was encompassed seven times. It was regarded as important by magicians when casting spells, and witches in early times are said to have enjoined the sick to dip their shirts seven times in running water. Second, the running water of a stream or river was necessary to carry away the evil-spirit that caused the disease.

In a recipe of the seventeenth century written by a certain John Dougall of Edinburgh, for a person suffering from convulsions, it is recommended to take cuttings of the sick person's nails, some hair from the eyebrows and a halfpenny, wrap them altogether in a cloth which had been round the patient's head and place the package in a gateway, where four lanes meet. The first person who found and opened it would then take the disorder and relieve the afflicted one. It was even thought that a disease could be transferred from a living to a dead person, as instanced in the directions given for relieving a man from a boil. The boil was to be poulticed for three days and nights, after which the poultices and cloths used were to be placed in the coffin with a dead person and buried.

In Lancashire, there was a common belief that warts could be transferred by rubbing each with a cinder which was then to be wrapped in paper and laid where four roads meet. The person who opened the packet would thus take the warts away from the sufferer.

In Devonshire, a child could be cured of whooping-cough by putting one of its hairs between slices of bread and butter and giving it to a dog to eat. If the dog then coughed, it was a sign that the ailment had been transferred from the child to the animal.

A curious cure for a "crick-in-the-neck", or cuts in various parts of the body, was to twist a piece of willow round the affected part in order to draw it away; while gout was believed to be relieved by transferring the disease to an old pine tree.

Persons suffering from toothache were recommended to bite the first fern they came across and to place a small piece of the stem in the decayed tooth; then, after it had been extracted, to bury it.

The transference of an ailment was usually accompanied by uttering some words of adjuration, as recommended in a cure for fever. In such a case, the sufferer was placed reclining in the branches of a plum tree and the words were then repeated as follows:

Climbing plant, stand! Plum tree, waver!

and so the fever would be relieved and pass to the tree.

Mannhardt records the names of some of the demons which in Germany were identified by the peasants with nearly all the maladies of plants, and states that the country people believed that the same demon could cure the disease. Diseases could be healed by transplantation if the affected part was covered for a while with a piece of fresh beef, until the sweat entered into it. The meat was then given to a dog or cat to eat.

A splinter of a blackthorn or willow, cut from under the bark, if used to prick the gums round an aching tooth till it bled, was to be replaced in the tree and bound up; in so doing the pain would be relieved.

Paracelsus was a believer in the transplantation of disease and stated: "There is a great difference between the power that removes the invisible causes of disease and which is magic, and that which causes merely external effects to disappear." He expressed his belief in a principle he called *mumia*, which he declared had great curative power. "This *mumia* or vehicle of life is invisible and is a spiritual substance containing the essence of life. The hair, blood or excrements of the human body continue to remain for a while in a sympathetic relationship with the *mumia* contained in it." He observed that "the *mumia* could be extracted from the diseased part of a person by a microcosmic magnet, and that when mixed with earth and a herb planted in it, the *mumia* in the magnet would be extracted by that plant and lose its diseased matter". It was necessary that the selected plant should be one that bore the signature of the disease from which the patient was suffering, in order that it might attract the specific influence from the stars. In this fantastic manner Paracelsus connected his *mumia* or "vehicle of life", with the doctrine of signatures and astrology.

Chapter V

HEALING BY SYMPATHY

ONE of the most curious beliefs in connection with the practise of medicine in early times, was the cult which came to be known as "Healing by Sympathy". This reached its height in the seventeenth century and its chief exponent was Sir Kenelm Digby, a man of some ability and learning.

It is difficult to conceive in these days how such a wild and fantastic delusion could be advocated and spread by such intellectual men as Van Helmont, Descartes and later by Madame de Sévigné.

The basis of the idea was a belief that certain ills of the body could be cured by applying the remedy to the object, such as a weapon, which was the cause of the malady. Thus, for instance, if a man was wounded by a knife or sword, the weapon which caused the wound was treated with a powder or ointment having "sympathetic" virtues, instead of the remedy being applied directly to the patient.

Sir J. G. Frazer was of the opinion that the germ of the idea could be traced to the commandment in the Pentateuch, "Thou shalt not seethe a kid in its mother's milk", an early prejudice against boiling milk, as it was supposed to cause suffering to the animal that gave it. Thus, if suffering could be conveyed to an animal, healing was similarly capable of transference.

A like idea is put forward by Pliny in the statement that "if any person shall be sorry for a blow he has given another afar off or near at hand, he shall presently spit into the middle of the hand with which he gave the blow, and the party that was smitten shall presently be free from pain".

Healing by "sympathy" was advocated in the sixteenth century by Paracelsus, who argued that it was the weapon that inflicted the wound which was to be anointed, and not the wound itself. He stated that the "Sympathetic Ointment" he recommended would be effective, no matter how far away the stricken person might be. He safeguarded his assertion by saying that, if an artery had been severed, or if the heart, the brain or the liver had suffered a lesion, his application would not answer.

He insisted, however, that the wound was to be kept properly bandaged, and the bandages were to be first moistened with the patient's urine. The application of the remedy to the weapon was to be repeated every day, in the case of a serious wound or every second or third day when the wound was not so severe, and the weapon was to be wrapped after anointment in a clean linen cloth and kept free from dust or draughts, or the patient would have much pain. He declared that "the anointment

34

of the weapon acted on the wound by a magnetic current through the
air direct to the healing balsam which exists in every living body, just as
the sun passes through the air". His formula for the "Sympathetic
Ointment" was an extraordinary one and runs as follows:

Take four ounces each of boar's and bear's fat, boil slowly for half an
hour, then pour on cold water. Skim off the floating fat, rejecting that which
sinks (the older the animals yielding the fat, the better). Take of powdered
burnt worms, of dried boar's brain, of red sandal-wood, of mummy, and of
bloodstone, one ounce each. Then collect one drachm of the moss from the
skull of a man who died a violent death (one who had been hanged preferably)
and had not been buried. This should be collected at the rising of the moon,
and under Venus if possible, but certainly not under Mars or Saturn. With
all these ingredients, keep in a closed vessel. If it becomes dry on keeping, it
can be softened with a little fresh lard or virgin honey. The ointment must
be prepared in the autumn.

Another curious compound which was employed in the treatment
of healing was the "Sympathetic Egg". It was prepared by taking an
empty chicken's egg and filling it with warm blood, drawn from a healthy
person. The egg was then carefully sealed and placed under a broody
hen for a week or two, so that its vitality should not be impaired. It was
then to be heated in an oven for some hours at a temperature sufficient
to bake bread. In order to effect a cure, this egg was placed in contact
with the affected part and then buried. It was assumed that it would
inevitably take the disease with it, as healthy and concentrated blood was
said to have a stronger affinity for disease than a weaker sort.

Sir Robert Talbot gave an account to the Royal Society, in the time
of Charles II, of a cure he effected with the aid of the "Sympathetic
Powder". He told the Fellows that "an English mariner who had been
stabbed in four places while at Venice, bled for three days without
intermission". He sent for some of the man's blood and mixed "Sympathetic Powder" with it. At the same time a man was sent to bind up the
patient's wounds with clean linen. On visiting the mariner soon afterwards Talbot found all the wounds closed and the man much comforted.
Three days later, he was able to call on Sir Gilbert to thank him but even
then, "he appeared like a ghost with no blood left in his body".

Van Helmont, Descartes, Baptista Porta and others were believers
in healing by sympathy. The first-named, in his *De Magnetica Vulnerum
Curatione* (1644) relates the story of a man in Brussels who, having lost
his nose during a combat in Italy, consulted Tagliacozzi, the famous early
plastic surgeon, who provided him with another, taking the necessary
strip of flesh from the arm of a servant. Thirteen months afterwards
the man found that his new nose was getting cold and then it began to
putrefy. It transpired that the servant from whom the flesh had been
taken had died and this, according to Van Helmont, accounted for Tagliacozzi's failure.

Goclenius and Fabricius Hildanus were also believers in the weapon-salve, after having heard Sir Kenelm Digby give a discourse on it at the University of Montpellier in 1658.

Digby, whose name is chiefly connected with the "Sympathetic Powder and Ointment", dabbled in politics, religion and science, and was an extraordinary character who played a prominent part in affairs in the Stuart period. His father, Sir Everard Digby, was involved in the Gunpowder Plot, was charged with treason and executed.   Kenelm, who succeeded to the title, became a favourite with King James I, who gave him a commission to fight against the Spaniards, and for a year or two he scoured the seas and captured French, Spanish and Flemish ships. On his return to England he was courted by society as a hero, and his plausibility soon made him a favourite.

During his discourse on "Healing by Sympathy", given before a great assembly of scientific men at the University of Montpellier, Sir Kenelm related the case of Mr. Howell who, in endeavouring to part two of his friends who were fighting, had his hand cut to the bone and applied to Sir Kenelm for aid.

"I told him," said Digby, "that I would willingly serve him, but if haply he knew the manner I would cure him, without touching or seeing him, it may be he would not expose himself to my manner of curing. Howell replied: 'The wonderful things which many have related unto me of your way of medicine, makes me nothing doubt at all of its efficacy.' I asked him then for anything that had the blood upon it; so he presently sent for his garter wherewith his hand was first bound, and dissolving some vitriol in a basin of water I put in the garter observing in the interim what Mr. Howell did. He suddenly started as if he had found some strange alteration in himself. I asked him what he ailed? 'I know not what ails me; but I find that I feel no more pain; methinks that a pleasing kind of freshness, as if it were a wet, cold napkin did spread over my hand, which hath taken away the inflammation that tormented me before.' I replied: 'Since then that you feel already so good effect of my medicáment, I advise you to cast away all your plasters, only keep the wound clean and in a moderate temper betwixt heat and cold.'   To be brief, there was no sense of pain afterward, but within five or six days the wounds were cicatrized and entirely healed."

In these words Digby gave away the chief secret of his treatment, for in keeping the wound clean and ceasing to apply the so-called "weapon-salves" and powders, he effected the cure which had been ascribed to them. When it is said that these horrible compounds usually consisted of human fat, blood, mummy and a moss found growing on skulls, it cannot be wondered at that the wounds usually became septic, sometimes with fatal results.

When the case of Howell became known and the Duke of Buckingham had testified to the genuineness of the cure, Digby became famous. He claimed that he obtained the secret remedy from a Carmelite monk in

Florence, but, after his death in 1682, George Hartman, his laboratory assistant, declared that *he* was the discoverer of the cure, which he prepared by "dissolving good English vitriol in a little warm water, filtering the solution and then evaporating it till fair large green crystals had formed." They were then crushed and dried in the sun until they whitened. Then he crushed them coarsely and again dried them in the sun.

Digby's explanation of the action of his powder was that the rays of the sun extracted from the blood and vitriol associated with it the spirit of each, in minute atoms. At the same time the inflamed wound was exhaling hot atoms and making way for a current of air. The air, charged with the atoms of blood and vitriol, was attracted to it and acted curatively.

Clarendon alludes to Sir Kenelm as "a person very eminent and notorious throughout the whole course of his life; very extraordinary person and presence; a wonderful, graceful behaviour; a flowing courtesy and such a volubility of language as surprised and delighted". Lady Fanshawe met him at Calais with the Earl of Strafford and others, and says: "Much excellent discourse passed but as was reason, most share was Sir Kenelm Digby's."

Madame de Sévigné, who showed an interest in many matters connected with healing, in a letter to her daughter written in January 1685, thus expressed her belief in the "Powder of Sympathy". She tells her that "a little wound which was believed to have been healed had shown signs of revolt; but it is only for the honour of being cured by your 'Powder of Sympathy'. The *Baume Tranquille* is of no account, now half dried and cured." On February 7, 1685, she wrote again: "I am afraid the 'Powder of Sympathy' is only suitable for old-standing wounds. It has only cured the least troublesome of mine."

Rudolph Goclenius in his *De Magnetica Curatione Vulneris* (1608), says that the treatment consisted in anointing the weapon which had inflicted the wound with the *unguentum armarium* of the patient's blood and human fat, the wound itself being wrapped in wet lint. This doctrine was supported by Robert Fludd, the philosopher, in 1619, and by Van Helmont in 1621, who attributed the cure to animal magnetism.

The Church held that the weapon-cure was wrought by magic of the devil and this view was held by William Foster in his *Hoplocrisma*, or *A Sponge to wipe away the Weapon Salve* (1631).

In 1690 Lemery, the French chemist, expressed his doubts about the "Powder of Sympathy" and in 1773, Baumé boldly declared its pretensions were absolutely illusionary. This ended the belief in the "healing by sympathy" that held sway in the seventeenth century and even influenced the literature of the period. Of such allusions we quote Hudibras as follows:

> For by his side a pouch he wore
> Replete with strange hermetick powder
> That wounds nine miles point blank would solder

By skilful chemist, at great cost
Extracted from a rotten post.

.   .   .   .

'Tis true a scorpion's oil is said
To cure the wounds the vermin made;
And weapons dress'd with salves restore
And heal the wounds they made before.

In *The Tempest*, the sympathetic treatment is clearly referred to when Hippolite has been wounded by Fernando, and Miranda, instructed by Ariel, visits him. She says:

Anoint the sword which pierced him with this weapon salve and wrap it close from air.

Lastly, Sir Walter Scott refers to the delusion in the *Lay of the Last Minstrel*, in the lines:

But she has ta'en the broken lance
And washed it from the clotted gore
And salved the splinter o'er and o'er.

Chapter VI

HEALING BY TOUCH

THE personal power of healing by touch in early times was attributed to the gods and, by natural association of ideas, became a divine right of kings. The practise is said to have been a survival of a rite performed by the priest-physicians in the temples of Egypt and Babylon. It originated in the belief that certain individuals were born with powers superior to those possessed by others, so that even a touch of the hand or a glance from the eye of such persons was sufficient to heal and to receive a share of their power.

There was a general belief in some parts of this country, especially in Wales, that a seventh son had this power of healing by touch, as Lupton declares: "It is manifest by experience, that the seventh male child by just order (never a girle or wench being born between) doth heal only by touching (through a natural gift), which is a special gift of God given to Kings and Queens."

Plutarch tells us that Pyrrhus, King of Epirus, cured colics and affections of the spleen by laying sufferers on their backs and passing his great toe over their bodies. Suelin further relates that when the Emperor Vespasian was at Alexandria, a poor blind man came to him, saying that the god Serapis had revealed to him that if the Emperor would touch his eyes with his spittle, his sight would be restored. Vespasian became angry and would have driven the man away but some of those around him urged him to try and exercise his power. At length he consented and cured the man of his blindness and others of lameness. The Emperor Adrian is said by Coelius Spartianus to have cured sufferers from dropsy by touching them with the tips of his fingers ; and the Eddas tell how King Olaf healed the wounds of Egill, the Icelandic hero, by laying-on of hands and singing proverbs.

The miracles of Christ and His disciples in healing the sick and restoring sight to the blind by touching them, bear some relation in another sense to curative power by faith. For instance there is the account of the healing of the leper recorded in St. Luke v, 12–13, and the remarkable story of the woman who had issue of blood for twelve years, who came behind unseen by Jesus and touched the edge of His garment. Yet He was aware of it, saying: "Somebody hath touched me, for I perceive that virtue has gone out of me" (St. Luke viii, 46). Further, Christ passed His power on to His disciples after the Resurrection and said: "They shall lay hands on the sick and they shall recover" (St. Mark xvi, 18).

The miraculous power of healing is supposed to have been conferred on monarchs through the medium of the Holy Oil, with which they were anointed at their coronations. Robert the Pious (970–1031), son of Hughes Capet, is said to have exercised this miraculous power, although there is a tradition that Clovis received it on the date of his conversion, A.D. 496. On that occasion, the Holy Oil was said to have been brought direct from heaven in a phial carried by a dove and the healing power was conferred at the same time. It is interesting to note that the anointing oil used at the coronations of our kings and queens today, is preserved in an ampulla of gold in the shape of a dove which forms part of our royal regalia.

Early chroniclers declare that the healing was a prerogative peculiar to the sovereigns of England and the first records of its exercise begin with the account given by William of Malmesbury of its practice by Edward the Confessor (1042–1066), from whom the hereditary right is said to have descended to all his successors to the English throne.

William tells the story of the Confessor and:

"a young woman who had a husband about the same age as herself, but having no child got into an ill state of health by an overflowing of humours in her neck which broke out in great nobbs. She was commanded in a dream to apply to the King to wash it. So to Court she goes and the king being at his devotions all alone, doi'd his fingers in water and dabbel'd the woman's neck and he had no sooner taken away his hand than she found herself better. the loathsome scabb dissolved but the lips of the ulcers remaining wide and open. She remained at Court till she was well which was in less thann a week's time; the ulcers being so well closed, the skin so fair, that nothing of her former disease could be discovered and in less than a year's time she was brought to bed with Twins."

The disease with which the healing was chiefly associated was struma or scrofula, later called "King's Evil". It was a disorder very common in England from the Middle Ages down to the seventeenth century and was mainly due to malnutrition. Edward the Confessor, however, appears to have exercised his healing power in other directions, and a story is recorded of his meeting with a "cripple, much diseased, whom he carried on his back to St. Peter's Church in Westminster, thereupon he was immediately cured of all his maladies". It is stated in the *Computus Hospitii* of Edward I, that a small sum of money was given by the King to those he healed.

Shakespeare alludes to the Confessor's "healing touch" in *Macbeth* (Act iv, sc. iii), and thus describes how the "Most pious Edward wrought the miracle of cure".

The doctor says:

> There are a crew of wretched souls
> That stay his cure; their malady convinces.
> The great assay of art; but at his touch
> Such sanctity hath Heaven given his hand
> They presently amend.

Macduff asks: "What's the disease he means?" to which Malcolm replies:

> 'Tis called the Evil;
> A most miraculous work in this good King;
> Which often since my here remain in England,
> I have seen him do. How he solicits Heaven
> Himself best knows; but strangely visited people,
> All swoln and ulcerous, pitiful to the eye,
> The mere despair of surgery, he cures,
> Hanging a golden stamp about their necks,
> Put on with holy prayers; and 'tis spoken
> To the succeeding royalty he leaves
> The healing benediction.

The "golden stamp" refers to the gold coin given to the sufferer after he had been "touched", which later became known as a "touch-piece". This practise is said to have been set up in the time of Henry VII. The Angel-noble, a current coin of the period, was the one first chosen for the purpose and after being pierced and threaded with a white ribbon, was suspended round the neck of the recipient. This coin bears the figure of St. Michael slaying the dragon, which is believed by some to symbolize an angel exterminating the disease.

After the reign of Queen Elizabeth a special coin was struck, reduced in size, and the inscription was changed to "SOLI DEO GLORIA". The "touch-piece" was apparently worn as an amulet to prevent the return of the disease, as some coins, like the money of St. Helena, were used as charms to ward off attacks of epilepsy, mention of which is made in the Wardrobe accounts of Henry III.

From the time of Charles I special smaller coins were struck of gold, silver and even copper, "for," says Wiseman, "the King's fortunes had fallen so low, that he could not give gold 'Touch-pieces'."

Certain Kings of France, including Philip I and Henry IV, claimed the right of healing by touch. Louis XIV also practised it extensively, and is said to have touched 1,600 persons on Easter Sunday in the year 1686. While touching the afflicted he is stated to have repeated the words: *Le Roi te touche, Dieu te guerisse,* giving to each person fifteen sous and every foreigner thirty sous.

Laurentius, physician to Henry I of France, asserts that this gift of healing belonged only to the Kings of France and that it was first practised by Clovis in the year 481, when he discovered his power accidentally, and "caused the disappearance of a painful chronic swelling from the neck of his follower Lanicesut by laying his hand upon it".

English chroniclers, however, maintain that the Kings of France only derived their power from their alliance to the English royal line, and this contention aroused much bitter controversy in former times. The French kings continued to exercise the rite down to 1776.

After the time of Edward I, no mention is made by the chroniclers of this country to the "healing", until the reign of Henry II, when Peter de Blois, who was chaplain to that monarch, records that "his master touched and cured scrofula". Gilbertus Anglicus, who is said to have lived in the time of King John, in his *Compendium Medicinae*, refers to the practise as an ancient one and says: "the disease was called King's Evil, because the king cured it."

The next allusion to the performance of the rite is made by John of Gaddesden (1280–1361) who is said to have been the first English physician employed at Court. Writing on scrofula and enumerating the various methods of treatment for the disease about 1320, he recommends that in case of these failing, the patient should repair to the King to be touched.

Bradwardine, Archbishop of Canterbury, who lived in the reigns of Edward III and Richard II, mentions the practise of the rite; and Sir John Fortescue, who was Lord Chief Justice of the King's Bench in the time of Henry IV and Chancellor to Henry VI, alludes to the King's healing by touch and attributes the power to the unction of the hands of the sovereign with the Holy Oil at the coronation.

The special form of religious service instituted in Henry VII's time was continued down to the year 1719 and was included in the English Prayer Book until that period.

It begins with the words: "THE CEREMONIES FOR HEALING THEM THAT BE DISEASED WITH THE KING'S EVIL IN THE TIME OF KING HENRY VII." After the liturgical portion there is a note:

the King shall be crossing the sore of the sick person with an angel of Gold Noble and the sick person to have the same angel hang'd about his neck and to wear it until he bee full whole.

Then the following prayer was to be said secretly after the sick persons be departed from the King, at his pleasure:

Almighty God, Ruler and Lord by whose goodness the blind see, the deaf hear, the dumb speak, the lame walk, the lepers cleansed, and all sick persons are healed of their infirmities; by whom also the gift of healing is given to mankind and so great a grace, thro' Thine unspeakable goodness towards this Realm is granted unto the Kings thereof, that by the sole imposition of their hands a most grievous and filthy disease should be cured, mercifully grant that we may give thanks therefore for this Thy singular benefit conferr'd on us, not to ourselves but to Thy name let us daily give glory and let us always exercise ourselves in piety, that we may labour not only diligently to conserve but every day more and more to increase Thy grace bestowed upon us; And grant that on those bodies soever we have imposed hands in Thy name, thro' this Thy vertue working in them and thro' our ministry may be restored to their former health, and being confirmed therein, may perpetually with us give thanks unto Thee, the Chief Physician and Healer of all diseases, and that henceforward they may so lead their lives as not their bodies only from sickness but their souls also from sin may be perfectly purged and cured.

Although Queen Elizabeth is said to have been averse to the practise, and the Roman Church denied that she possessed the healing power, she is reputed to have "touched a great number of people" when she came to the throne.

Richard Wiseman exults: "that the gift was not taken away upon our departure from the Church of Rome", for it was regarded as a proof of rightful sovereignty. Richard Smith tells us that Queen Elizabeth was accustomed to make the sign of the Cross with her finger on the scrofulous swellings, a practise which was not followed by her successors, until James II revived it. From the Queen's own words, it is apparent she disliked the practise of the healing and on one occasion, being importuned by many persons suffering from the disease, she exclaimed: "God only could relieve them from their complaints."

The method of applying the touch appears to have varied with individual sovereigns, and before Elizabeth's time there is simply mention of the sores being touched. Elizabeth contented herself by making the sign of the Cross on the afflicted part, but her successors, James I, Charles I and Charles II, are said to have performed the rite by "stroking" the swellings.

William Clowes, who was one of Elizabeth's surgeons, in his book entitled, *A Right Fruteful and Approved Treatise for the Artificiall cure of that Malady called in Latin Struma* and in English, *"The Evil" Cured by Kings and Queens of England,* describes the disease as "one repugnant to nature which grievous malady is known to be miraculously cured and healed by the Queen's most Royall Majesty even by Divine inspiration and wonderfull worke, and power of God above man's skill, arte and expectation".

The Stuart kings appear to have had a special predeliction for exhibiting their power of touching, and Charles I is said by contemporary writers to have excelled all his predecessors in the exercise of the Divine gift, for, says one: "it is manifest beyond all contradiction that he not only cured by his sacred touch both with and without gold, but likewise effected the same cure by his prayer and benediction only". He certainly must have "stroked" a very large number of people, for Wiseman records that when the king's fortune had fallen so low that he could not give gold pieces, he was the first to have special touch-pieces struck for the purpose, of silver and even copper.

After the Restoration, multitudes of people flocked to London to receive the benefits of the Royal touch, and in his performance of the rite, Charles II must have exceeded all his predecessors. This may have been due to the suspension of the rite during the time of the Commonwealth, although John Browne states that "that method had been tried by the late usurper Cromwell, but without success".

Charles II touched several thousands of sufferers every year, and in 1682 he performed the rite on 8,500 people. Parish registers were kept of such cases as had received certificates and were touched for the King's

Evil. From the public register kept by Thomas Haynes, Serjeant of His Majesty's Chapel Royal, from 1660 to 1664, 23,601 were touched and again from 1667 to 1684, the number reached 68,506. So great indeed was the increase in the number of applicants that it was soon found necessary to place some restriction upon them.

That none may approach the Royal Presence but such as are really troubled with the Evil, [says Browne], several officers were appointed for this great ceremony. Among the first of which are his Majesty's Chirurgeons-in-Waiting, who are to take in certificates and deliver out tickets in order to a healing.

For this purpose metal tokens of copper or brass, about the size of a penny, were issued. When applying for tickets, patients were bound to bring with them certificates signed and sealed by their ministers or churchwardens declaring that they had never been previously "touched" by the King.

Faith in the King's power naturally played an important part in the healing, and Browne asserts that:

the healing held on Good Friday do carry a strong faith with some people who, unless they can be touched by the King that time, their belief is so weak and tender, that they do not presume and suppose any other time in the year is so fitting.

The performance of the rite was preceded by a Royal Proclamation; the following is the text of one issued on March 26, 1616.

BY THE KING
A Proclamation concerning The King's Evil

Whereas such people as repair to His Majestie for healing of the King's Evil have in former times forborne to approach or offer themselves to the former kings of this realme during the summer time, in respect of danger and inconvenience, which order hath bene of late neglected, and such people useth to repair indifferently at all times. Therefore His Majestie doeth declare and forbid that hereafter, no such person make their repaire up for healing betweene the Feastes of Easter and Michaelmas for the which although it had been ynough for His Majestie to have signified His pleasure for recontinuing the said order unto the Clearke of the Closet or His Chirurgeons in that behalfe. Yet His Majestie doubting that some such weake and infirme persons may come from remote parts and thereby leese their travaile, is pleased out of his goodnesse to publish this Order by His Highesse Proclamation.

Given at our Palace of Westminster ye 26 day of March in the fourteenth yeere of Our Reigne of Great Britaine, France and Ireland.

GOD SAVE THE KING

The service of the Healing was carried out with great solemnity and

☙ By the King.

☙ A Proclamation concerning *The Kings Euill.*

Hereas ſuch people as repaire to His Maieſtie foȝ healing of THE KINGS EVILL, haue in foȝmer
times foȝboȝne to appȝoch oȝ offer themſelues to the foȝmer Kings
of this Realme, during the Summer time, in reſpect of danger,
and inconuenience, which oȝder hath bene of late neglected, and
ſuch people vſeth to repaire indifferently at all times : Theȝe-
foȝe his Maieſtie doeth declare and foȝbid, That hereafter no ſuch perſon make their repaire vp foȝ healing, betweene the Feaſts of Eaſter and Michaelmas, foȝ the which although it had bene ynough foȝ His Maieſtie to haue ſignified His pleaſure foȝ recontinuing the ſaid oȝder vnto the Clearke of His Cloſet, oȝ His Chirurgions in that behalfe;
Yet His Maieſtie doubting that ſome ſuch weake and infirme perſons may come vp
from remote parts , and thereby leeſe their trauaile, is pleaſed out of His goodneſſe, to
publiſh this Oȝder by his Highneſſe Pȝoclamation.

Giuen at our Pallace of Weſtminſter the 26.day of March,in the foureteenth
yeere of Our Reigne of Great Britaine, France and Ireland.

God ſaue the King.

☙ Imprinted at London by Robert Barker, Printer
to the Kings moſt Excellent Maieſtie.
ANNO DOM. 1616.

TOUCHING FOR THE KING'S EVIL.
A Proclamation issued by King James I in London, 1616.

usually took place on a Sunday. In winter, it was always held at White-hall, but in summer it was sometimes held at Windsor. Browne gives us the following description of the ceremony in 1672:

The tickets being delivered out, His Majestie does generally appoint the day of Healing of which the Chirurgeon is to acquaint those who are to be Touch'd, the which for the most part does happen on Sundays or other days it matters not which, the effecte of his Cure being as good at one time as another. The Day being come, before His Majestie doth approach to his Royal Chair, which is generally after morning prayers, the Chief Officer of the Yeomen of the Guard doth place the sick people in very convenient order for their approaching the King without trouble or noise. The which done, His Majestie enters His Royal Chair, uncovered, at whose beginning there are generally two chaplains attending; one of which reading the ceremonies appointed for this Service, His Majestie all the while being surrounded by his Nobles and many other spectators. The Sick and Diseased people being kept back by the Chirurgeons till the appointed time, where, having made three obeisances, they do bring them up in order. The chief-in-waiting delivering them one by one to the King to be touched the which done, the other receives him or her from him, and this method is used throughout the whole number which come to be healed.

Close enquiries were made into the success of the practise by investi-gators at the time, some of whom were by no means believers in any actual royal virtue, but who yet admitted unhesitatingly the reality of many of the claimed cures. Some persons are said to have been cured immediately they were touched, while others did not get rid of their swellings until they had been treated a second time. Cases are related of persons who had been quite blind for several weeks and were even obliged to be led to Whitehall yet recovered their sight immediately on being "touched"; others, unable to walk, were carried on their beds and after the rite are said to have received immediate relief.

William Beckett, F.R.S., a well-known surgeon, in 1732, and Dr. Douglas, Bishop of Salisbury, in 1754, both admit that cures did result from the King's touch, and the latter states that he knew a man personally who had been healed. Beckett points out how likely it was that "the excitement of the visit to the Court both in anticipation and realization, and the impressive ceremony there conducted, would in many instances so affect the constitution, causing the blood to course through the veins more quickly as to effect a cure".

The following interesting account of the ceremony is taken from *Mercurius Politicus* of June 21–28, 1660:

Saturday being appointed by His Majesty to touch such as were troubled with the Evil a great company of poor afflicted creatures were met together, many brought in chairs and baskets and being appointed by His Majesty to repair to the Banqueting House. His Majesty sat in a chair of State where he "stroked" all that were brought to him and then put about each of their necks a white ribbon with an angel of gold on it.

In this manner His Majesty "stroked" above 600 and such was his princely patience and tenderness to the poor afflicted creatures, that though it took up a very long time, His Majesty who is never weary of well-doing was pleased to make enquiry whether there were any more who had not been "touched". After prayers were ended, the Duke of Buckingham brought a towel and the Earl of Pembroke a basin and ewer, who after they had made obeisance to His Majesty kneeled down till His Majesty had washed.

The Parliamentary Journal for July 2–9, 1660, says:

The Kingdom having been for a long time troubled with the Evil by reason of his Majesty's absence, great numbers have lately flocked for cure. His sacred Majesty on Monday last touched 250 in the Banqueting House, among whom, when his Majesty was delivering gold, one smuggled himself in out of hope of profit, which had not been "stroked", but his Majesty quickly discovered him, saying, "This man hath not yet been touched"; His Majesty hath for the future appointed every Friday for the cure, at which 200 and no more, are to be presented to him who are first to repair to Mr. Knight, the King's Surgeon, being at the "Cross Guns" in Russell Street, Covent Garden, over against the Rose Tavern, for their tickets.

Samuel Pepys, as might be expected, found his way to the Banqueting House to see the ceremony on April 13, 1661, and says in his *Diary*: "There I saw the King heale, the first time I ever saw him do it; which he did with great gravity but it seemed to me an ugly office and a simple one."

Evelyn, who witnessed the Healing on July 6, 1660, states:

His Majestie began first to touch for ye evil according to custome, thus His Majestie sitting under his state in ye Banqueting House, the chirurgeons cause the sick to be brought or led up to the throne, where they, kneeling, ye King "strokes" their faces or cheeks with both his hands at once, at which instance a chaplaine in his formalities says: "He put his hands upon them and he healed them." This is said to every one in particular. When they have been all touched they come up again in the same order and the other chaplaine kneeling, and having angels gold strung on white ribbon on his arme, delivers them, one by one, to his Majestie who puts them about the necks of the touched as they passe, whilst the other chaplaine repeats, "That is ye true light who came into ye world."

"The eagerness to obtain certificates from the chirurgeons was so greate," says Evelyn, "that on March 8, 1684, there was so greate a concourse of people with their children to be touch'd for the Evil, that six or seven were crushed to death by pressing at the chirurgeons door for tickets."

Charles II was importuned by the afflicted even when out walking, and Ashmole tells us that:

a man named Evans, who was in such a loathsome condition that none could be found willing to recommend him for a certificate, placed himself in St.

James's Park where he knew the King walked. Upon his approach he fell on his knees exclaiming, "God bless your Majesty." Whereupon the King gave him his hand to kiss, upon which Evans availed himself of the opportunity to apply it to his dreadfully ulcerated nose which from that time improved and ultimately recovered.

It is, however, a significant fact that, according to the bills of mortality of the period, more people died from scrofula during the reign of Charles II than at any previous time.

John Bird, who was a firm believer in the efficacy of the Royal touch, was of the opinion that the King's healing power was not confined to one disease but that rickets could also be cured. In support of his belief he wrote a book entitled, *Ostenta Carolina, or the Late Calamities of England with the Authors of them*:

The Great Happiness and Happy Government of King Charles II. Ensuing, miraculously foreshewn by the Finger of God in two Wonderful diseases, the Rickets and King's Evil, wherein is also shown and proved. That the Rickets after a while shall seize no more children but quite vanish through the Mercy of God and by means of Charles II. That King Charles II is the last of the kings which shall so heal the King's Evil. Delivered by the hand of the Lord on his unworthy servant and His Majesty's subject John Bird, and by him made Publicke for the Glory of God, Honour of the King and comfort of the People of God. London 1661.

Bird's prophecy, however, was not fulfilled for James II continued to practise the healing like his predecessors, and according to Bishop Cartwright on August 28, 1687, "he touched 350 persons at one sitting". On another occasion he is said to have performed the rite on some 800 sufferers, in the choir of Chester Cathedral.

William III, of the House of Orange, when he came to the throne of Britain, is said to have considered the rite "a silly superstition", and could only be induced to perform the ceremony once, when he remarked to the patients who were brought to him, "God give you better health and more sense."

But Queen Anne revived the ancient custom and performed the rite both in London and in Oxford. On March 17–30, 1714, she touched 200 persons, among whom was Samuel Johnson who had been brought to London from Lichfield by his mother to be touched by the Queen— it is said at the instance of Sir John Floyer, at that time a noted physician in Lichfield. Boswell gives the following account of the visit:

His mother yielding to the superstitious notion, which it is wonderful to think prevailed so long in this country as to the virtue of the regal touch; a notion which was encouraged and to which a man of such enquiry and such judgment as Carte could give credit, carried him to London where he was actually touched by Queen Anne. (He was then about two or three years old.)

Mrs. Johnson, indeed, as Mr. Hector informed me, acted by the advice of Sir John Floyer. Johnson used to talk of this very frankly and Mrs. Piozzi has preserved his very picturesque description of the scene as it remained upon his fancy. When asked if he could remember Queen Anne, "He had," he said, "a confused but somehow a sort of recollection of a lady in diamonds with a long black hood."

The cure, however, was not effective in Dr. Johnson's case, for he suffered from the disease all his life. He left the original touch-piece given to him by the Queen to Dr. Taylor, Prebendary of Westminster, at whose death it passed into the possession of the Duke of Devonshire and it is now preserved in the British Museum.

Sergeant-Surgeon Dickens, Queen Anne's surgeon, relates a story of a young woman whom, at her request, he brought to the Queen to be touched. After the performance, he says, he impressed on her the importance of never parting with the gold piece which was given to all patients. She promised always to retain it and in due course she was cured. In time, thinking all risk had passed, she disposed of the touch-piece; the disease returned. She confessed what she had done penitently to Dr. Dickens and by his aid she was touched again and once more she was cured.

On February 28, 1712, a little more than two years before Queen Anne's death, the following proclamation appeared in the *Gazette*:

It being Her Majesty's royal intention to touch for the Evil on Wednesday the 19th of March next and so to continue weekly during Lent, it is Her Majesty's command that tickets be delivered the day before at the office in Whitehall and that all persons shall bring a certificate signed by the Minister and Churchwardens of their respective parishes, that they have never received the Royal touch.

Queen Anne was the last British Sovereign to touch for the "Evil". There is no record of any of the Georges attempting the rite, although the young Pretender, Charles Edward, when claiming to be Prince of Wales, "touched" a female child at Holyrood House in 1745; and after his death in 1780, his brother Cardinal of York still touched at Rome and special silver touch-pieces were struck for them.

A curious instance of how these traditions linger on, is the belief that certain relics of Charles I still have the power of healing. Thus, the shirt, said to have been worn by the King on the scaffold, which is embroidered with the royal cypher "C.R." and a crown, and still stained with blood, is yet preserved in the parish church at Ashburnham, in Kent. As late as 1860, people suffering from scrofula were brought to the church to "touch the relic", in the hope of being cured.

Chapter VII

HEALING IN ANCIENT BRITAIN

THE magical and medical practices of early Britain have come down to us through folk-lore and manuscripts and we know that like nearly all races, ancient and modern, the people developed something of herb-lore frequently mixed with magical material.

After the decline of the Roman power in Britain, the greater portion of the practical knowledge of healing known to the ancient inhabitants of these islands must have disappeared, but with the influx of the Teutonic races a new era dawned, as they brought with them to England a self-acquired knowledge of the properties of herbs or worts which they employed in healing. This empirical knowledge, which was largely intermixed with magical practices, charms and incantations, formed the basis of the medicine of the Anglo-Saxons. Their lore is full of references to the use of water in healing, and many allusions to the running streams which they endowed with curative powers occur in their manuscripts. They had the idea that disease was caused by the arrows or darts of mischievous supernatural creatures who wandered everywhere and loved to shoot their envenomed weapons at passers-by, as well as by demoniac possession. There were also the water-elves, who lived in marshy and wet land and attacked mankind. Many of these beliefs came from the civilizations of the Tigris and Euphrates which had persisted throughout the ages.

The early religious belief of the Anglo-Saxons consisted fundamentally of a crude, fearful worship of the forces of Nature, but with the introduction of Christianity into England by Augustine in 597, people began to emerge from this state and started to develop a literature of their own. The northern runes, the beechen tablet and the scratching implement were superseded by the Roman Alphabet and the written word, inscribed on skin or parchment with style and ink.

The Christian missionaries coming from the more civilized Roman Empire no doubt brought with them some knowledge of the medicine of their country and from Greece also, the fountain head of the healing art in Europe, learning filtered through, all of which began to exert a certain influence on medicine in Britain.

During the eighth century, great monasteries were founded, first at Winchester, then at Malmesbury and later at Glastonbury. These became the chief centres of learning and the cradle of the arts. Their libraries contained manuscripts, original and in the vernacular, and others copied from the learned books in Latin and Greek introduced from other parts of Europe. It is noticeable that in the writings of Anglo-

Saxon origin, we often find the protection of Christ invoked, while the pagan spells and incantations are derived from foreign sources.

Until the close of the tenth century we have little reliable knowledge of the healing art in early Britain, but from the scanty relics of Anglo-Saxon literature that remain, we are able to gather some idea of its practice. We know that great faith was placed in charms and incantations in curing disease, but these were generally accompanied by the administration of drugs; and behind the superstitious practises there existed a real practical knowledge of the healing-art, which rested mainly on a knowledge of the properties of the herbs from which the *materia medica* was chiefly drawn.

The earliest medical text written by an English hand is a small, fragment of the ninth century found at Echternach, now in the Biblothèque Nationale in Paris. It contains the device called the "Sphere of Pythagoras", but we also have in this country several Anglo-Saxon manuscripts dealing with medicine which give us a good idea of the knowledge of the period.

The Anglo-Saxon practitioner of healing was known as the Leech, an appropriate name in one sense which was probably derived from the medicinal use of the leech for letting blood, one of the earliest methods of treatment. The Leeches were not exclusively of the priestly caste like the Druids, although they apparently received their early training in the monasteries, where the sick were brought to be treated.

From contemporary drawings we are enabled to form some idea of the appearance of the Anglo-Saxon practitioners. Thin and grave in mien, the Leech, as became a man of learning, is represented as with full moustache and beard and is attired in the frock or Anglo-Saxon tunic, with a decorated border and girdle reaching to his knees. His legs are bare but his feet are covered with pad-hose and a soft boot with a roll-down top. In some of the representations his head is covered by a pointed cap of the Phrygian type and from his shoulders hangs a half-length cloak or mantle.

The *Medicinale Anglicum*, the earliest Anglo-Saxon manuscript dealing with medicine, is supposed to have been written by a scribe called Cild for a patron or colleague named Bald, and this manuscript is known as the *Leech Book of Bald*. The author refers to his library and tells us that "he loved his precious volumes more than fees or stored wealth".

In the course of his treatise he refers to two other Leeches who were apparently both teachers. One named Oxa, he states, "taught this Leechdom", and the other called Dun is mentioned as the originator or instructor of a special method of treatment. It is evident from many parts of the book that Bald was familiar with the works of some of the early Greek fathers of medicine and from allusions made to King Alfred, the book was written either in the lifetime of that monarch or shortly after his death.

The manuscript copy of the *Medicinale Anglicum*, now in the British

Museum, is believed to have once belonged to the famous Abbey of Glastonbury, for a list of books of that foundation given by Wanley contains mention of it; and when it was rebound in 1757, the words *Medicinale Anglicum* were found inscribed on one of the fly-leaves in almost illegible characters. The following lines are written at the end of the second book:

> Bald is the owner of this book which he ordered Cild to write
> Earnestly I pray here all men in the name of Christ,
> That no treacherous person take this book from me
> Neither by force, nor by theft nor by any false statement.

The book itself is a definite and complete work consisting of 127 folios written on vellum and is divided into two parts. The plan adopted by the writer is first, a rough classification of the members and limbs of the body and second, the affections and diseases to which they are subject. Beginning with an epitome of the various leechdoms recommended for the affections of the head, ailments of the eyes, ears, throat, nose, the mouth, lips and other parts of the face are treated and so throughout the body down to the feet. The final chapters contain the methods recommended for treating diseases prevalent at the period, such as fevers, humours, paralysis and smallpox.

In studying the *Leech Book of Bald* one cannot fail to be struck by the significant terms which are used in the descriptions of several diseases. Thus in connection with epidemic and other diseases which were noticed to spread with rapidity, the expression "Flying venom" is used which well contrasts with what are now called air-borne germs; and the term, "venomous swellings" probably refers to bubonic plague. Smallpox, which is called pocked disease, is the Anglo-Saxon word signifying pustule and was evidently prevalent at the period, as instanced in the following leechdom:

> Against pockes; very much shall one let blood and drink a bowlful of melted butter; if they (the pustules) strike out, one shall dig each with a thorn and then drop one-year alder-drink in, then they will be seen.

This treatment was evidently intended to prevent pitting and serves to identify the disease.

Struma, or what was later known as King's Evil, was called "neckratten", or purulence in the neck, in Anglo-Saxon times, and the following treatment was employed:

> When first the neckratten begins to exist, smear it with gall of a beeve or best of an ox; it is a tried remedy; in a few nights it will be whole. If thou wouldst know if it be neck-purulence, take an earthworm entire, lay it on the place where the annoyance is and wrap up fast above with leaves; if it be neckratten the worm turneth to earth, if it be not he, the patient, will be

whole. Again for neckratten take coriander and beans sodden together and lay on; soon it removes the disease.

In another leechdom for the same disease, a burnt water-crab reduced to powder and made into an ointment with honey was recommended as a sure cure.

Yellow jaundice, which was known to the Anglo-Saxon leeches as "The Gall disease, from which cometh great evil", was thus diagnosed: "When the patient's body all becometh bitter and as yellow as good silk and under the root of his tongue there be swart veins and pernicious and his urine is yellow."

The last observation is interesting as one of the few instances in the leechdoms which may be regarded as clinical reference to the appearance of the urine as an aid to diagnosis.

The potions against poisons given in the leechdoms are many and show the dread of poisoning that existed at the time owing largely, no doubt, to the imperfect knowledge of toxic substances. Thus:

against poison put in Holy Water, betony, and after the small attorlothe drink the water and eat the worts, or as an antidote to any poison "boil the netherward part of Bishopwort and Lupin or the netherward part of Spring-wort, Everthroat, and clote in ale; give to drink frequently."

That powdered glass was supposed to be a poison is shown in a leechdom, for: "ana-worm which grows in a man. If the worm eat through to the outside and make a hole, take a drop of honey, drop it in the hole, then have broken glass ready ground, spread it on the hole, then as soon as the worm tastes it, he will die."

From this account of the anaworm it seems probable that maggots or bot-flies which usually infest cattle are referred to.

For the bite of an adder it is directed to wash a black snail in Holy Water and give it to the sick person to drink. For bronchial affections, or what is termed "lung disease, host or cough" treatment by inhalation is thus suggested: "Take snails, apple and brimstone and frankincense of all equally much, mingle with wax, lay on a hot stone and let the patient swallow the reek through a horn and afterwards eat three pieces of old lard or butter."

For a cough, there is quite an excellent leechdom the recipe for which is given as follows: "Boil in honey alone, horehound, add a little barley meal. Let the patient eat at night fasting and when thou givest him drink or brewit, give it him hot."

Hemiplegia was known to the Anglo-Saxon leeches as the "Half-dead disease" and is described as that which "comes on the right side of the body, or the left where the sinews are powerless and are afflicted with a slippery and thick humour, evil, thick and mickle". The treatment consisted in blood-letting, warmth and a purging wort-drink and rubbing in a salve composed of old salt grease, some horse-marrow, goose or hen's fat and good worts.

The method of treatment for typhus fever, or "lent addle" as it is termed in the leechdoms, was by incantation accompanied by medicine, which consisted of a drink composed of "Feverfue" the herb, "ram's fall" (*Menyanthes trifoliata*), fennel and waybread.

Let a man sing many masses over the worts, souse them with ale and Holy Water, boil very thoroughly. Let the person drink a great cupfull as hot as he may, before the disorder will be on him; say the names of the four gospellers and a charm and a prayer. Again, a divine prayer: "Thine hand vexeth, Thine hand vexeth."

Liver troubles were evidently common and receive considerable attention. Thus it is stated:

For all liver diseases and of its nature, increment and of the six things which work the liver pain and curing of all these, the first is swelling that is puffing up of the liver; the second the bursting of the swelling; the third is wound of the liver, the fourth is a burning heat with sensitiveness and with a sore swelling; the fifth, a hardening of the maw; the sixth, is a hardening of the liver without soreness.

Following a description of the organ, it is recommended for a swelling of the liver to let blood from a vein on the left side then, after a bath, a salve of oil and rue, dill and marche. This was to be applied on wool "swathed up fast" for about three nights. For an abcess of the liver "when the purulent swelling bursteth", warm and fresh goat's milk should be given to the patient.

A strange cure for a man possessed of devils is thus given in the leechdoms. For "fiend, sick man or demoniac, when a devil possesses the man or controls him from within with disease". The drink is to be drunk out of a church bell.

It consisted of githrife, cynoglossum, yarrow, lupin, betony, attorlothe, caaock, flower-de-luce, fennel, church-lichen, lichen of Christ's mark or cross and lovage. "Work up the drink off clear ale, sing seven masses over the wort, add garlic and Holy Water and drop the drink into every drink which he will subsequently drink and let him sing the Psalm, *Beati immaculati* and *Exurgat* and *Salvum me fac deus*; then let him drink the drink out of a church bell and let the mass priest after the drink, sing this over him *Domine, sancte pater omnipotens*".

The religious element in connection with the administration of drugs is shown in a leechdom for the "Phrenzied":

Give bishopswort, lupin, bonewort, everfern (*Polypodium vulgare*) githrife and elecampane when day and night divide; then sing thou in the church litanies that is the names of hallows or saints and the Paternoster.

With the song go thou that thou mayst be near the worts and go thrice about them and when thou takest them, go to church with the same song and sing twelve masses over them and over all the drinks which belong to the disease in honour of the twelve apostles.

For epidemic diseases which were known to the Anglo-Saxons as "flying venom", both charms and religious rites were employed. Thus for every venomous swelling on a Friday, "churn butter which has been milked from a neat or hind all one colour and let it not be mingled with water. Sing over it nine times a litany and nine times the Paternoster and nine times this incantation, *A crae aecrae aerm aernem madre, aercume het aernem, aeradopice.*"

Again, among the charms recommended to be carried as a protection against smallpox is one consisting of the name of "St Nicasius" to be written on a piece of parchment: "St Nicasius had a small variola and asked of God that whoever should carry his name written . . . 'Oh St Nicasius, bishop and martyr, pray for me . . . a sinner and by thy intercession defend me from this disease'. "

Another charm mentions the name of Longinus, who according to tradition was the Roman soldier who pierced the side of Christ while on the Cross. It reads: "For a stitch, write a cross of Christ and sing thrice over the place these words and a Paternoster; *Longinus miles lancea ponxit Dominum et restitit sanguis et recessit dolor.*" This charm was also much favoured throughout the Middle Ages for healing wounds or for staunching blood and is found in the *Compendium of Medicine* of Gilbertus Anglicus.

As a cure for headache, the sufferer is recommended to take "the lower part of the cross-wort and put it on a red fillet and bind it round the forehead". Red, the colour of blood, was favoured by the Babylonians for their charms 2,000 years before the Anglo-Saxon period. They believed that a three-fold cord on which twice seven knots had been tied, when fastened round the head would banish headaches. Red was sacred to Thor, and in Eire farmers often tie a piece of red cloth round their cows' tails to prevent them from being ill-wished; while in the Highlands of Scotland, dairy maids sometimes carry a little cross made of rowan twigs with their red berries, bound together with red worsted in order to prevent the witches from injuring their cattle, or turning the milk sour.

In another leechdom for headache, it is directed to "Delve up way-bread without iron ere the rising of the sun and bind the roots about the head with cross-worts by a red fillet. He will soon be well." Yet another method of relieving the pain in the head, eye troubles, temptations of the fiend, for night visitors (goblins), for spring disease, nightmare, for fascinations and evil incantations, the sufferer is directed to seek in the maw of young swallows for some little stones. Thus we have the origin of the linseed poultice, which combined with the powdered bark of the slippery elm was commonly employed in domestic medicine down to the twentieth century.

Honey was generally employed for dressing wounds, and for this purpose was specially prepared by first warming before the fire and then mixing it with a little salt. Thus, the leechdom says: "For cleansing a wound take clean honey, warm it at the fire, then put in a clean vessel, add salt to it and stir it until it is the thickness of pottage. Smear the wound with it."

It is noticeable that cleanliness is specially enjoined throughout the operation, and the use of honey was thus recommended by Hippocrates and other early Greek physicians.

Operations were performed for abscess on the liver and harelip, and the actual cautery was extensively used by the Anglo-Saxon leech for many disorders, from gout to headache.

Bleeding was resorted to in cases of paralysis and special directions were laid down for the right seasons for "letting-blood".

Other references to surgery in the Anglo-Saxon leech books are not numerous but there is evidence that the use of splints was known, in a leechdom for a broken limb. For a salve:

if the shanks be broken it is directed to take bonewort (probably violet or pansy), pound it, pour the white of an egg out, mingle these together. Lay this salve on the broken limb and overlay with elm rind; apply a splint; again, always renew these till the limb be healed.

For the eyes when swollen, it is recommended to get "a live crab, put his eyes out and place him alive into water. Put the eyes upon the neck of the man who needs. He will soon be well."

This leechdom is interesting as the use of crabs' eyes as a curative agent survived until the eighteenth century when the small concretions, called the "eyes", found in crabs, were employed as external as well as internal remedies.

Chapter VIII

Anglo-Saxon Herb-Lore and Wort-Cunning

As far as our knowledge goes, the choice of the herbs and plants employed for curative purposes was due chiefly to some uncommon and striking property attributed to them in magic ritual and their action having been proved by actual use, they took their place as healing remedies. Thus, those having strong odours like valerian, rue, and sage, aroused curiosity on account of their powerful smell. In Greek mythology the herbs that produced delirium and death, such as mandrake and opium, were attributed to the divine witches, of whom Hecate and Circe were the chief and from tradition these plants and their properties passed into literature. Manuscripts on botany, first mere descriptions like those given by Theophrastus in the sixth century B.C., who alludes to 500 plants, were succeeded by illustrations for their identification, and the earliest of these dates from a little later than the first century of the Christian Era. It was written by Crateuas who not only collected but depicted the herbs and plants he described.

Then came the work of Pedanius Dioscorides (A.D. 40–90) who described 600 plants and herbs which were figured in a manuscript of the sixth century. This was followed by a Latin work based on Dioscorides, bearing the name of Apuleius about A.D. 400. The manuscript copy of the sixth century now in Leiden became the first printed herbal.

The Anglo-Saxon version of this work known as the *Herbarium of Apuleius Platonicus*, illustrated with drawings, dates from about the eleventh century and is now in the British Museum.

Early botany was inseparable from medicine and was largely influenced by superstition in the form of magic and astrology. The plants were believed to exercise a potent effect on vegetable life and certain kinds were only to be gathered when the Sun, Moon, or the planets were in certain positions. But under all the illusions of incantations, amulets and charms linked with astrology, there existed a real and sincere belief that rested mainly on a knowledge of herbs which had been proved from experience to be of value and benefit to suffering humanity.

The Anglo-Saxons drew their *materia medica* chiefly from the plants which grew around them and their knowledge of herb-lore, or wort-cunning as it has been called, which had come down to them from the earliest traditions of past ages, was considerable.

In their gardens they grew rue, hyssop, fennel, mustard, elecampane, celandine, lupin, flax, rosemary, coriander, savin, and many other worts, whose properties they had studied and whose virtues they had proved. Some were used when freshly gathered and others after they had been dried. From the latter we have the origin of the word drug derived from

the Anglo-Saxon word "drigan", to dry. Many of the herbs employed
by the Anglo-Saxon leeches 1,000 years ago are used in medical
practice today. Physicians of the twentieth century still prescribe
henbane, colchicum, camomile, marshmallow, horehound, white poppy,
hop, celandine, savin, rue, pennyroyal, marjoram, coriander, dill, fennel,
hellebore, foxglove, liquorice, elder, violet, dog-rose, serpentary, stavesacre,
and many others. On the other hand, some herbs which were regarded
by the Anglo-Saxons almost with veneration for their healing virtues,
are now almost forgotten, or but rarely used.

Betony, for instance, was credited with extraordinary virtues and
recommended for at least twenty-nine diseases. It was a magical herb
and worn as an amulet against magic and ghosts. Vervain (*Verbena
officinalis*), too, was regarded as a magical plant and was known to the
Anglo-Saxons as "Ash-throat", the dried root being used as a charm when
suspended from the neck to heal strumous ulcerations. "Against all
poisons", enjoins a leechdom, "take dust of this same wort, it is said
sorcerers use it for their crafts." Its reputation has survived to the
present day, for only a few years ago a child was brought to a hospital
in East Norfolk suffering from strumous ulcerations, with a charm formed
from verbena roots hung round its neck.

The flower of the camomile, still used as a fomentation and taken
internally when infused in boiling water, was regarded as a herb of magic.
It was taken as a tonic and as an aromatic and stomachic in cases of
jaundice, thrush and ague.

The elder, endowed with magical properties, was universally esteemed
and many supernatural traditions are associated with it. It was one of
the sacred trees of Scandinavia and the Danes believed that Hylda-moer
(*elder mother*), dwelt in the tree and that her permission had to be asked
before any of the branches could be cut off. In Lower Saxony, the
woodman, before lopping it, had to go on his knees and pray, "Lady Elder
give me some of thy wood, then I will give thee some of mine when it
grows in the forest." In Sweden, no injury was allowed to be done to the
elder, and pregnant women were told to kiss it before their confinement.

There was an aversion to the wood being used for making cradles, in case
the "Lady Elder" might take revenge on the baby which was laid in one.

The ancient Prussian god of the earth was supposed to live under an
elder, and it was believed to act as a protection against witches. The
healing properties attributed to it were many and it was used in cases
of epilepsy as an amulet, and for transference of disease. In Denmark
it had a reputation for curing ague and toothaches, and in Eire a twig
cut into nine parts and threaded was worn to ward off epileptic attacks.
It was given internally for dropsy, jaundice, green-sickness and externally
when mixed with bull's fat for tumours, scalds, burns, bites of mad dogs,
and for swellings. The berries were regarded as sudorific and diuretic,
and useful in urinary troubles, gravel and stone.

To setewale, the old English name for valerian, was attributed the power of inspiring love and it was given internally as a diuretic in jaundice, rickets and disease of the nervous system.   Of it Chaucer wrote:

Ther springen herbes grete and smale
The Licoris or any Setewale.

Among the peasantry in the north of England it was so venerated, that "no broths, pottage or physical meats are worth anything if Setewale were not at an end", and there was a well-known couplet:

They that will have their heale
Must put Setewale in their keale.

The Anglo-Saxon name for the common houseleek was "sinfull" and when made into an ointment it had a reputation for healing bedsores, for which purpose it is still used in some parts of the country.
The leechdom reads:

For all gatherings of the ill-humour from the body take this wort which is named semper vivum and by another name sinfull and lard and bread and coriander, pound all together in the manner in which thou wouldst work a poultice and lay it on the sore.

The Anglo-Saxon leeches recognized the narcotic properties of henbane, which they called "hennebelle" or "Belene" and for sore ears they recommended sufferers to "take juice of this same wort and warm it and drop it in the ear; it, in a wonderful manner puts to flight the sore of the ears and also likewise though there be worms in, it kills them."   It is not surprising, owing to its ancient reputation, that they used it to relieve toothache; the leechdom says: "For sore of the teeth, take roots of the same wort, seethe in strong wine and sip it so warm and hold it in the mouth; soon it will heal the sore of the teeth."
They were also aware of the demulcent properties of horehound (*marrubium vulgare*), and administered it for lung diseases and colds, in the same way it is used today as a domestic remedy for bronchial troubles.   Thus we read:

for colds in the head and in case a man breaks heavily (makes great efforts to clear his throat of phlegm) take this wort, which the Romans call marrubium and also the English call horehound, seethe it in water, give it to them that break heavily; it will heal them wonderfully.   For Lung disease; take this same wort seethe it in honey, give it to swallow he will be wonderfully healed.

The healing properties of the medicated bath were known also, and recommended as follows:

For ache of loins and sores of the thighs take this same wort, pulegium and pepper of either alike much be weight; pound them together and when thou be in the bath smear them where it most troubleth.

Chapter IX

THE HEALING ART IN ANCIENT WALES

As early as the year 430 B.C. there is evidence that the art of healing was cultivated and encouraged in Wales and it is thus mentioned in the laws of *Dyvnwal Moelmud*, which date from about that period. Medicine, commerce and navigation are therein called the three civil arts, each of which had a peculiar corporate privilege. The art of healing is further said to have been included among the "nine rural arts known and practised by the ancient Cymry, before they became possessed of cities and sovereignty, or before the time of Prydain ab Aedd Mawr", about a 1,000 years before the Christian era.

At that time, it is stated that the priests and teachers were the *Gwyddoniaid*, or men of knowledge, who combined the healing of the body with the teaching of religion. To them the inception of the healing art in Wales is attributed. They studied the arts of astrology, theology and medical botany and from that knowledge treated the sick and afflicted. It was during the time of *Prydain* that the *Gwyddoniaid* became divided into three orders which consisted of the Druids, the Bards and the Ovates, each of which had its peculiar duties as well as privileges. Healing, astrology and religion were intimately associated with the Druids who reverenced the Moon and appealed to it in time of difficulty or trouble. They believed in its influence on man as well as inanimate objects and plant life and were adepts in magic, especially in divination. The most solemn rite of divining was carried out by accurately examining the entrails of sacrificed victims and judging from their appearance, whether the gods were favourable to their desires. They divined also from the fall and convulsions of the limbs of the animals and from the flow of blood immediately after the victim had received the fatal blow.

The Ovates studied the natural sciences, "save when meditation gives place to holy rites; then, in the grove, each order has its rank and station", while the Bards were proficient in music, poetry and oratory.

It is thought probable that the Druids acquired some knowledge of healing from Greek sources through the Phoenicians who traded with Britain, for in later times the name of Hippocrates is mentioned and his works were highly esteemed by the physicians of *Myddfai* who flourished about the sixth century.

To their influence much of the folk-lore of early British medicine may be traced. In their practice they called both magic and religion to their aid and endowed many herbs and plants with mysterious properties, while they also had a belief in astrology. They recognized the value of preventive treatment and, as a protection from fevers, they anointed the body with vervain and attributed to that herb the power to procure friendship and to obtain all the heart desired. To ensure its magical properties, it was necessary to gather it with certain ceremonies at the rise of the dog-star, when both the sun and moon were beneath the horizon. Before uprooting the herb, it was necessary to propitiate the earth by a libation of honey and during the whole operation, the left hand only was to be used.

After being lifted from the earth, the herb had to be waved aloft and then the leaves, flowers and roots dried separately in the shade. The magical properties of vervain were recognized in Welsh witchcraft, as it formed one of the ingredients in the mystical cauldron of Ceridwen.

Further, mention must also be made of "All heal", or the mistletoe, so highly venerated by the Druids, for nothing was held more sacred. It was only to be approached in the most reverent and devout manner, for they believed that whatever grew on the oak tree was sent from Heaven and was a sign that the Deity had made a choice of the tree. Its gathering was made the occasion of a great ceremony which always took place on the sixth day of the moon. The proceedings in the oak grove have often been described. Briefly, after preparing the sacrifice and feast under the tree, two white bulls were brought up, whose horns had been bound for the first time. The Arch-Druid robed in white then mounted the tree and with a golden sickle cut the mistletoe which was received in a white cloth. The victims were then sacrificed and prayers offered to the deity to render his gift favourable to those to whom it was distributed. Mistletoe was believed to be especially valuable in cases of sterility and to render fruitful every animal to whom a decoction of it was given, while it was also regarded as a protection against all poisons.

Another plant highly esteemed by the Druids was hedge hyssop (*Lycopodium Selago*) which, like mistletoe, was gathered with great care. Nothing made of iron was allowed to touch it, nor was the bare hand thought worthy of that honour. A peculiar vesture or sagus was employed by the right hand and it was further necessary that this vesture should be holy and that it should have been taken from some sacred person privately, and with the left hand only. The gatherer had to be a Druid and clothed in white, whose bare feet had been washed in pure water. He had first to offer a sacrifice of bread and wine before proceeding to gather the plant, after which it was carried from the spot where it grew in a clean new napkin.

In the *Kadir Taliesin*, the *selago* is called "the gift of God", and in modern Welsh is still termed *Gras Dawor*, "the grace of God".

It was used in the treatment of eye-troubles, and as a charm was carried on the person as a protection against misfortune. Marsh-wort, or *Samolus*, was believed to possess supernatural powers and according to the Druids was able to ward off and cure certain diseases,

There can be little doubt that the Druids studied the properties of many plants and were skilful in the treatment of some diseases; but how far their medical knowledge extended, there is but slight evidence to show. Borlase asserts that they had a knowledge of anatomy, based on the bodies of living men and animals—but we have no evidence to support this statement. Their system of medical treatment, apart from superstitious rites, was distinctly rational. They first devised the means most likely to operate and then called in the aid of religion, which was largely influenced by the peculiar beliefs of the time.

For internal diseases and chronic disorders, they appear chiefly to have combined the use of the cold bath, exercise and change of place with the administration of herbs and plants. To these must be added drinking from certain wells, the waters of which they believed to possess special healing properties. They devised general directions for the preservation of health in the form of short maxims or aphorisms commending cheerfulness, temperance, exercise and early rising.

Following the Druidical period came the references to healing in Wales made by Taliesin, who was chief of the Bards in the sixth century. Taliesin was something of a physiologist and held that "there are three intractable substantial organs of the body viz: the liver, the kidneys and the heart". Further, there were three intractable membranes; the dura mater, the peritoneum, and the urinary bladder. "There are three tedious complaints," he continues, "disease of the knee-joints, disease of the substance of the ribs and phthisis, for when purulent matter has formed in one of these, it is not known when it will get well." Between the sixth and the tenth centuries little is known, for the country was torn by feuds and wars until the time of *Howel Dha* or Howel the Good, who lived about the year A.D. 930. He prescribed a code of laws in some of which references are made to the practioners of medicine of the time. Mention is made of the office and privileges of a "mediciner" or physician to the Royal Court and to his allowances and fees. His duties chiefly consisted in administering medicines gratuitously to all within the palace and to the head of the household.

He was entitled to receive the following fees "For applying a tent—24 pence ; for an application of red ointment—12 pence ; for an application of herbs to a swelling—4 legal pence, and for letting-blood—4 pence". He was free to travel the road and out of the road along with the messenger of the sick, and entitled to take another's horse to procure aid for a person in danger, without being required to make amends.

In the early part of the thirteenth century when Rhys Gryg, who was a great soldier, flourished, he had a domestic physician named Rhiwallon attached to his suite, assisted by his three sons, Cadwgan, Gruffydd, and Einion. They lived at Myddfai in Carmarthenshire. Under the patronage of Rhys Gryg these physicians made a collection of recipes applicable for healing various diseases of the body, "as a record of their skill, lest no one should be found with the requisite knowledge as they

THE HEALING ART IN ANCIENT WALES 63

were". Many of these recipes had been handed down by word of mouth from one generation to another since the time of Howel the Good and others, there is little doubt, are of an earlier period. The "Physicians of Myddfai", however, put them into writing for the first time and so this early record of medicine has come down to us today.

This interesting manuscript consists of 188 paragraphs dealing with anatomy, physiology, pathology, medicine and surgery, from which may be gathered a knowledge of the healing of the time. The first part deals with the treatment of various diseases such as pneumonia, fevers, ascites, peritonitis and others. In surgery, the general practice seems to have been to attempt the removal of any tumour or diseased condition, first by drugs given internally and, when these failed, to resort to the knife or the cautery. Lithotomy and trepanning are specially mentioned and the ligaturing of haemorrhoids was practised.

The following are examples of some of the aphorisms recorded:

There are three bones in a man's body which when fractured will never unite again and neither of these exists when a man is born, namely, a tooth, the knee-pan, and the os frontis. The physicians three master difficulties are a wounded mammary gland, a wounded knee-joint and a wounded lung.

For medical treatment 175 plants, herbs, flowers, and roots are mentioned including foxglove, poppy, valerian, peppermint and broom, all of which continue to be used in medicine today. These were administered in the form of infusions, decoctions, pills, or ointments. Besides the remedies, a number of other recipes are included. Thus for eczema, an ointment of honey of ivy, fox-marrow and white resin is recommended. Others are as follows:

For deafness: ram's urine, eel's bile and the juice of ash expressed and placed in the ears. For a punctured wound: take the dung of a bull and apply thereto. To induce sleep: take poppy heads bruised in wine. For falling sickness: burn a goat's horn, directing the smoke upon the patient. He will forthwith rise. Before he has risen from the ground, apply dog's gall upon his head and the disease will not attack him any more.

As a measure of cleansing the body, an enema or emetic was recommended to be employed every month.

Rhiwallon and his sons, usually called the "Physicians of Myddfai", were granted lands and privileges by Rhys Gryg, Lord of Llandovery, for their maintenance "in the practice of the art of healing so they should benefit all those who sought their help". The descendants of this historic medical family continued to practise medicine in Wales without a break until the middle of the eighteenth century and the last of the family died in 1743.

A further light is thrown on the history of healing in ancient Wales by another manuscript, said to have been compiled by Howel the physician, "who was a son of Rhys, who was a son of Llewellyn whose father was Philip the physician, a lineal descendant of Einion". It is believed to have been written about the end of the fifteenth century and is divided into 815 paragraphs. A large proportion of the work is devoted to dietetics with directions for the regulation of diet in health and disease. It mentions emetics, purgatives, suppositories and cordials, while bleeding is recommended if necessary. The work begins with a number of conjectures as to the exciting causes of various disorders of which the following may be taken as examples:

Fever is excited by excess of heat and cold. Eruptive poison in the blood or tumours are produced by irregularities of eating and drinking; obstructions in the stomach, veins or other hollow vessels of the body, so that the food and drink, blood or humours cannot pass on as usual. A boil, carbuncle or plague are occasioned by the entrance of poison into the system. From these proceed all fevers and diseases incident to the human body and by the aid of active remedies they are cured.

Gout is attributed to a "desiccation of humours into a calcareous earth". Paralysis, to the blood becoming sluggish or viscid in the veins, while brain-fever is stated to be occasioned by water under the fontanelle pressing upon the brain or membranes. Eight hundred plants, herbs, roots and flowers are mentioned, many of which are used in medicine today. Among inorganic bodies alluded to are copper sulphate, alum, mercury, sulphur, antimony and lead, while a number of animal substances such as the fat of boars, cats and geese are embodied in the applications.

Among the curious remedies recommended are the following:

For worms in children: take the child's hair, cut it as small as you can and mix as much as will stand on a golden crown with the pulp of a roasted apple. With this you will kill the worm.

To extract a tooth without pain: take some newts, by some called lizards, and those nasty beetles which are found in ferns in the summer time. Calcine them in an iron pot and make a powder thereof. Wet the forefinger of the right hand and insert it in the powder and apply it to the tooth frequently, refraining from spitting it off, when the tooth will fall away without pain. It is proven.

For pain in the eye: take the gall of a hare, of a hen, of an eel and of a stag with fresh urine and honeysuckle leaves and then inflict a wound upon an ivy tree, mix the gum that exudes from the tree therewith, boiling it quickly and straining it through a fine linen cloth. When cold, insert a little thereof in the corner of the eye and it will be a wonder if he who makes use of it does not see stars in mid-day, in consequence of the virtues of this remedy.

For Stranguary and Stone: take the blood and skin of a hare and make a powder thereof; mix with the cyder of red-rinded apples, mead or beer and drink it with either. Let the patient drink this only. If you should wish to prove this, take a spoonful of the powder with water and put it in a hole made in an acid stone and by next day it will have certainly dissolved it.

Here is a recipe for an ointment for general use:

Take gander's fat, the fat of a male cat, and red boar's fat and three drams of blue wax (cupriated wax), water-cress, wormwood, the red straw-berry plant and primrose. Boil them in pure spring water and when boiled stuff a gander with them and roast them at a distance from the fire. The grease issuing from it should be carefully kept in a pot. It is a valuable ointment for all kinds of aches in a man's body and is like one that was formerly made by Hippocrates. It is proved.

An interesting addition to this manuscript is a list of the "essentials of a physician". These are:

I. A lancet to bleed or open an abcess; also a knife somewhat larger.
II. A steel or silver spatula to spread a plaster.
III. A pipe and a bladder to inject to the urinary organs or Rectum.
IV. His plasters, his ointments, his pills, his powders, his potions, carefully preserved to meet any demand or occasion.
V. A garden of trees and herbs where such herbs, shrubs and trees as do not everywhere grow naturally may be kept cultivated and where foreign trees and plants, which require shelter and culture before they will thrive in Wales, may be grown.

Finally, some sound advice is offered to the young physician before starting to practise. He is exhorted to submit to a careful preliminary training and a final examination, so that he "as physician may be skilled in the judgement and science of the wise and skilful physicians who have preceded him". He is to be kind, gentle, mild, meek, intelligent, wise, and gentlemanly in act and deed, in word and conduct, being careful not to shame those whom he has to examine, particularly when he has to examine women. He should always have his case of instruments, emetics and antidotes about him in case of need. He should be constitutionally and habitually devotional, so that the blessing of God may be upon him and what he does, and that he may be conscientious to do what is right and beneficial in the practice of his art.

These were the ethics laid down for the practitioner of the healing art in Wales, in the fifteenth century.

Chapter X

THE HEALING ART IN ANCIENT EIRE

IT has been stated that "the practitioners of the healing art in Eire are the legitimate heirs of what has been termed the oldest professional culture of which there is record in the living language of any European nation". Certainly there is considerable evidence, from a number of early manuscripts, of the high character which distinguished early Celtic medicine, and although some of it is in legendary or mythical form, it is not unworthy of consideration. Like other races of antiquity, the Irish had their great traditional physicians. The one of whom we have the fullest record was Diancecht, who is mentioned by Cormac MacCuilleanain in A.D. 831–903 and also in some manuscripts of the eighth century.

His name signifies "Vehement Power" and wonderful stories are recorded of his skill in healing and it is probable that he was a Druid of profound knowledge and ability. The earliest account of his healing is mentioned in connection with the Battle of Moytuma, fought in the County of Sligo between the Firbolgs and the Tuatha De Danaans, where it is stated that he prepared a bath of herbs and plants in the rear of the contending forces, into which the wounded were plunged and are said to have come out healed, owing to the action of the *Slan Ici*, regarded as a sovereign remedy for all diseases.

In the great battle said to have been fought about 487 B.C., in which the older Firbolgian rule in Eire was overthrown by the Tuatha De Danaan race, King Nuada lost his arm and the physician Diancecht staunched the blood and dressed the wound. Miach, the son of Diancecht, had an artificial hand wrought in silver for the monarch, who afterwards bore the name long remembered in history of *Nuada of the Silver Hand*. This substitute, says an early Gaelic chronicler, "was so exquisitely fashioned and with such mobility i1 every joint and finger, as though it was the natural hand".

The same chronicler goes on to state that "twenty seven years after, in a conflict known as the second Battle of Moytura, King Nuada of the Silver Hand fell, and according to tradition, Diancecht, who was present with his son and daughter, Airmedh, prepared a great healing bath, with the principal herbs and plants of Erin and over it pronounced incantations during the contest. Soldiers wounded in the fight were at once plunged into the bath and when they emerged were whole and fit, and able to fight the enemy again and again."

Another tradition in which the healing-bath plays a part comes from the period after the Milesian invasion, when Crionthan, the Governor of Leinster, applied for help to his northern allies the Picts and they sent

66

him one Trosdale, a famous Druid, who was renowned for his skill in healing. Accordingly, the historian states, "at the next battle which was fought on the banks of the Slaney, Trosdale arranged a bath of milk at the rear of the army, into which the wounded soldiers were plunged". He was also credited with the power of making a bath of "the milk of white-faced cows, which would render the body of him who bathed in it invulnerable to the wounds of poisoned arrows".

An interesting story is related of the palaces of Tara and Emaniah, to which a building was attached called "the House of the Crimson Branch". Near it was the Royal Hospital called the *Bearg*, or the "House of Sorrow", where the sick and wounded were lodged and attended with special care.

Several early historians record that in the second century B.C., Josina, who became King of Scotland, was educated in Erin and wrote a treatise on the "Virtues and Powers of Herbs" the knowledge of which he gathered in that country, where he was instructed by the physicians.

At that period many of the leeches took apprentices, who lived in their houses and were instructed in the mysteries of their art. For this instruction a fee was paid which included their keep, clothes and lodging, covering the period while "at their learning". We are told also, that the leech, like his prototype of later times, carried a bag which was called *Les* and a leech without his medicine bag was termed a "Fer-bolg". The Liaig or Leea, (radically the same as the old English leech), ranked with the higher craftsmen and the workers in the precious metals and belonged to the Ollavesor, the highest order of their particular caste. According to the *Book of Glendalough*, the physician had a separate seat assigned to him at the royal banqueting table and by the Brehon laws was entitled to his food and that of four of his pupils or apprentices at the house of his patient while the latter was being healed but "at the cost of the transgressor, if the wounds were caused maliciously". If a man was maliciously or accidentally wounded he was removed to the house of a leech, who examined his wounds and gave certificates as to their character, upon which depended the legal liabilities of the person who had inflicted the wounds. If the leech thought he could cure the wounded man, he gave security for his proper treatment and in return received security for his fees, which varied according to the rank or status of the patient. Thus, for healing a bishop, the leech was entitled to receive 42 cows and so downwards through various grades to the "houseless, homeless man, the houseboy or slave" for whom the reduced fee of two cows was deemed sufficient.

For every cow killed for his chieftain's family, the kidneys were assigned to the "physitian" and for every sheep, the shoulders were given to the "astronomer".

The Celtic physicians gave due attention to cleanliness, and appreciated the value of pure water and free ventilation, when treating the sick or wounded. The leech's house, under the provision of the Brehon laws, was the appointed place where the sick were to be treated until the fifteenth century, when it is stated that wounded men, including the chiefs of Septs or tribes, were frequently taken to the house of the leech to be healed. These houses were ordered to be built either on the bank of a running stream, or with such a stream passing through the precincts of the house. They were ordered to be provided with four doors, with the object of allowing all that took place within to be open to inspection and, further, to permit one door being left open whichever way the wind blew.

Baths played an important part in medical treatment for the cure of rheumatism and skin diseases, and the water of certain wells was believed to cure those suffering from epilepsy and nervous troubles. Such was the well of the Virgin *St Athracht* or *Attracta* at Tuberaraght, near the shore of Lough Talt. Cormac's glossary mentions the old *foth rucud*, the bath used for "Bathing sick persons, and it is for lepers it is oftenest practised."

Epilepsy was called *galar poil* or "Paul's Sickness", from a belief that St. Paul, after one of his visions, had a seizure of the disease. There is also a record that St. Gamin of Inez Celtra died in A.D. 653 of *teine brurr*, "fire of swelling", which is descriptive of St Anthony's Fire or erysipelas. According to Zeuss's glossary of the eighth century, cancer was expressed by two words *tuthle* and *ailse* and diarrhoea was called *brunnech*. A pestilence or plague was denoted by several words, those mostly used being "tamor" and "tamp"; in later times "plaig" was the name applied to plague.

Ancient records show that in Celtic times, Eire was visited by several plagues, and the first of these is said to have destroyed a whole colony of the Tuatha De Danaans at Howth, in the year 118 B.C. There was another visitation in A.D. 554 and again in 576, when it was called "lepra". The coincidence of this period with that of the great plague of Justinian which began in A.D. 540 and ravaged Europe for nearly half a century, leaves no doubt as to its identity.

In the year A.D. 946, a strange disease which was called *Readhibudh* or "Furious Death" broke out and attacked both men and cattle. It was generally ascribed to magic and appears to have been contagious. From the *Book of the Four Masters*, A.D. 986, we learn that "Druidical or Magic Sickness" caused by demons, ravaged the eastern part of Eire and "caused mortality of men plainly before peoples eyes". Again in 1084, a great pestilence broke out, which is said to have killed a fourth of the men in Eire. It began in the south and spread over the country. It is thus recorded by a chronicler:

The cause of this pestilence was due to demons which came out of the northern hills, to wit three battalions and in each battalion there were thirty and ten hundred and two and as Oengus Oc, the son of Dagda, related to Gilla Lugan, who used to haunt the fairy mound every year of "semain night". Even so they were seen by Gilla and wherever their heat or fury reached there their venom was taken. For there was a sword of fire out of the gullet

of each of them and every one of them was as high as the clouds of heaven.
So that is the cause of the pestilence.

During the fourteenth century Eire was visited by the "black death"
and also by a scrofulous disease which attacked the skin and joints. It
was known as *fiolun*, a name which was sometimes applied to scurvy or,
it has been suggested, may have been applied to the form of the disease
known in Britain as the "King's Evil".

Leprosy appeared in Eire at an early date and became prevalent in
the sixth century when it was sometimes known as *clam* or *Brosc* but
usually as *lobor*. St. Patrick is said to have healed lepers and among
the accounts of miracles performed by other saints and healers leprosy
is often mentioned.

It is evident from early records that medicated baths were frequently
employed in the treatment of disease, as instanced in the bath used
by Diancecht to heal the wounded after the Battle of Moytura, and again
by Trosdale at the Battle of the Slaney. They were also used in a
certain skin disease and in *Cormac's Glossary* reference is made to bathing
for sick persons.

Sweating-houses, or hot vapour baths, were used by leeches in parts
of ancient Eire and the remains of these structures, known as *Tigh
nalluis*, are still to be found in the northern parts of the country. They
were built entirely of stone and were from five to seven feet long inside,
with a very low door through which to creep. They were usually built
remote from habitations and near a pool of water. When about to be
used, a great fire of turf was kindled inside until the interior became like
an oven, after which the ashes were swept out and the patient, after
wrapping himself in a blanket, crept inside and sat down. When the door
had been sealed he was supposed to remain there until profuse perspiration was produced. Immediately on emerging he plunged into cold
water, after which he was briskly rubbed until a warm glow was
obtained.

In surgery, there is evidence that certain operations were performed
such as trepanning, an account of which was written in A.D. 637 concerning a young Irish chieftain named Cennfaelad, whose skull was
fractured by a blow from a sword. It is stated that the "injured portions
of the brain and skull were removed, which so cleared his intellect and
improved his memory, that he became a great scholar, and this after
twelve months treatment at the school of *Tomregan* in County Cavan,
where he was cured". The legend accounts for the sudden improvement
in his condition by stating that his "brain of forgetfulness" was removed.

In the record of the death of King Concobar Macnessa it is stated that
"the surgeon stitched up the wound with thread of gold, because his
hair was gold-coloured".

It appears that wounds were usually treated with decoctions or
poultices of herbs mixed with honey, similar methods being used for

broken limbs, and there is a reference to splints for fractures and amputation is advised for gangrenous limbs. Venesection and cupping were practised and an operation for hare-lip is described. Cupping or scarification was performed by the leeches with an iron instrument called a *gipne* and a case is mentioned in the Acallamh, where a physician named Bebinn had the venom drawn from an old unhealed wound on Cailte's leg, by two fedans or tubes, by which means the wound was eventually healed. It is stated that these were the fedans of Nudarn's daughter Binn from which it may be inferred that they were something more than simple tubes and were a special contrivance designed by Binn for the operation. Binn, we are told, was a woman physician who also treated Cailte for a disorder by the administration of five successive emetics which she prepared by steeping certain herbs in water and so restored him to health.

Mention must be made of the "healing stones" in which great faith was placed as curative agents and which were carefully preserved. One was kept in the family of the Fitzgeralds from an early period. The stone was sometimes called the *clock-omra*, or murrain stone, as it was usually employed to cure murrain in cattle and hydrophobia in human beings. A similar talisman was treasured in the MacCarthy family; and another healing-stone was preserved in a church near Buckross in Donegal, to which the sick were brought, on account of its healing properties.

Richardson in his *Folly of Pilgrimage* tells us of a wooden statue of a woman carved and painted, in the possession of the house of O'Herbebys, which was sent for by the sick people in the locality in order to cure them. Offerings of sheep were sometimes made to it and sacrificed with peculiar ceremonies.

Large stones with holes on their surface called *brash*, or "Bullan Stones", in which water had accumulated in the cavities, were visited by persons suffering from rheumatism who would place their knees in the larger holes, at the same time offering gifts in the smaller ones. The water found in the holes was also said to be efficacious in eye-ailments.

Much superstition surrounded childbirth, and pregnant women were taught to kneel before the *brash*, or "Bullan Stones", and to pray for safe deliverance; there is, however, record of the Caesarian operation being performed on Eithne, the daughter of Eochaidh Feildlech.

As might be expected, Eire was rich in herbs to which healing properties were attributed, and magic and charms entered very largely into the treatments prescribed by the physician. Diancecht is said to have recognized fourteen disorders of the stomach, for which he administered mostly vegetable remedies. One of his recipes known as "Diancecht's porridge" has been handed down and is said to be the oldest known in Eire. It was for the relief of "colds, phlegm, sore-throats, and the presence of evil things in the body", such as worms, and it advised hazel buds, dandelions, chickweed and wood-sorrel, to be boiled together with oatmeal and to be taken morning and evening, when the cold or other trouble will disappear. The use of a poultice of yellow baywort was also recommended to be tied round the neck for "throat-cats" or sore throats. Diancecht also prescribed "white frankincense beaten up with white wine to restore the memory", and an excellent cordial, to be made up with one part of gentian and two parts of centuary bruised well together and mixed with water to drink, while saffron he considered a most notable tonic.

Probably the earliest of the Irish manuscripts on healing and medicine is the one in the library of the convent of St. Gall in Switzerland, which is said to date from the eighth century. It consists of prayers, charms and incantations for the healing of various diseases, including one for long life, others for headache and diseases of the urine. For the pain in the head the invocation is to the "eye of Isaia, the tongue of Soloman, the mind of Benjamin, the heart of St. Paul and the faith of Abraham", ending with *Sanctus, sanctus, Dominus, Deus Sabaoth.* Added to this:

say this thing every day for thy head against headache; after repeating it place thy spittle upon thy palm and put it on thy temples and at the back of thy head and say the Pater thrice thereupon and draw a cross with thy spittle on the top of thy head and on thy head also draw the form of the letter U.

Another manuscript of the tenth century records Diancecht's "Elixir of Life" which he bequeathed to his people, by which everything to which it was applied should be made whole. It reads:

A preservation for the dead, the living, for the want of sinews, for the tongue tied, for swelling in the head, of wounds from iron, of burning from fire, of the bite of the hound; it preventeth the lassitude of old age, cures the decline, the rupture of the blood vessels, takes away the virulence of the festering sore, the poignancy of grief, the fever of the blood—they cannot contend with it—he to whom it shall be applied shall be made whole.

The religious influence in these monastic manuscripts is shown in another ancient book entitled *Medicina Antiqua* which begins:

The age of the Lord when this book was made was a thousand and three hundred years and twice twenty years and twelve years more. The book was finished in the year that Shane Oge, the son of Cu-Aithne was killed and it was written in the house of the son of Dermod O'Meaghere. These things are gentle, sweet, profitable, of little evil which have often been testified by us and our instructors. . . . I implore every doctor at the beginning of the work (of curing) that he remember the Father of Health (God) that the work is finished prosperously and let him not be in mortal sin and let him beseech the patient not to be so either. And let him implore the Heavenly Father above all, who is the Physician and the "Balsam-Giver" above all, for the diseased to end his work prosperously and to save him from shame and discredit at that time.

The acquaintance of the early physicians of Eire with Greek and other classical literature is evidenced in several versions of the works of Hippocrates and Galen, which were written in the eighth century.

Another source of information on the practice of healing at an early period in Eire are the books of the hereditary physicians, who were attached to the great families where medicine and healing was distinctly an hereditary office, descending from father to son. These practitioners kept books where they recorded the recipes and prescriptions of their predecessors, which were believed to be proved by experience. Some of the recipes were copied from other early documents, as may be judged from the introduction to one written in the year 1352. It begins:

May the merciful God have mercy on us all. I have here collected practical rules from several works for the honour of God for the benefit of the Irish people and for the love of my friends and kindred. I have translated them from Latin into Gaelic, from the authority of Galen in the last book of his *Practical Panteon* and from the book of the *Prognostics of Hippocrates*. These are things gentle, sweet, profitable and of little evil, things which have often been tested by us and our instructors. I pray God to bless those doctors who will use this book and I lay it on their souls as a conjuration, that they extract not sparingly from it; that they fail not on account of neglecting the practical rules herein contained, and more especially that they do their duty in cases where they receive no pay on account of the poverty of the patients. I implore every docor that before he begins his treatment, he prays God the Father of Healing to the end that his work may be finished prosperously.

About 1600, when Camden wrote, it is stated that there was no territory in Eire without its hereditary physician, the majority of whom were men of ability and learning. Although the practice of physic and surgery was hereditary in families it never descended in regular succession, only the most distinguished and eminent of the tribe being called upon. Among the earliest of these were the O'Lees. Lee or MacLee was the name of the hereditary physician of Brian Boroihme about 1055 and the O'Lees became the hereditary doctors of the O'Flaherties of West Connaught. The manuscript book of the O'Lees was written on vellum and dated about 1443. It is partly in Latin and partly in Gaelic. The pages are curiously ruled and divided, so that the script forms patterns resembling astrological figures. It is a complete system of medicine, treating among other matters of:

putrid fevers, abcesses and pustules, of wounds, poisons and hydrophobia, of affections of the brain and other parts; of the period of life and the time of the year when certain diseases become common and of the temperature or cardinal point that influences them.

The O'Hickeys were the hereditary physicians of the O'Briens of Thomond, Co. Clare, the MacBriens of Arra, the MacNamaras of Clare, and the O'Kennedys of Ormond. The name of Hickey, like that of Liagh, indicated their calling, being the Irish word signifying "embalming", or "curing". Their book, written about 1303, is a translation of Gordon's *Lily of Medicine*.

The book of the O'Shiels was transcribed in 1657 from an earlier manuscript and consists partly of translations from ancient authors, and partly of dissertations on the medicinal properties of herbs. The O'Shiels were the hereditary physicians of the M'Coughlans of Devlin and of the MacMahons of Oriel. The book of the MacAnlega was transcribed in 1512 from an earlier copy by Melaghlin MacAnlega, who says it was lent to him by one of the O'Mulconrys. The name MacAnlega means the son of the physician and the book is a commentary on ancient classical writers on medicine. The O'Nealans were also hereditary physicians to the Dalgass or Militia of Thomond, from which came the old Irish saying that "if a person was too ill to be cured, the physician of the Royal Militia could not raise him".

The reputation of these hereditary Irish healers long outlived that of most other professions and continued down to the seventeenth century.

In ancient Eire nearly all diseases were attributed to the *Meillteorcacht* or "fairy strokes", a belief similar to that which prevailed among many primitive peoples who attributed disease to demons or evil-spirits.

Sir William Wilde, who made a list of diseases known to the Irish from the early manuscripts, records seventy-five which were known to the Celtic leeches. These include smallpox, known as *bolgoch* or pustule disease, and consumption known as *angobracht* or *anbobracht*, which according to *Cormac's Glossary* is a person without *bracht* or fat; in the Brehon Code "one who has no juice or strength". Diseases of the bladder or kidneys were called *galar fuail*, literally disease of the urine, ophthalmia, *galar sula* or disease of the eye, and the word *crupan* is still used in some parts of Eire to describe a paralytic affection of cattle. There is a record of an early Irish king called *Aed Baridnech* or *Aed* of the "Shivering disease" which was probably ague, while palsy was known by the words *crith* (shaking) and *lam* (a hand).

The ancient code known as the Brehon Laws which are contained in the *Seanachos Mor* gives us an idea of the regulations concerning physicians in Eire from the fifth to about the twelfth century. They define the amount of fees to be paid for particular operations or treatment. Also, the physician was to receive the same joint of meat as the king; his person was to be regarded as sacred; his possessions inviolate; no impost was to be levied on him; an honourable maintenance and certain proportions of land were to be his, without any disturbing cause whatever to interfere with the enjoyment of his rights and properties. So highly were they esteemed that Tighermas gave them the right to wear the same number of colours in their clothes as princes of the blood, and Aldergordh directed that they should wear gold rings.

The treatment of the patient proceeded with great deliberation, and exemplary was the penalty imposed on the person who caused the wound or sickness. The physician was not only entitled to his food while in attendance on the patient and until he was restored to health, but the four pupils who waited on him had also to be fed at the cost of the transgressor. A limit was given to the time for the cure. Thus, for a wound in the hand or arm, the period was one year, a wound on the leg a year and a quarter, and for a wound on the head, three years was allowed to make a perfect cure. Although the physician enjoyed such privileges he had great responsibility and if he was convicted of negligence or unskilfulness, he was liable to be called upon to pay for the food consumed by himself and his pupils and to refund all fees previously paid.

In the ancient book of Lecan compiled in 1417 from earlier documents, a further light is thrown on the medicated baths of tradition. It is stated that Las Mhagh (now called Lusmagh) was so named on account of the plain, or field of herbs, out of which Diancecht brought every healing plant which could be found to Slainge's Well, Achadh Abba at Mugh Tuiredh, when the great battle was fought in which the well or bath was used to heal the wounded. Diancecht, it is said, subsequently died from plague, while with the army, and an early manuscript now in the library of Trinity College, Dublin, further states that "jealous of the superior knowledge possessed by his son he slew him, and from his grave arose a number of herbs all efficacious for the cure of disease". Baths of milk were believed to prevent poisoned wounds, and so we learn that after a battle in which the men of Leinster participated, the physician advised that "thrice fifty cows of the plain were to be milked into one pit and every one of the wounded men had nothing more to do than lie in the new milk and then the poison would affect him not".

For centuries, students from all parts of Europe flocked to the Irish schools of medicine, and from these institutions came such men as Aleuin, the founder of the University of Pisa, Johannes Scotus Erigena, the first professor of philosophy at Oxford, and many others who became famous.

An interesting light is shed on the conditions of medical practice in Eire in the sixteenth century, in the *Diary of Thomas Arthur*, who was a member of an old Limerick family, born in 1593. He began to practise in the reign of James I and kept a Diary from 1619 to 1663. In 1620 he records:

The amount of my fees for this year is £74 1 8, for which and other gifts conferred on me unworthy I am, I return boundless thanks to Almighty God. I went to Dublin on the 3rd of May to Mr. George Secton (gonorrhoea laborantem) who being thoroughly cured, gave me a horse of the value of £8 and £5 in gold. I then went to the Lady of Arthur Chichester, the Treasurer of this kingdom then living at Carrickfergus, whom when labouring under dropsy and forewarning her of her death, which happened within a few days after my prognosis, I attended upon. He gave me on May 25th, £5 10.

Other fees he records range from two shillings to five pounds, and it was apparently often customary to pay the doctor a lump sum fee, when the patient was cured.

The Irish peasantry had an intimate knowledge of the healing properties of herbs and plants which had been handed down from an early period, but some of the remedies they employed were of a curious nature. This may be judged from the following, culled from a Gaelic manuscript of the fourteenth century:

For baldness: let calcine a raven, his ashes boil in sheep's suet and rub to the head and it cures. With mice, fill an earthen pipkin, stop the mouth with a lump of clay and bury beside a fire, but so as the fires not too great reach it not. So be it left for a year and at a year's-end, take out whatsoever may be found therein, but it is urgent that he who shall lift it have a glove upon his hand, lest at his finger ends the hair comes sprouting out.

For paralysis: take a fox with his pelt and with his inwards; boil him well till he part from his bones and the patient's body being well scoured first, bathe the limbs or even the whole person in his broo.

For falling sickness: put salt and white snails into a vessel for three nights, add seven woodbine leaves; mix to a paste and poultice for nine days. A plaster of mandragore and ground-ivy placed on the head and if the patient sleeps, will do well, if not he will not.

For dysentry: woodbine and maidenhair should be boiled in new milk with oatmeal and taken three times a day.

For the liver: leaves of plantain, wild sage, shamrock, dockleaf, valerian and the flower of the daisy, plucked by the person before sunrise and fasting on Monday or Wednesday, while saying a "Hail Mary" and a "Paternoster." They should be boiled and strained and a glassful of the liquor taken twice a day, the residue of the herbs being carefully burnt.

Another recipe in which shamrock forms an ingredient is one given for lumbago, as follows: "Take dog-fern roots with shamrock well-cleaned and powdered and mixed with butter on a May-day morning, with holy salt and made into a paste not to be washed off but left on till cured." For toothache, this charm should be said: "May the thumb of chosen Thomas in the side of guileless Christ heal my teeth without lamentation from worms and from pangs."

Saliva was regarded as efficacious against hostile spells and the diseases occasioned by them, and in West Meath it was believed to have the power of curing burns, if taken from a person who had acquired the virtue, by drawing a lizard across his tongue, in the direction contrary to the scales of the reptile. It will, therefore, be seen from the strange mixture of magic and religion, incantations and charms found in Irish folk-medicine, that these had a certain psychological as well as a remedial action. The incantations had some efficacy in soothing nerves, and the plants had, in certain cases, definite remedial effects, while the religious element exerted a powerful influence on the sick person.

When the leech could do no more and death claimed the victim, he appears to have been always ready to take part in the "keens" or lamentations for the dead which formed so characteristic a feature of an Irish funeral.

Chapter XI

FOLK-MEDICINE IN BRITAIN

FOLK-MEDICINE may be described as the use of herbs and plants by the people in primitive times, when nearly every tribe and race had its own traditionary healing lore. In those days this knowledge was chiefly confined to the wise-men and women, who prepared and administered the remedies which had been found of value in the treatment of the various disorders which afflicted suffering humanity. This traditionary lore was at first handed down from generation to generation by word of mouth; then, as time went on, it was committed to writing and formed the basis of the books on domestic medicine and the recipe manuscripts collected and recorded by housewives down to the close of the eighteenth century.

In the preparation of some of these remedies, magic and astrology played important parts and were believed to influence their properties. For before a plant could work its healing powers, due regard had to be paid to the planet under whose influence it was supposed to be for, as Aubrey observes, "if a plant be not gathered according to the rules of astrology it hath little virtue in it".

Michael Drayton adds to this:

> Besides in medicine, simples had the power
> That none need then the planetary hour
> To help their workings, they so juiceful were.

Although a great deal of superstition has been interwoven with folk-medicine, there is a certain amount of truth in the claims made for the many remedies which for centuries, with more or less success, have been employed by the peasantry, both at home and abroad.

Thus, for instance, in Cornwall, club-moss was believed to be most effective in all diseases of the eyes, if gathered on the third day of the moon, when it was seen for the first time. The gatherer was directed to take the knife with which it was to be cut in his hand, show it to the moon and repeat the words:

> As Christ healed the issue of blood
> Do thou cut what thou cuttest for good.

When the sun was setting, the gatherer was then to wash his hands and cut the club-moss while kneeling and wrap it in a white cloth. Afterwards it was to be boiled in water taken from a spring nearest the place of growth and the resulting decoction was then ready to be used as a fomentation for the eyes, or for swellings.   An ointment was also made from club-moss after it had been mixed with butter made from the milk of a new cow.

The ceremony described for the gathering was similar to that performed when collecting other plants, and is partly pagan as regards the phase of the moon, while the prayer shows how the rite was afterwards christianized.

It is well-known, and a fact still recognized, that plants to be employed for medicinal purposes are most active and best gathered just before coming into flower.

The Romans, when gathering the first anemone of the year, uttered the words: "I gather thee for a remedy against disease," for they believed the anemone to be a protection against sickness and it is thus referred to in the lines:

> The first spring bloom anemone she has doubtless wove
> To keep him safe from pestilence where he should rove.

Another plant of classic interest was the peony, or "healing plant" of the Greeks, which was associated with Asklepios their deity of medicine. It is supposed by some early writers to have been named after Paeon, the first physician of the gods and a pupil of Asklepios, who attributed to it remarkable virtues.   According to the mythological story, Paeon first received the flower from the mother of Apollo on Mount Olympus and with it cured Pluto of a wound he had received in a combat with Hercules. Paeon's success in healing aroused so much jealousy in Asklepios that he secretly compassed his death, but Pluto transferred his body into the flower which he called Peony.

The ancient Greeks believed it was a plant of divine origin caused by an emanation from the moon, for it shone during the night, drove away evil spirits and protected the habitations of man.   This gave rise to a belief that evil-spirits and demons avoided the places where it grew and it became customary to wear small pieces of the root, fashioned like beads to be worn round the neck, to protect the wearer from evil influences. This superstition persisted until recent times in the form of necklaces of beads turned from peony root which were placed round the necks of babies especially when teething, to prevent convulsions.   Known as the "Anodyne necklaces" they were exploited and advertised in the seventeenth and eighteenth centuries.

Peony had also a wide reputation for curing epilepsy, which virtue thus is referred to by Lord Bacon: "It hath beene long received and confirmed by divers trialls that the root of the male piony dried and tied to the necke doth helpe the falling sicknesses and likewise the incubus we call the mare."

Charms played a prominent part in the prevention of the evil effects caused by the bites of venomous reptiles and some of the early and curious spells are worth recording.   Here is one believed to be of great antiquity which was employed to counteract the effect of the bite of an adder. "Lay a cross, formed of two pieces of hazel-wood, softly on the part, repeating these words three times:

> Underneath this hazel in mote,
> There's a braggotty worm with speckled throat,

Nine double is he; now from 9 double to 8 double; and from 8 double to 7 double; and from 7 double to 6 double; and from 6 double to 5 double; and from 5 double to 4 double; and from 4 double to 3 double; and from 3 double to 2 double; and from 2 double to 1 double; and from 1 double to no double; no double hath he!"

This ancient charm for the bite of a venomous adder is supposed to have originated from the tradition that St. Patrick, when he drove the snakes from Eire into the sea, held a rod of hazel-wood in his hand.

The part that numerals played in folk-medicine is shown in many old customs connected with healing. Thus, in Devonshire, poultices had to be made of *seven* different kinds of herbs. To cure an infant of thrush it was directed to take *three* rushes from any rushing stream and each was then to be passed separately through the mouth of the child and afterwards thrown back into the water. As the current bore them away so it was believed the ailment would leave the child.

In some parts of the country, a person who suffered with dizziness was told to run after sunset, naked, *three* times through a field of flax, when the flax would at once "take the dizziness to itself". This and the following cure show a connection with the ancient belief in the transference of disease. In Sussex, where ague was at one time prevalent, the sufferer was told to eat *nine* sage leaves fasting, *nine* mornings in succession or go early in the morning to an old willow tree and after making *three* knots in one of the branches say:

> Good morning, old one,
> I give thee cold; Good morrow, old one.

Charms to take warts away are innumerable and in many, numbers play a part. Thus it was recommended to tie as many knots on a hair as were warts to be removed and then throw the hair away. In Eire it was customary to take *nine* leaves of dandelion and eat *three* on *three* successive mornings. In Cornwall where bramble leaves are used to apply to scalds or burns, *nine* leaves were to be moistened with spring water and applied to the injured part, but while this was being done, for every bramble leaf it was necessary to repeat the following lines three times:

> There came three angels out of the East
> One brought fire and two brought frost.
> Out fire! and In frost!
> In the name of the Father, Son, and Holy Ghost.

The prevalence of certain diseases and ailments in early times is evidenced in the many cures that have come down to us from past centuries. Epilepsy, for instance, which was originally ascribed to demoniac possession, was generally treated by charms and incantations, and from the time of the Apostles who cast out the devils religious rites played a prominent part. In the fourteenth century, great faith was placed in the following charm:

> Gasper with his myrrh beganne
> The presents to unfold
> Then Melchior brought frankincense
> And Balthasar brought in gold,
> Now he that of these holie Kings
> The names about shall beare
> The Fallyng yll by Grace of Christ
> Shall never need to feare.

Every man and woman bearing this writing about them with good devotion saying every day three paternosters, three aves and one creed, are assured of being free from attack.

Among other remedies for epilepsy we find shavings of rhinoceros horn and human blood. Charas says: "In the month of May take a considerable quantity of healthy young men's blood, let blood in that season who are not red-haired. Distil it twice and spread on plates and dry in the sun or oven."

Other strange cures for the same disease were "Water of Swallows" made by distilling 40 live swallows, castoreum one ounce, in 3 lb. of white wine; one to three ounces being given to the patient every morning for 40 days; also "Compound Water of Magpies" which was prepared by taking six young magpies, half a pound of white dung of a peacock, 5 ounces of mistletoe of the oak and 5 ounces of fresh cowslip flowers, distilled with 5 lb. each of white and Spanish wine. Four ounces of this was to be taken morning and evening, in the last days before the full and new moons. Another remedy which had a universal reputation for epilepsy and hysteria was "Salt of Coral" prepared by dissolving coral in vinegar and distilling it. A "Salt of Pearls" was prepared in the same manner, using lemon juice instead of vinegar. Another method was to bruise the pearls and pour the lemon juice over them. "When dissolved add some May dew and decant the solution." This is described by a sixteenth-century writer as "a most noble cordial for convulsion and falling sickness for it purifies and keeps the body sound, comforts the brain, memory and heart".

Another remedy prepared from birds was the volatile "Salt of Ravens" which was made by taking "a whole raven, dried, gently chopped into bits, head, bill, feathers, claws, bones and entrails, then placing them in an earthen retort in a reverbatory furnace and distilling with a gentle fire". The dose was from eight to twenty grains. For an epileptic fit it was customary to anoint the soles of the feet, nostrils and nape of the neck with "Oil of Kites". It was claimed this remedy would prevent the fits, if applied "three days before and after the full and new moons". To prepare it, it was necessary to take four young kites from the nest and, after plucking them, to boil them in a mixture of black-cherry water, peony roots, castor, rue, rosemary, lavender, St. John's-wort flowers, valerian root and olive oil. They were to be boiled until they came to a mash and then were to be pressed.

During the Middle Ages coins of all kinds, which bore the impression of a cross, were commonly worn as charms around the neck, and among those used thus for epilepsy were certain silver tokens called the "money of St. Helena" which bore a cross on one side and an image of the saint on the other. In Berkshire, a ring made from a piece of silver collected at a Communion service was believed to avert attacks. A variation of the charm was to have a ring made from five sixpences collected from five different bachelors, which were to be conveyed by the hand of a bachelor to the smith, who was also to be a bachelor; but none of the persons from whom the coins had been obtained were to be told the purpose for which they were to be used. Another charm in which money played a part was to beg 30 pence from 30 poor widows and exchange them with a clergyman for half a crown, taken from a Communion plate. Having done this, the sufferers were bidden to walk nine times up and down the aisle of the church, then pierce the coin and wear it round the neck.

Fevers of various kinds, including malaria, were very common in some parts of the country, especially in the eastern counties. A general charm employed in the fourteenth century was for a priest to repeat the following words:

I forbid the quaking fevers, the sea fevers, the land fevers and all the fevers that ever God ordained; out of the head, out of the heart, out of the back, out of the sides, out of the knees, out of the thies. Frae the points of the fingers to the nebs of the taes. Out sail the fevers, go some to the ill, some to the hope, some to the stone, some to the stock. In St. Peter's name, St. Paul's name, and all the saints of heaven. In the name of the Father, Son, and Holy Ghost.

Another charm found in a manuscript of the fourteenth century was to be written on a laurel leaf thus:

+ *Ysmael* + *ysmael* + *adjuro vos per angelum ut so oretetur iste Homo.* Ley thys lef under hys head that he wote not there of and let him ete Letuse oft and drink Ip'e seed small grounde in a motter and temper yt with ale.

There was an ancient belief that the application of heat to the soles of the feet would reduce a fever from the head; thus for typhus fever, live pigeons split open are recommended to be placed on the soles of the feet or the "skirt of a sheep recently killed". In Norfolk, the spleen of a cow was employed for this purpose.

Certain insects sometimes entered into the composition of the folk-remedies, as instanced in the "Water of Pismires" given for tertian ague. The recipe reads, "Of the larger pismires gathered in May or June, 1 lb., Honey 2 lb., Spring water 1 lb. Mix and distil. The dose is a spoonful."

For what was termed "pestilent fevers" the spirit of woodlice was recommended which was prepared as follows: "Take an earthen retort, fill it almost full with millipedes and distil. With the first degree of heat will come the phlegm, the second the oil, and the third the volatile salt. Mix together and distil again. The spirit may be given to a drachm."

For all kinds of fevers and agues the "Spirit of Vipers" had a universal reputation. For its preparation, the viper's flesh was to be dried and then shred in small pieces and put into an earthen retort and placed in a reverbatory. "Distil with gentle fire and drive with phlegm, drop by drop." Rolsincius advises the dried flesh with the dried hearts, livers, heads and tails distilled all together, "so you will have spirit", he says of "oil and volatile salt; the salt sticking to the neck and sides of the receiver". The result was declared to possess powerful curative pro-perties and to be a sovereign remedy for fevers, epilepsy, tremblings and hysteria as well as asthmas, coughs, and diseases of the chest and lungs, for "it strengthens the stomach, helps digestion, the liver, spleen and bowels and is one of the greatest sudorifics in the world".

A more attractive remedy for hectic fevers and lung troubles was "Jelly of snails". It was made by taking "twelve garden snails, free from shells and cleansed, add new milk from a red cow 2 lb., and boil to one half, then strain and add rose-water 1 ounce, sugar-candy half an ounce and mix for a draught".

For quartan fevers, the livers of frogs are recommended which were to be prepared by drying them on cole-wort leaves in a closed vessel, then reducing them to powder, of which thirty grains were to be taken, in any vehicle.

For asthma, shortness of breath and coughs, a preparation with the curious name of "A body without a Soul" was administered. It con-sisted of orris root one drachm and a half, musk three grains and sugar six ounces. When the whole was mixed and reduced to powder it was given in wine or water.

Elias Ashmole who suffered from ague, writing in his *Diary* on April 11, 1681, says: "I took early in the morning a good dose of the elixir and hung three spiders about my neck and they drove my ague away. *Dea gratias.*" A spider enclosed in a walnut shell and worn suspended from the neck was frequently employed as a charm against attacks of ague, while cross-oaks or oaks growing at cross roads were believed to possess healing power for the same disease. In east Norfolk, a popular remedy was to take as much snuff of a candle as would lie on a sixpence and after mixing it with honey, to swallow it at bedtime.

A Sussex remedy was to eat *seven* sage leaves while fasting for *seven* mornings, while in Suffolk it was customary to bury a handful of salt in the ground. Some charms were regarded as infallible in more than one disease and the following was employed for ague, as well as toothache:

Peter sat at the gate of Jerusalem and prayed and Jesus called Peter, and Peter said, "Lord I am sick of ague" and the evil ague being dismissed, Peter said, "grant that whosoever weareth these lines in writing, the evil ague may depart from them and from all evil ague, Good Lord Deliver us."

In contrast with the written charm, chips from a gallows upon which several persons had suffered the extreme penalty of the law, worn in a bag round the neck, were likewise regarded as infallible cures. Among the saintly personages appealed to by sufferers from ague were St. Petronilla (said to be the daughter of St. Peter) and Sir John Shorn, an Augustinian canon of Dunstable, in the thirteenth century.

Coughs due to various causes have always been a common ailment, and folk-remedies for them were innumerable. Charms both spoken and written were popular throughout the country, and among them great faith was placed in the "Judas ear", a fungus sometimes found growing in elder stumps. This charm was as follows:

> For the cough takes Judas ear
> With the parynge of a Peare
> And drink them without feare.
> If you will have remedie
> The syppes are for the hyckocke
> And six more foe the chyckocke
> Thus my pretty pyckocke
> Recover by and by.

In the northern counties another cure was to shave the patient's head and hang the hair on a bush, so the birds could carry it away and with it the "cough" to their nests. In Devonshire and Cornwall the procedure was varied by placing the hair cut from the person's head between two slices of bread and butter which were then given to the dog to eat. Both of these cures are relics of the ancient belief in the transference of disease from man to animals or birds.

For whooping-cough it was customary in Cheshire to catch a frog and hold it for a few minutes inside the child's mouth. The idea underlying this cure was that frogs croaked and the choking caused by the cough resembled the sound. Thus the ailment in some parts was called "Frog-in-the-throat", hence the remedy. In Norfolk, the sufferer was made to drink some milk which a ferret had lapped, while in Suffolk the hair of the eldest child of the family was cut into small pieces, then placed in milk and given to the affected children to drink. A favourite remedy in Lancashire was to boil the cochineal insect in a quantity of water and dose the

sufferer with the decoction, a teacupful at a time.   Another cure was to
pass the afflicted child *three* times under the stomach and *three* times over
the back of a donkey, or to hold a spider over the sufferer's head and
repeat the words:

> Spider as you waste away
> Whooping cough no longer stay

The spider was then to be placed in a little bag and hung over the mantel-
piece till it died.   Here again we have the perpetuation of the idea that
disease could be transferred from the sufferer to another living creature.

Another interesting development of the idea was the custom of passing
the afflicted child through an arch, formed by the bough of a tree.   In
Oxfordshire, mothers were told to go into the fields alone and seek in the
hedges a wild rose, or bramble which had bent to the ground and become
rooted like a bow.   The child was then to be taken to the spot on *nine*
mornings and passed *nine* times through the arch, after which it would be
cured.   Sometimes a cleft in a tree was used for the same purpose.   The
whole proceeding symbolized rebirth or re-entry into life, through which
the body was purified and so freed from disease.   It is interesting to note
in connection with these cures that the number nine was a numeral
denoting power, wisdom, mystery and protection, and was used by the
early priest-physicians in healing.   It was the product of *three* and so
associated with intellectual and spiritual knowledge.

In some parts it was customary to collect *nine* star-stones (quartz)
from a running stream, taking care not to interrupt the passage of the
water.   These were to be placed in a quart of water, taken from the stream
in the direction in which it ran and made very hot, after which the liquid
was to be bottled and given to the patient, a wineglassful at a time, for
nine successive mornings.

Dr. Plowright, who practised in East Anglia for many years, says: "In
1904 it was customary to cure by charms in the district where I lived, and
many chronic diseases were assigned by the people to witchcraft.   One
of the common curative methods employed was to burn a small bottle of
the patient's urine on the fire at night.   The bursting of the bottle or
blowing out of the cork, signified the expulsion of the devil or evil spirit
causing the disease and their exit from the body up the chimney."

Sticking the back of a toad full of pins arranged in the form of a circle
and double curved line and then burying it, while still alive, in a wide-
mouthed bottle near the window, was another method employed in cases
of haemiplegia.

Professor Byers tells us that in Ulster, as in England, (see above),
it was customary when children were suffering from whooping-cough, to
pass them three times under and over a donkey's back or body.   Another
cure was the giving of two articles of food, such as bread and milk or bread
and cheese, which had to be obtained from two first cousins who were

married.   A cure for mumps was to place a donkey's bridle and blinkers on the child's head and the bit in its mouth.   The patient was then to be blindfolded and led to a stream or well and made to drink three times in the name of the Trinity, the charmer repeating his incantation the while. The sufferer was then led back, the bridle removed and it was pronounced cured.

There were many cures for ringworm which was very common among children.   The earliest of these were the charms which were to be said over the heads of the kneeling sufferers.   One ran:

> Ringworm white,
> Ringworm red,
> I command thou wilt not spread.
> I divide thee to the east and west
> Or the north and to the south.
> Arise in the name of the Father, Son and Holy Ghost.

Another was to make the child affected take a pinch of ashes between the forefinger and thumb and hold it to the affected part on three successive mornings while fasting, saying:

> Ringworm, ringworm red!
> Never mayst thou spread or speed,
> But aye grow less and less
> And die away among the ase (ashes).

In some cases three sticks were put in the fire and, when glowing, were passed round the affected part, one after the other, while saying:

> Ringworm, ringworm, don't spring or spread
> Anymore; go thee ways down to the dirt.

Still another cure was to pass the child through the hopper of a corn-mill.

It has been found that many of the earliest charms which passed from one county to another, often became altered.   In Somersetshire, the last mentioned was phrased:

In the name of the Father, Son and Holy Ghost.
There were three angels came from East to West
One brought fire and another brought frost
And the third was the Holy Ghost.
Out Fire! in Frost! In the name of the Father, Son and Holy Ghost. Amen.

This charm was to be repeated *three* times, after which the affected part was to be blown on *thrice*.

A similar charm was employed for burns, (see also page 79), which were also to be blown on *thrice*:

> Here comes I to cure a burn sore
> If the dead knew what the living endure,
> The burn sore would burn no more.

In Scotland, the following words were repeated:

> Thir sairs are risen through God's ware
> And must be laid through God's help.
> The mother Mary and her dear Son
> Lay thir sairs that are begun.

Another cure for ringworm used in Scotland was a decoction made from sun spurge (*Euphorbia helioscopia*), popularly known as Mare's milk.

In Hampshire, for whooping-cough great faith was put in a drink of new milk from a cup made from the variegated holly, while in Sussex, the excrescence found on the briar, known as "Robin redbreast's cushions" were used for the same disease.

For the skin trouble commonly called shingles, it was customary to in Surrey to scrape the "Crombe", a kind of lichen that gathers on old bells exposed to damp and rub it over the part affected. Professor Gwynn Jones states, "it is a common belief in South Wales that shingles can be cured by certain persons blowing on the affected part, especially if the person who blew was descended from one who had eaten the flesh of an eagle". It is difficult to account for this belief, although the breath of human beings and some animals were formerly believed to have curative virtues. There is a tradition that the Romans believed that the aged could be rejuvenated by being breathed on by young girls, while Dr. Beddoes, a well-known physician of the last century, expressed his belief that the breath of cows had a beneficial effect on persons suffering from chest and lung diseases. In some country districts also, it was commonly believed that the breath of cattle was helpful in cases of consumption, and sufferers were often recommended to live over a shed where cows or goats were kept.

For consumption and diseases affecting the heart and lungs there was an old remedy, dating from the sixteenth century, prepared by distilling together the blood of a calf, newly killed, three pounds; of Venice turpentine ten ounces; liquorice root one pound; raisins, stoned, twelve ounces and fresh figs one hundred; garden snails seventy, orris root six ounces and white bread-crumbs one pound. It was directed to take two ounces daily for fifteen days.

The flesh of vipers had a universal reputation as a restorative and a preventive of plague, in ancient and comparatively modern days. From the times of Mithridates it formed an important ingredient in many medicinal preparations and viper broth, fat, and viper wine and bread are still employed in some parts of the continent, while in the seventeenth century Viper lozenges were included in the London Pharmacopoeia.

The vipers employed in medicine were the common variety which in this country are called adders (*Vipera communis*). Antonius Musa, physician to Octavius Caesar, is said to have been one of the first physicians to have recommended the flesh of vipers in medicine and in Galen's time it was regarded as a nourishing diet in certain wasting diseases.

Charas, the famous French chemist, wrote a treatise on the use of vipers medicinally, which was published in 1669. In it he declares that the head of the viper, grilled and eaten, would cure its bite, or hung round the neck would cure quinsy. He claimed that the skin, fastened round the right thigh of a woman, was an excellent aid to childbirth and that viper fat was a valuable application in gout and for tumours.

Madame de Sévigné was also a believer in the curative virtues of vipers, and writing to her daughter in 1679, she says, "Madame de Lafayette is taking viper broth, which much strengthens her sight." Six years later she declared to her son: "It is to vipers I am indebted for the abundant health I now enjoy. They temper, purify and refresh the blood." She recommended him to get M. de Boissy to send him ten dozen vipers from Poitou and to take two every morning. The heads were to be cut off, the bodies scalded, cut into small pieces and used to stuff a fowl.

In 1724, Quincy in extolling the virtues of vipers says, "they restore free perspiration and render the skin smooth and beautiful, while they cure itch, leprosy and the worst skin eruptions". Viper wine was a popular tonic in the eighteenth century and was believed to cure sterility. Viper broth was made by boiling a chicken together with a middling-sized viper, from which the head, skin and entrails had been removed, in a quart of water. In making the wine, it was necessary first to drown the live viper in the liquid and then allow it to macerate for some days. Viper bread was prepared by taking an ounce of the dried flesh reduced to powder and mixing it with three ounces of sarsparilla, 8 lb. of wheat flour and the yolk of one egg. A little yeast should then be added and milk to make into a paste. It was then cut into four little cakes and baked in the oven.

In Scotland, a decoction made from sea-southernwood and mugwort was regarded as efficacious for a consumptive cough; while in Eire, a decoction made from St. Fabian's nettle, crocus, betony and horehound was a never failing remedy. In Cardiganshire, Wales, where magic was often mixed with folk-medicine, for heart-troubles the patient was directed to go to a smithy and procure a piece of steel and obtain some yarn and saffron. The saffron and steel were to be placed in a pint of old ale and a piece of the yarn was then to be soaked in it. After a while, the yarn was to be taken out and wound round the sufferer's wrist; he was then to drink the ale. If, after a lapse of a few days, the yarn was found to have lengthened, it was regarded as a sign that the patient would recover. It is not to be wondered at that hæmoptosis, or bleeding from the nose, was considered a serious and alarming symptom and was at first treated with magical rites. One charm ran:

Christ that was born in Bethlehem and was baptised in fludd Jordan and water is mild; the child is meeke and mild as the flud so stood. So staunch thou the blood of this person and bleed no more, by the virtue of the Father, Son and Holy Ghost. Obey to my bidding and staunch thou blood without any more delay. This, Lord's Prayer three times over and this three times over and the creed at the latter end.

Another popular charm was to repeat the passage from Ezekiel xvi, 6: "And when I passed by thee and saw thee polluted in thine own blood, I said unto thee when thou wast in thy blood, Live." The dying words of our Lord, "It is finished", were also esteemed as a charm for stopping bleeding at the nose, if written on the forehead of the sufferer with his or her own blood.

In Norfolk, it was customary to place a skein of scarlet silk round the neck, which was then tied with nine knots in the front. If the patient was a male, the silk was to be applied and the knots tied by a female, or if a woman, the knots were to be tied by a man. In some parts of the country it was usual to snuff up the nose the powder of a stone found in the head of a carp, or plug the nostrils with the fur of a hare.

The ailment commonly known as sore-throat naturally came into the domain of folk-medicine. St. Blaise was generally regarded as the patron saint who healed all affections of the throat and so, to remove a bone that had stuck in the throat, the sufferer was enjoined to call on the Deity and remember St. Blaise. A popular method was to hold the person affected by the throat and pronounce the words: "Blaise the martye and servant of Jesus Christ commands thee to pass down." A ceremony called the "Blessing of the Throats" is, at the present day, performed at St. Ethelreda's in Ely Place, Holborn, on February 3 every year, in which the protection of St. Blaise is invoked to heal all persons present who are suffering from throat affections. The crypt of the church is usually crowded and those actually afflicted are asked to come forward. While kneeling at the altar, the officiating priest holds branched candles under the chin of each and while touching the affected part, the following prayer is repeated. "By the intercession of the Blessed Virgin Mary and through the merits of the Blessed Blaise the martyr, may our Lord deliver you from all ills of the throat."

In some parts of Eire, a repetition of the first fourteen verses of St. John's gospel called *In Principio*, was regarded as of exceptional power in exorcising the "sore-throat demon". In other parts of Eire, a more rational treatment was employed, which consisted of tying a cabbage-leaf round the throat, while the juice squeezed from the stalk and leaves, mixed with honey, was given to relieve hoarseness. A syrup made with the leaves of agrimony was taken for the same purpose.

For quinsy, there was a general belief in Cornwall that a toad, placed in a bag and worn by the sufferer round the neck would give relief, or failing that, some dust taken from the floor of the patient's room, when moistened with saliva, was to be rubbed on the neck.

At a period when rabies resulting from a bite from a dog or other animal was a real danger and terror, as well as throwing the sufferer bodily into a pond or lake, treatment was carried out by the administration of madwort (the root of balaustrium), mixed with storax, cypress nuts, soot and olive oil, which is said to have first been recommended by Cardinal Richelieu. Beetroot, boxleaves, cabbage, cucumbers, black-currants and foxglove were also given, and in Russia, the leaves of the *genesta sentoria*. Besides the vegetable products mentioned, the liver of a male-goat, the tail of a shrew mouse, the brain and comb of a cock, pounded ants and a soup made from cuckoos were employed and, as an example of the doctrine of "similitudes", the liver of a mad-dog or a wolf, washed in wine and dried in a stove, should also be mentioned as a remedy!

Ophthalmia appears to have been common in this country in the Middle Ages and many curious remedies are recommended for soreness of the eyes. Among them were scrapings from certain stones, especially if they came from a church. In certain parts of Wales, for instance at Penmynydd, a fourteenth-century tomb and also, at Clynnog, some stone columns are said to have been seriously damaged, owing to the depredations of people who had visited the churches and scraped at the stones to obtain pieces which they used as a cure for sore eyes. A piece of one of the statuettes on the west front of Exeter Cathedral was chipped off within the last part of the nineteenth century. This, when powdered and mixed with lard, was believed locally to be effective for all kinds of sores. It was known as St. Peter's stone, as it was always scraped from the figure of that apostle. The story is told of a man who walked from Teignmouth, some eighteen miles away, in order to fling stones at one of the statuettes until he brought down the arm of one, which he carried off with the object of using it for making eye-salves. At Marston St. Lawrence, in Northamptonshire, there was a common belief that rain which fell on Holy Thursday (Ascension Day) was "Holy Water" which came straight from heaven and so was most efficacious for healing all eye troubles. For dimness of sight it was recommended to smear the eyes with the fat of a fox or child's urine mixed with honey, while fumitory juice was employed for the same purpose.

Among the popular remedies for gout and rheumatism were horseradish, crane's bill and herb-gerard, while mole's feet were also tied to the garters. Burdock leaves, or a potato or chestnut (that must be stolen), carried in the pocket, were regarded as most efficacious. For sprains in arms or legs, it was customary in some parts of the country to call in a person who was practised in "Casting the wrested thread". The thread had to be spun from black wool, in which nine knots had been made, and this was tied round the affected part. While the operator was placing it over the limb he had to repeat the following charm:

The Lord rade (rode)
And the foal slade (slipped)
He lighted
And she righted;

Set joint to joint
Bone to bone
And sinew to sinew.
Heal in the Holy Ghost's name.

Warts naturally came in for treatment by magic or incantation and many methods of banishing these excrescences were practised in various parts of the country.   In some counties, rubbing them with eel's blood was common, and in others pricking the wart with a thorn from a gooseberry bush was customary.   In Oxfordshire and Buckinghamshire, it was recommended that the sufferer should go out into the garden and find a black slug, with which he was to rub the underside of the warts.   The slug was then to be impaled on a thorn and as it died, so the warts would disappear.   Another method which had to be practised when the moon was at the full, was to take an empty dish outside the door and go through a pretence of washing.   While doing so, look at the moon and say, "In the name of the Father, Son and Holy Ghost—I wish the wart away."

Then there was the charm of transference, which was carried out by taking a piece of string and making a number of knots in it, corresponding to the number of warts to be cured, and laying it under a stone.   Whoever should tread on the stone, it was said, would attach the warts to himself and so take them away.

For the painful swelling commonly known as "White leg", in Devonshire it was customary to place bandages round the swollen limb and while this was being done, the following charm had to be repeated nine times followed by the Lord's Prayer:

As Christ was walking he saw the Virgin Mary sitting on a cold marble stone. He said unto her, "If it is a white ill-thing or a red ill-thing or a black ill-thing or a rotten ill-thing or a cold creeping ill-thing, or a sore ill-thing, or a smarting ill-thing, or a swelling ill-thing, let it fall from thee to the earth in My Name and the Name of the Father, Son and the Holy Ghost. Amen."

The common ailment known as cramp in the legs is dealt with in connection with Cramp-rings, but besides the rational methods of treatment, such as sulphur carried in the pocket and garters of eel-skins worn at night when in bed, there were several charms for the ailment that are worth recording.

In some districts it was customary, directly the attack was felt coming on, to say: "I spread the pain in the name of the Father, Son and Holy Ghost.   If it is a pain in the name of the Lord, I spread it out of the flesh, out of the sinews and out of the bones affected."   Sometimes to relieve the acute pain, a candle was immediately lighted and the affected part pricked with a pin which was then stuck in the candle. As the flame reached it, the pain was said to disappear. In Lancashire, a poker was placed under the bed or the shoes or slippers, so arranged as to just peep from beneath the counterpane. This was believed to avert the attack.

In the northern counties, for erysipelas it was customary to wear round the neck small pieces of elder, gathered from a tree on which the sun never shone ; while in the Highlands of Scotland, if half of the ear of a cat was cut off and the blood allowed to drop on the affected part it was believed to prevent the rash from spreading. For the same disorder, oil of toads was employed, prepared by taking four live toads and boiling them in olive oil and straining it. In place of this, an oil of frogs was regarded as equally efficacious, made by boiling twelve live frogs in olive oil for an hour and then expressing the juice from them.

From a leech book of the ninth century, for headache it is recommended to take the juice of elder-seed, cow's brain and goat's dung dissolved in vinegar or to apply to the forehead a decoction made from swallow's nests, boiled in water.

In conclusion, mention should be made of a curious restorative highly esteemed in the northern counties and known as "Cock broth". According to the recipe:

Take an old cock, well wearied with running till it falls down. Then kill him. Pull off his feathers. Embowel him. Then stuff his body with hyssop, parsley, borage, bugloss, thyme, sweet majoram, onions and lemon juice. Chop all small, then stuff him and boil him. Strain and make savory with salt and drink liberally from two to three quarts a day.

The testicles taken from a live horse or a boar, cut in pieces and washed in white wine, then dried and powdered, were credited with similar virtues.

Pomanders to cheer the heart, prevent epilepsy and apoplexy were carried to avert those diseases and what were called "evil airs". A favourite recipe for one consisted of styrax 6 drachms, gum benzoin 1 ounce, labdanum 2 drachms, damask rose leaves 80 grains, red rose leaves 80 grains, musk, ambergris of each 10 grains. Add mucilage of tragacanth made with damask rose-water sufficient to make into a paste, then roll into balls. The balls could be stitched into the clothing or held to the nose. They could also be made into pills and taken every night for the diseases mentioned. When made into little beads and threaded, they were sometimes worn as necklaces.

The Anodyne necklaces to be worn by children when teething, to prevent convulsions, were made of small, round pieces of male peony and henbane root, with holes bored through and then threaded on a string, or a piece of silk. (See page 78.)

Chapter XII

THE DOCTRINE OF SIGNATURES AND ITS INFLUENCE ON HEALING

WHETHER or not the so-called "Doctrine of Signatures", or "Similars" as it is sometimes termed, originated in Egypt or Babylonia, the belief that certain signs, forms and shapes existed in animals and in plants that indicated their powers and virtues in the healing of disease, is one of great antiquity.

It was an ingenious system elaborated for discovering, from certain marks or appearances in the various portions of a plant's structure, the medicinal properties it possessed.

Writers on medicine and botany of the sixteenth and seventeenth centuries, including Crollius and Kircher, state their belief that sure marks signs and indications are to be seen not only in animals but also in plants, from which their properties in healing can be inferred.

The famous Kircher observes:

Since one and all of the members of the human body under the wise arrangement of Nature, agree or differ with the several objects in the world of creation, by a certain sympathy or antipathy of Nature, it follows that there has been implanted by the providence of Nature, both in the several members and in natural objects, a reciprocal instinct, which impels them to seek after those things which are similar and consequently beneficial to themselves, and to avoid and shun those things which are antagonistic, or hurtful.

Hence has emanated that more recondite part of medicine which compares the "Signatures or Characterisms" of natural things, with the members of the human body, and by magnetically applying like, produces marvellous effects in the preservation of human health.

Crollius in his treatise on the doctrine, declares that it is the most useful part of botany and states that

the occult properties of plants; first, those endowed with life, and second, those destitute of life; are indicated by resemblances; for all exhibit to man by their "signatures and characterisms", both their powers by which they can heal and in the diseases in which they are useful. Not only by their shapes, form and colours, but also by their actions and qualities, such as by their retaining, or shedding their leaves. They indicate what kind of service they can render to man, and what are the particular members of his body, to which they are specially appropriate.

The old herbals, the chief source of medical botany in the Middle Ages, are full of the doctrine and its application to healing, largely founded on the folk-medicine of an earlier period, in which it played a part.

William Coles in his *Art of Simpling* (1656) observes:

The mercy of God which is over all His works, maketh grass to grow on the mountains and herbs for the use of man, and hath not only stamped upon them a distinct form, but also given them particular signatures whereby a man may read, even in legible characters, the supposed medicinal virtue attached to it.

It is probable that the doctrine of signatures was evolved from the curious resemblance observed in ancient times between the leaves, flowers and roots of plants and herbs and parts of the human body, as in the case of the mandrake root which, on account of its frequent likeness to the human form, was believed to prevent sterility and promote fecundity. This is instanced in the use of the fruit, given in the book of Genesis, when the barren Leah went out to meet her husband with the words, "Thou must come in unto me this night, for surely I have hired thee from Rachel by giving her some mandrakes Reuben found."

The general rules that seem to have guided the believers in the doctrine were: First, herbs or plants, or their seed, flowers or fruit, which resembled some organ or member of the human body in figure, colour, quality or consistence, were considered to be adapted to that organ, or member, and to possess medicinal properties specially applicable to it. Second, all herbs or plants that in flowers or juice bear a resemblance to one or other of the four humours, *i.e.* blood, yellow-bile, phlegm, and black-bile, were deemed suitable for treating the same humours by increasing or expelling them.

All yellow-hued plants, if edible, were thought to increase yellow-bile. In this category were included melons, crocus and other yellow-flowered plants with a sweet flavour. Plants of dull or blackish hue, brownish or spotted, were held to be good in the treatment of black-bile, some having a tendency to increase it and others to arrest it and carry it off. Plants bearing white flowers and having a thick juice resembling phlegm or rheum were believed to increase the humours they represented, while milky plants were supposed to increase and induce milk in nursing mothers. Some plants of red colour were believed to increase the blood and others to correct and purify it, while plants of a mixed colour, as they united in themselves a diversity of temperaments, were thought to produce a diversity of effects and believed to possess and exercise a double virtue.

Plants whose decoction or infusion, as well as colour and consistence, was like some humour of the human body were declared to be appropriate for the purpose of evacuating that humour by attraction, or increasing it by incorporation.

Some plants were even deemed to represent certain diseases and judged to be helpful in their cure. Thus for calculus, those which represented stones, like the root of white saxifrage, nuts and the shells of nuts, were given in such cases. Spotted plants were administered to eradicate spots and scaly plants to remove scales. Plants which exuded gums or resins were considered to be good for the treatment of pus or matter, while swelling plants were given for tumours and those that shed bark for the cleansing of the skin. In short, accordingly as plants and herbs showed peculiarities in their actions, so they were supposed to operate on the human body. Sterile plants such as fern, lettuce, willow and savin, were believed to conduce to sterility, while fecund plants were said to promote fertility. Evergreen shrubs or plants and those that were long-lived were supposed to increase bodily vigour and so induce longevity.

To follow out the doctrine more fully, with regard to colour and appearance; the root of the cheldonium infused in white wine until it was yellow, was considered a sure remedy for jaundice. The herb lungwort, spotted with tubercular scars, was recommended in cases of consumption, while liverwort, shaped like the human liver in its green formation, was used for biliousness. Blood-root, so-called from the red colour of its roots, was given for dysentery, or "bloody flux" as it was generally termed ; and the corolla of the Canterbury bell, commonly known as "throat-wort" was employed for bronchitis. Prunella or brown-wort, on account of its brownish leaves and purple blue flowers, was given in quinsy, while pimpinella, saxafraga and other plants which grow in cracks in rocks and are so-named "break-stones" were used in cases of calculus. Burst-wort was used for ruptures and scorpion grass as an antidote for the stings of venomous insects. Briony root, on account of its resemblance to the feet of a dropsical person, was employed for dropsy, while the moon-daisy was recommended for insanity. Birth-wort, kidney-wort, nipple-wort and spleen-wort were given for diseases of the organs their names imply on account of their fancied resemblance to the various parts.

Similitude in shape and form is instanced in the use of hound's tongue, so-called from the shape and softness of its leaves, that was supposed to tie the tongues of hounds, so they could not bark ; while garlic was regarded as a war plant for soldiers, on account of its acute and tapering leaves of lance-like form. The little germander speedwell, with its blue flower so like a tiny eye, was known as "eye-bright" on account of its supposed value in making a water to improve the sight, and in Wales it was known as the "Eye of Christ".

William Turner, author of the first English Herbal printed in 1551 and called the *New Herbal* was a firm believer in the doctrine of signatures and constantly alludes to it in his descriptions of plants and herbs. He says:

God hath imprinted upon the plants, herbs and flowers as it were Hieroglyphicks, the very signature of their vertues as the learned Crollius and others well observe, as on the nutmeg being cut resembles the brain, the red poppy-flower resembles at its bottom the setling of the blood in the pleurisie and how excellent is that flower in disease of the pleurisie and surfeits hath sufficiently been experienced. In the heliotrope and the marigold, subjects may learn their duty to their sovereign, which his sacred Majesty King Charles the First mentions in his princely meditations, walking in his garden in the Isle of Wight, in the following words:

"The Marigold observes the Sun
More than my subjects me have done."

Jean Adrien Helvetius, the French physician who introduced ipecacuanha into medical practise in 1686, compiled a list of classified herbs and plants which, in his time, were considered by the learned in herb craft to form the basis of the system embraced in the doctrine of signatures and in it epitomizes the results of the researches of the earlier botanists. He emunerates the members and organs of the human body and the various herbs and plants to be used in treating them for disease. The following will give an idea of his classification although the complete list is much more extensive.

The Head—Geranium, Walnuts, Marjoram, Poppy, Rose. The Hair—Asparagus, Fennel, Vine roots, Flax, Goat's beard. The Eyes—Euphrasy, Daisy, Mallow, Cornflower. The Ears—Bear's ear, Gentian, Viper's bugloss, Hypericum. The Tongue—Horse-tongue, Adder's-tongue, Hound's-tongue, Hart's-tongue, Frog-bit, Salvia. The Teeth—Sunflower seed, Toothed moss, Toothed violet, Dandelion. The Heart—Motherwort, Strawberry, Peony, Rose, Iris. The Lungs—Lung-wort, Beet, Lettuce, Scabious, Valerian, Rhubarb. The Liver—Liver-wort, Endive, Aloe. The Bladder—Bladder-wort, Black hellebore, Nasturtium. The Spleen—Spleen-wort, Agrimony, Devil's-bit, Broom. The Stomach—Cyclamen, Acorus root, Chives, Radish, Ginger. The Kidneys—Kidney-wort, Jasmine, Lupin, Beans, Currants. The Intestines—Navel-wort, Dodder, Fenugreek, Chamomile flowers. The Hands, Fingers and Nerves—Garlick, Briony, Fig, Tormenttilla, Lupin, Melon, Plantain, Satyrion, Currants.

We may conclude from the observations of the early botanists recorded in the herbals, how belief in the doctrine of signatures was carried on from ancient times and continued through the Middle Ages. In the monastic gardens plants and herbs were cultivated by the monks for their medicinal virtues. Even down to the eighteenth century, we find that John Ray, the famous botanist (1627–1705), who separated flowering from flowerless plants in his *Methodus Plantarum* (1682), apparently considered there was some reason for the doctrine.

Howbeit, [he observes], I will not deny but that the noxious and malignant plants do, many of them, discover something of their nature by the sad and melancholick visage of their leaves, flowers and fruits. One observation I shall add relating to the virtues of plants, which I think there is that there are, by the wise dispensations of Providence, such species of plants produced

in every country, as are made proper and convenient for the meat and medicine of men and animals that are bred to inhabit therein. Insomuch that
Solander writes, that from the frequency of the plants that spring-up naturally
in any region, he could easily gather what endemical diseases the inhabitants
there are subject to. So in Denmark, Friesland and Holland, where the
scurvy usually reigns, the proper remedy there of Scurvy Grass, doth plenti-
fully grow.

There can be little doubt that the signatures of some plants were
observed after their properties had been discovered, as in the case of the
poppy, which was appropriated in the doctrine to brain disorders, on
account of its fruit being shaped like a head. But its narcotic properties
had been known to the ancient Egyptians and Greeks from a much
earlier period. Roses also, which were recommended in disorders of the
blood in the Middle Ages on account of their colour and healing virtues,
rhubarb and saffron for diseases of the liver, were all employed by the
Arabs in early times. That the seeds of henbane were used by the
Babylonians and Assyrians as a remedy for toothaches is evidenced from
cuneiform tablets inscribed over 2000 B.C.; but the later botanists
declared they were employed because the seed receptacle resembled the
formation of the jaw. The Babylonians believed that the kernels of the
seeds, after being placed in the cavity of a decayed tooth, bred worms
which were the cause of the pain.

The signatures of certain plants also simulated to some extent the
diseases they were supposed to cure. Thus the lily-of-the-valley on
account of its flower, hanging like a drop, was deemed a remedy for
apoplexy; wolves' livers were recommended for liver troubles, foxes'
lungs for pulmonary diseases, and dried worms, powdered and mixed
with milk, were given to expel worms.

In conclusion Culpeper adds this quaint caution: "Have a care you
use not such medicines to one part of your body which are appropriated
to another, for if your brain be overheated and you use such medicines
as cool the heart or liver, you may make mad work."

Chapter XIII

TRADITIONARY HERBS OF HEALING

SOME of the historic plants and herbs employed in healing in ancient times originally gained their reputation, not so much for their inherent remedial virtues, as for their supposed magical powers, which had been associated with them in mythological tradition. Probably the best known of these was the mistletoe, on which the name of "All-heal" was bestowed by the Druids who had a considerable knowledge of herb-lore. They believed it to be a cure for all diseases that afflicted mankind and regarded it as a Divine gift of peculiar sanctity, only to be gathered with befitting ceremonies on the sixth day, or at the latest the sixth night of the sixth moon, after the winter solstice, when their year commenced. Pliny declared that the Druids held nothing more sacred than the mistletoe and the tree on which it was produced, providing this was an oak.

They make choice of groves of oaks on their own account, nor do they perform any of their sacred rites without the leaves of these trees, so one may suppose that for this reason they are called by the Greek etymology Druids; and whatever mistletoe grows on the oaks they think is sent from Heaven and is a sign of God Himself as having chosen that tree. This however, is rarely found but when discovered is treated with great ceremony. They call it by a name which in their language signifies the curer of all ills and having duly prepared their feast and sacrifices under the tree, they bring to it two white bulls, whose horns are for the first time tied. The priest dressed in a white robe ascends the tree and with a golden pruning-hook cuts off the mistletoe, which is received into a white sagum or sheet; then they sacrifice victims, praying that God will bless His own gift to those on whom He has bestowed it.

The Druids attributed marvellous curative virtues to mistletoe and after being placed in water, the liquid was distributed to those who deserved it, to act as a charm against the evil spells of witches and sorcerers. If any part of the plant should come in contact with the earth it was considered as ominous of some great disaster impending. Besides its healing virtues, it was believed to be an antidote to all poisons. During the Middle Ages, when it was to be gathered by the people, it was still believed that if it was not cut with suitable reverence, the gatherer would be punished for his neglect.

Aubrey relates how some persons cut the mistletoe from an oak tree in Norwood to sell it to the apothecaries in London and "one fell sick shortly afterwards and, soon after, each of the others lost an eye, while a rash fellow who ventured fell on the oak itself and broke his leg shortly afterwards". After the gathering, it became customary at times to deck the houses with mistletoe-boughs, so that the spirits of the forest might shelter among them during the cold winds and frosts of winter. In Worcestershire, farmers used to take a bough and present it to the cow that first calved after New Year's Day, to preserve it from ill-luck and disease and bring good fortune to the dairy. Medicinally, the twigs dried and powdered were used in the treatment of epilepsy and the leaves and berries, after being dried and powdered, were given for forty days together as a cure for apoplexy, palsy and falling-sickness. It was not only administered internally but a sprig was worn round the neck as a talisman against witchcraft.

It was used all over Europe, especially in the countries of the North. There is a Scandinavian legend that the Apollo of the North, Baldr, was rendered immune by his mother Friggand and proof against all injury by the elements fire, air, earth and water; Loki, the evil-spirit, however, being at enmity with him, fashioned an arrow out of a branch of mistletoe (which proceeded from one of the elements) and gave it to Hödr, the blind deity, who threw the dart at Baldr and struck him down. The gods decided to restore Baldr to life and, as a reparation for his injury, the mistletoe was dedicated to his mother Friggand. To prevent it again being used adversely to her, it was placed under her sole control, so long as it did not touch the earth, the Empire of Loki. It is said that from this reason the custom arose of suspending a bough of mistletoe from beams and ceilings, so that whenever persons of opposite sexes passed under it they could give one another a kiss of peace and love, in the assurance that the plant was no longer an instrument of mischief. An echo of these legends survived until the seventeenth century, for Clusius the botanist observes that a sprig of the sacred plant worn round the neck is a talisman against witchcraft, always providing that it was not allowed to touch the earth, after it had been gathered.

There is a tradition in Sweden that a knife with a handle made of wood from the mistletoe would ward off epilepsy, and for other complaints, a piece worn round the patient's neck, or made into a ring and worn on the finger, was equally effective.

The next in importance of the traditionary remedies was Mugwort, a species of wormwood (*Artemisia, mater herbarum*). The name is supposed to have been derived from Artemis, one of the titles of the goddess Diana, and from the earliest times it had a reputation for relieving ague and disorders peculiar to women. It was used in incantations to drive away lurking devils and counteract the effects of Evil-eye. Pliny says, that "if the wayfarer ties this herb about him, he will feel no fatigue and can not be hurt by any poisonous medicines nor by any wild beast, not even by the Sun itself".

It is mentioned in the *Herbarium* of Apuleius Platonius, the longest of the Anglo-Saxon medical manuscripts, believed to have been written between A.D. 1000 and 1050. According to tradition it says that "the herb was first found by Diana and given to Cheiron the Centaur, who discovered its properties and passed them on to man". It is recommended to be taken to "put to flight devil-sickness and for sore-feet, sore-thighs, gout, fevers, soreness of the stomach and quaking of the sinews. Put in the shoe the traveller will not become weary, if when he gathers it before sunrise he first repeats these words: *Tollam te, Artemisia, ne lassus sim in via*. When this is said loudly, the herb may be pulled up."

Another classic herb which derives its name from Cheiron the Centaur, who lived in a cave on Mount Pelion, was Centaury, the well-known blue-bottle of our cornfields. Cheiron is said to have cured himself from a wound he had accidentally received from an arrow, poisoned with the blood of the hydra. Barthelemy tells how

when Anacharsis visited the cave of Cheiron on Mount Pelion, who taught mankind the use of plants and herbs as medicine, he was shown a plant which grew near it, the leaves of which he was informed, were good for the eyes but the secret of preparing them was in the hands of one family only, to whom it had been lineally transmitted from Cheiron himself.

In Lucan's *Pharsalia* the Centaury is mentioned among the plants to be burned to drive away serpents, owing to the beneficial fumes given off as it is consumed. Its employment is thus described:

> Beyond the farthest tents rich fires they build
> That healthy medicinal odours yield;
> Their foreign Galbanum dissolving fries,
> And crackling flames from humble wallwort rise;
> There centaury supplies the wholesome flame
> That from Thessalian Cherion takes its name.

Betony, another herb held in high esteem in early times, was credited with marvellous virtues with which the Romans were well acquainted. Pliny asserts that "serpents would kill one another if surrounded by a ring composed of Betony", and Antonius Musa, physician to Augustus, wrote a treatise on its excellence and declared it would cure forty-seven different ailments. Owing to its magical properties, there was a belief that a house near which Betony was sown would be free from all mischief, and there was an ancient saying that "when a person is ill he should sell his coat to buy Betony". It was praised by all the old herbalists and Turner remarks in his *British Physician* (1687):

It would seem a miracle to tell what experience I have had with it. This herb is hot and dry, a plant of Jupiter and is appropriated to the head and eyes for the infirmities thereof it is excellent, as also for the breast and lungs; being boiled in milk and drunk, it takes away pains in the head and eyes. *Probatum*. Some write it will cure those that are possessed of devils or frantic, being stamped and applied to the forehead.

He gives a list of between twenty and thirty complaints which Betony will cure and then says: "I shall conclude with the words I found in an an old manuscript under the virtues of it, 'More than all this have been proved of Betony'." Gerarde says "it was used as a remedy against the bitings of mad dogs and venomous serpents, being drunk and also applied to the hurts and is *most singular* against poyson". Franzius went so far as to state that the wild beasts of the forest, aware of its surpassing virtues, availed themselves of its efficacy when wounded.

In Italy at the present time there are several proverbs relating to Betony: "May you have more virtues than Betony" is one, and another, "Known as well as Betony".

Other early medical writers recommend Betony for "sores of the eyes and ears, dimness of sight, flow of blood from the nose, toothaches, sore loins, internal injuries, indigestion and as an antidote to poisons and for drunkeness".

The common method of administering these herbs or worts was in the form of a simple decoction made with water, beer or wine, as shown in the following Leechdom: "Take roots of betony, seethe them in water to the third part, evaporating two-thirds of the water. Take of the same wort by three drachms weight, boil in water, then give it to him to drink."

There were few of the important herbs of antiquity round which so many legends and traditions clustered as Vervain, commonly known as Verbena (*Verbena officinalis*). From early times it was held as a symbol of enchantment and regarded as a plant of magic and healing. It was employed in divinations, sacrificial and other rites and in incantations. The Magi of the ancient Elamites or Persians employed it in the worship of the Sun, always carrying portions of it in their hands when they approached the altar. The magicians used it in their divinations and declared that by smearing the body over with the juice of the plant, a person would be able to make friends with his greatest enemy and cure any disease he wished. When they gathered vervain, it was always at a time when the Sun and Moon were invisible and they poured a libation of honey and placed honeycomb on the earth to atone for robbing it of so precious a plant.

The ancient Greeks called it the "Sacred Herb" and cleansed the festival table of Jupiter with it, before any great ceremony took place. The Romans regarded it as a plant of good omen and dedicated it to Venus. They employed it in religious rites and enjoined those who came to the temples to "Bring your garlands and with reverence place the Vervain on the altar".

They also purified their houses with it to avert evil-spirits and to make themselves, as they believed, invulnerable, they carried a blade of grass and a sprig of vervain about them. Virgil says it was one of the charms used by enchantresses, and those who worked their will were told to "Bring running water and bind the altars round with fillets, and with Vervain strew the ground".

Vervain was venerated by the Druids in Britain and in Gaul and sacrifices were offered when it was gathered. This took place in Spring and at the rising of the Great Dog Star. The root had to be dug up with an iron instrument and to be waved aloft in the air, the left hand only being used. The leaves and flowers were then picked off and with the stalks dried separately in the shade and after being infused in wine, were employed to heal the bites of serpents. In the Druidic processions to the gathering the white-clad herald carried a branch of vervain in his hand, and during the rite, the priests prayed for an hour in the temples, while holding sprigs of vervain in their hands.

In early Christian times, vervain as the "Holy Herb" became connected with the name of Christ. It was said to be found growing on Calvary, and afterwards was regarded as a sacred plant and thus saluted:—

> All hail, thou "Holy Herb" Vervain,
> Growing on the ground;
> On the Mount of Calvary
> There wast thou found;
> Thou helpest many a grief,
> And staunchest many a wound.
> In the name of Sweet Jesus,
> I lift thee from the ground.

The sacred character of Vervain was still maintained during the Middle Ages and it acquired a wide reputation for its healing properties, as well as being used in compounding charms and love-philtres. The juice was administered for plague and other parts of the plant were given as a remedy for different disorders. It was sometimes worn round the neck as an amulet and was believed to possess the power of combating witches. Its magical virtues in love-philtres were said to secure the affection of those to whom it was given and in some parts of northern France it was used for its curative properties for human beings as well as cattle, while the village maidens gathered it for its sweet smell and to aid their charms in attracting lovers.

Vervain and Rue were often associated and were probably the most frequently used ingredients in the mystic cauldron. Rue also entered largely into magic rites as well as being greatly esteemed for its remedial virtues. It is supposed that the root of the wild rue or *Moly* was the herb given by Mercury to Ulysses, as an antidote to the poisonous draught offered to him by Circe the enchantress.

In early times Rue (*Ruta graveolens*) was called "Herb of Grace" from the fact that the word means repentance, which is needful to obtain the grace of God. Dioscorides recommended the seed as an antidote to all deadly medicines, as well as to the bites of serpents, scorpions and the stings of wasps and the famous alexipharmic devised by Mithradates, King of Pontus, was composed of twenty leaves of rue with figs, walnuts and juniper berries.

It was one of the earliest plants cultivated in the English herb-gardens and is frequently mentioned in the Anglo-Saxon Leechdoms. Its strong aromatic smell and bitter taste, with the blistering quality of the leaves, caused it to be considered almost a "heal-all" and in a manuscript of 1305 it is described as

> Rew bitter a worthy gres (herb)
> Mekyl of mythand vertu is.

Even animals were supposed to have recognized its virtues, and Pliny tells us that "weasels eat it to prepare themselves for a fight with rats and serpents".

The herbalists of the sixteenth century recommended it to preserve chastity for, says Turner, "it quickenith the sight, stirs up the spirits and sharpeneth the wit. The very smell thereof is a preservation against the plague in the time of infection"; and old Tusser extols its virtues in the lines:

> What savour is better, if physicke be true,
> For places infected, than wormwood and Rue.

The several allusions to Rue by Shakespeare shows it was well known for its properties in his time, and in *Richard II* he makes the Gardener say:

> Here did she fall a tear; here, in this place,
> I'll set a bank of Rue, sour Herb of Grace
> Rue, even for Ruth, here shortly shall be seen
> In the remembrance of a weeping queen.

In *Hamlet*, Ophelia remarks:

> There's Rue for you; and here's some for me; we call it
> Herb—grace o' Sundays; O, you must wear your Rue with
> a difference.

Rue was the English word for sorrow and remorse and "to rue" was to be sorry for anything, or to have pity; we still say a man will rue a particular action, or be sorry for it, and so it was natural that a plant that was so bitter and had always borne the name of rue or ruth, should be connected with repentance. Thus we may suppose the "Herb of Repentance" became transformed into the "Herb of Grace".

Medicinally, when combined with Euphrasy, it was regarded as a valuable eye-lotion and in Italy, was recommended by physicians in the seventeenth century as a specific against epilepsy and vertigo, or when suspended round the neck it was believed to effect a cure. It is still greatly esteemed in that country as a protection against Evil-eye and witchcraft and representations of the plant in silver are often worn as charms to bring "good luck" to the wearer.

Parkinson, the famous herbalist of the seventeenth century, says: "Without doubt it is a most wholesome herb, although bitter and strong. Some do rip up a bead-rowl of the virtues of Rue but beware of the too frequent or over much use thereof", alluding no doubt to its properties as a powerful stimulant and narcotic.

Chapter XIV

PLANTS OF THE DEVIL

FROM the remote period when man discovered the properties of herbs and plants, those that were found to produce stupor, delirium and death were associated with spirits of evil, usually impersonated in the Devil himself.

In some cases, as instanced in the mandrake, his Satanic Majesty was believed to inhabit the plant and in others to work his evil influence through the root, leaves or flowers. All plants that were discovered to have poisonous effects on man or animals may be said to have been deemed "plants of the devil" and "banes to life". Thus, we have their properties often indicated in their names, such as wolf-bane, leopard's-bane, sow-bane and many others of a similar nature. Plants believed to bring death or ill-luck were dedicated by the Greeks in early times to Hecate and her daughters, Medea and Circe, as they were said to be used by them in working their enchantments and sorceries and were so employed by practitioners of the black art and witches down to the Middle Ages.

Some plants were specially named after the Evil One on account of their obnoxious odour such as Asafoetida, which was known as "Devil's dung", the poplar-leaved fig was called the "Devil's tree", the berry of the deadly nightshade the "Devil's berry" while the plant itself was known as "Death's herb". The fruit formerly bore the name of *dwale*, a word in Danish meaning "a deadly trance", suggestive of its effects.

Briony, the root of which sometimes bears a strong resemblance to the human form, was called the "Devil's cherry" in some countries, while the Petty spurge was known as "Devil's milk". Another name for the beautiful Clematis with its climbing tendrils was "Devil's thread", Indigo was known as "Devil's dye" and a species of ground moss was known as the "Devil's claws". "Devil's bit" was the name given to *Scabiosa succisa* on account of the legend that its stunted blackish root had originally been bitten short by the devil, owing to his spite against man and because he knew that otherwise it could be employed for many profitable purposes. Gerarde remarks of this root: "The greater part seemeth to be bitten away; ye old fantastic charmers report that the devil did bite for envy because it is a herbe that hath so manie good virtues and is beneficial to mankinde." Among them were those of preventing pestilence; the powdered root was applied to the plague buboes and also to the bites of venomous animals.

The *Nigella damascena* was called "Devil-in-the-bush" on account of its round capsules peering from a bush of finely divided involucre and the long arms of *Scandix pecton* were known as the "Devil's darning-needle", while the beans or seed vessels were termed "Venus's comb".

On account of its resemblance to an intestine, the Dodder was known as "Devil's gut", while the acrid milk of the Euphorbia obtained the name of "Devil's milk". Puff-balls or *lycopodium* were called "Devil's snuff boxes" on account of the fine particles they contain which, says Gerarde, "are very dangerous for the eies, for it hath beene often seene that divers have beene made blinde ever after, when some small quantities thereof hath been blowne into the eies".

The fungus *Exidia glandulosa* was known as "Devil's butter" on account of its poisonous properties, while in Russia De Gubernatis tells us that another species is called the "Devil-chaser" as it protects infants

The Mandrake:
from *Ortus Sanitatus*, 1491

Gathering Mandragora:
from a XIIth century MS.

from fright and drives away the Evil One. We are told that it is only necessary to hold up a sprig and the devil is compelled to flee.

Henbane was known in Germany as the "Devil's Eye", a name also applied to the stitchwort in Wales, while in some parts of the Principality the houseleek was known as "Devil's beard"; and in Norfolk, the stink-horn was "Devil's horn". In Eire the nettle is called "Devil's apron"; the convolvulus the "Devil's garter" and the *Ranunculus arvensis* the "Devil-on-both-sides". In Germany, mothers used to stop their children from eating mulberries by singing to them that the devil wants them for "blacking his boote"; and in some parts of this country the *Arum maculatum* is called the "Devil's Ladies and Gentlemen".

The hawk-weed (like the scabious) bore the name of "Devil's bit" because the root looks as if it had been bitten off. A species of ranunculus was known as the "Devil's coach wheels" and in some parts of the country ferns are said to be "Satan's brushes".

In Sweden, a rose-coloured flower grows and is known as "Our Lady's Hand". It has two roots shaped like hands: one of them is white, while the other is black but when both are placed in water, the black one sinks and is called "Satan's Hand" while the white one which floats, is known as "Mary's Hand".

Besides the plants associated with the devil by name, there were the poisonous herbs which caused stupor and death. The best known of these, the mandrake, (*Mandragora officinalis*), round which so many curious and weird legends cling, was in ancient times known as the "Devil's candle" on account of the glare its leaves were supposed to emit during the night. The mandrake was regarded as something more than a plant, and its root, which often resembled the human form, was accounted the habitation of a powerful evil spirit. Great danger and even death itself was believed to threaten the person who uprooted it, as it uttered terrible shrieks and groans and so the gathering of the dreaded plant was only performed with certain ceremonies. Its powerful narcotic properties were known long before the Christian era.

The aconite or monkshood, (*Aconitum nappellus*), has been known as a powerful poison from early times and was commonly called "Wolf's bane." From its root, the alkaloid aconitine is extracted, one of the most deadly poisons known. In ancient Greece, Wolf's-bane was credited with causing the fevers so prevalent in the neighbourhood of Corinth, while in the Far East, a species of the plant was employed to poison the arrow-heads used in warfare. The deadly nightshade, (*Atropa belladonna*), which Chaucer calls *Dwale*, always bore an evil reputation; it was also known as "Death's herb" and its fruit was termed the "Devil's berry".

Chapter XV

Herbs and Plants Dedicated to Saints

Ancient Greek and Roman legends tell us that certain herbs and plants were closely connected with various deities in pagan times, but with the Christian era they were often rededicated to saints. Trees also were assigned to with the gods and so we find the Alder was dedicated to Neptune, the Apple to Venus, the Ash to Mars and the Bay to Apollo, while the Beech was allotted to Jupiter Ammon. The Cypress was assigned to Pluto, Dittany to Diana, the Iris to Juno, Ivy to Bacchus, Myrtle to Mars and Venus, Narcissus to Ceres, Olive to Minerva, Poplar to Hercules, Poppy to Ceres and Diana and the Vine to Bacchus. It is difficult in some cases to account for the connection, but the association of Venus with the apple and the vine with Bacchus is obvious from the well-known legends concerning those deities.

In early Christian times, when the monks began to cultivate herbs and plants in the gardens of the monasteries and learnt to employ them for their healing properties, it can be seen how some came to be associated with particular saints. Beyond their medicinal virtues in some cases, certain flowers were selected for various religious festivals; in this way, in course of time, they became associated with some saint of the Calendar.

A Franciscan monk thus explained the idea of identifying certain plants with the saints and festivals.

Mindful of the festivals which our Church prescribes, [he says], I have sought to make these objects of floral nature the time pieces of my religious calendar. Thus, I can light a taper to our Virgin Mother at the blowing of the white snowdrop which opens its flower at the time of Candlemas. The lady's smock and the daffodil remind me of the Annunciation, the blue hair-bell of the Festival of St. George, the ranunculus of the Cross, the scarlet lychnis of St. John the Baptist's day, the white lily of the Visitation of Our Lady, and the virgin's bower of the Assumption.

The same writer goes on to say:

To St. Gerard was dedicated *Ægopodium Podagraria*, because it was customary to invoke this saint against the gout, for which the plant was deemed a remedy. To St. Benedict was assigned the water Avens, hemlock and valerian and such plants as were believed to be antidotes to poisons, for according to tradition the Saint's life was saved from a cup of poisoned wine, presented to him by a monk, by the vessel being touched with one of these plants, thus shivering it to pieces.

St. Christopher was associated with the baneberry and fleabane, and although St. George of England was connected with the harebell here, in other countries the peony was dedicated to him.

The St. Francis thorn or *eryngium* was dedicated to that saint owing to his having been tortured by its spines, while St. Anthony's nut (*Bunium fluxuosum*) or pig nut, was associated with him because he was regarded as the patron saint of the pig.

St. James's wort received its name owing to its efficacy in healing horses of which St. James was the patron, while the cowslip, or Herb Peter as it is sometimes called, was named from its supposed resemblance to a bunch of keys, the symbol of that saint.

The Campanula, commonly known as Canterbury Bell, was so-called in honour of St. Thomas of Canterbury, an allusion to the horse-bells of the pilgrims who journeyed to his shrine; and the "Root of the Holy Ghost" was the name given to the *Angelica sylvestris*. The pansy was called "Herb Trinity", on account of its having three colours in one flower.

Hemp agrimony was commonly known as the "Holy Rope", taking that name from the rope which was used to bind Christ, and the hollyhock was originally known as the "Holy Hock".

Many of the names of the saints associated with plants were given on account of their time of flowering corresponding to the festival of the saint celebrated in church. Flowering on the fête day, the herb or plant was believed to be particularly useful in protecting both men and women from evil-spirits and witches.

According to tradition, St. John the Baptist is associated with several plants, which were known as the "Herbs of St. John". He is supposed to have been born at midnight and so on the eve of his anniversary, precisely at that hour, the fern blooms and seeds and the seed is credited with the power of rendering its possessor invisible. In some countries, before daybreak on St. John's morning, the dew which has fallen on vegetation is collected with great care, as it is thought to possess marvellous virtues in preserving the eyes from all ailments. In certain parts it was also reputed to have the property of renewing the roots of the hair and of preventing baldness, while in others it was used as a lotion to beautify the skin and complexion. The dew was also administered internally to reduce fevers. The "Herb of St. John" (*Hypericum perforatum*) infused in olive oil, was believed to heal wounds and to be of great value in preserving those who gathered it from the effects of witchcraft and the Evil-eye. In the south-west parts of France, crosses made of St. John's herb are fixed on the front doors of the cottages on the eve of St. John, to keep witches away; and these are renewed from year to year.

The belief in the power of the herb was almost universal in Europe and in certain districts the villagers made garlands composed of white lilies, green birch, fennel, St. John's wort, wormwood and the legs of game birds, which they kept in their houses as a protection against evil spirits and witchcraft. Bauhin, the famous botanist, says that "the *hypericum* or perforated St. John's wort and the *Fuga daemonum* or 'Devil's flight' were especially effective in frightening away evil demons and acting as charms against enchantments, storms and thunder''.

The custom of placing sprigs of St. John's wort over the doors was also observed in some parts of Wales and Stowe, in his *Chronicle*, remarks that "on the vigil of St. John Baptist, everyman's door was shadowed with green-birch, long-fennel, St. John's wort, orpine and white lilies and such like, garnished upon with garlands of beautiful flowers. They also had lamps of glass with oil burning in them all night."

The leaves of some varieties of St. John's wort are marked with blood-red spots, which are said to appear on August 29, the day on which the saint is believed to have been beheaded. Besides those mentioned, the following were also included among the herbs of St. John, *Mentha Sarracenica, Centrum Galli, Androsaemon, Abrotanum, Sceophalaria* and the *Crassula Major.* The bright yellow flower symbolized the Sun "which disperses all evil spirits" and also the saint who "was a light to them that sit in darkness".

There is a curious tradition in the Isle of Man that if you tread on the St. John's wort after sunset, a fairy horse will rise from the earth and after carrying you about all night, will leave you in the morning wherever you may chance to be at sunrise.

The medicinal properties of St. John's wort are many, and it was formerly largely employed in nervous disorders or what was commonly termed "heart melancholy". For this purpose it was necessary to gather it on a Friday, "in the 'House of Jupiter' when he comes to his effectual operation" (about the full Moon in July), and when so gathered and hung round the neck, it was said to "mightily help the heart melancholy and drive away all phantastical spirits". The leaves of the herb are astringent and were used to make gargles and lotions, while they were also said to have the power of protecting the wearer against lightning, for which purpose the Dutch peasants gathered it before sunrise. Great faith was placed in its power of healing all kinds of wounds, hence its original name *Tutsan*, a corruption of its French name *la Toute—saine* or "All-heal".

The Sicilians make an ointment from the flowering tops by infusing them in olive oil and a similar salve was formerly much used in various parts of this country and was greatly esteemed by housewives for healing cuts and bruises.

The scarlet lychnis was dedicated to St. John in the Catholic Church and its flame-coloured flower was said to be lighted up for his day, while the carob tree was designated "St. John's bread" from a tradition that it supplied him with food in the wilderness. Currants, on account of their ripening at this time were popularly known as "berries of St. John" while the *Artemesia* was called "St. John's girdle" in Germany, and in Sicily the "Saint's beard".

The Roman Catholic Church had a complete list of flowers, one for each day, dedicated to particular saints on their feast-days, but mention need only be made here of a few that are not so widely known at the present time. Thus, the Clarimond Tulip was associated with St. Mark on April 25, the Red Campion with St. Philip and St. James on May 1, Midsummer Days with St. Barnabas, June 11, Yellow Rattle with St. Peter, July 29, Sun-flower with St. Bartholomew, August 24, the ciliated Passion Flower with St. Matthew, September 21, Michael daisy with St. Michael, *Floccose agaric* with St. Luke, October 18, and the Amaranth with All Saints on November 1.

The relics of certain saints and objects associated with them, still preserved and venerated in churches and monastic institutions in various countries, also played a part in healing, for many people retained many of the old superstitions. St. James's admonition to "anoint the sick with the healing Chrism oil and the sprinkling of Holy Water", was carried out for centuries after the early Christian era. In the blessing of the water, performed so that it might "avail for the casting out of devils and the driving away of diseases, in houses or places of the faithful and so in sprinkling therewith, they might be freed from all uncleanness and delivered from hurt. Let not the breath of pestilence therein abide, nor the destroying blast," says the admonition. In Italy, in the sixteenth century, the wine used at the Feast of St. John was blessed with some ceremony, as a protection against poison, and in someM ahommedan countries, water drunk from a metal cup, having certain characters and passages from the Koran engraved on the interior, was believed to possess the same virtue.

St. Hubert's mantle, preserved in the Abbey of St. Hubert in Belgium, was believed to prevent hydrophobia from attacking those bitten by mad dogs, if placed on the person's head, while his miracle-working stole is also said to work the cure by application. Close to the little church at Bascons, in the Landes district of France, is a well dedicated to St. Amand and on the anniversary of his martyrdom, pilgrims from all the towns and villages round flock to drink of the water which is believed to be a certain cure for eczema, and an oil that has been specially blessed and is dispensed in the church is used for the same purpose.

St. Chad of Lichfield was the patron saint of medicinal springs and his well in that city was long famous for its cures. Miracles are said to have been wrought by mixing dust from his shrine with the water and drinking it.

The Shift of St. Etheldreda, a patroness of Ely, which was once preserved in the church dedicated to her in Norfolk, was regarded as a cure for sore throat, or toothache, if placed on the affected part ; and in the Treasury of Durham Cathedral was once preserved in a small ivory pyx, a tooth of St. Genguphus, to which resort was also made to heal those suffering from epilepsy.

To come to more recent times, mention should be made again of the shirt of King Charles the martyr, stained with his blood and which he wore on the scaffold, that is still preserved in the church at Ashburnham and is believed by the faithful to possess healing properties.

Chapter XVI

PLANTS AND DRUGS USED BY SORCERERS SOME OF WHICH ARE EMPLOYED IN HEALING TODAY

MANY plants and herbs employed by sorcerers in the practice of the Black Art in early times are now used in healing. They were chiefly those which were known to possess the power of inducing stupor, sleep and delirium after their fumes had been inhaled. The sorcerers' dupes were thus induced to believe their hallucinations were the result of divine or supernatural agencies. According to Greek mythology, Hecate was believed to have a knowledge of the properties of every herb which she imparted to her daughters Medea and Circe the sorcerers, so they might carry on their evil tactics.

The Vedic magicians likewise were acquainted with many plants and herbs which they used in preparing their powerful philtres. It is said that among the Brahmins, the *Soma*, a sacred drink prepared from the potent juice of the *Asclepias acida*, or *Cyanchum Viminale*, was one of the means they employed for producing the ecstatic state, in which the votary appeared in spirit to soar above the terrestial regions and become united with Brahma. In the human sacrifices, it is said that the *Soma* drink, prepared with magical ceremonies and incantations, was declared to be a holy act. Other plants favoured by the Vedic magicians were the Mango, Champak, Jasmine, Lotus and Asoka, all of which were employed in making their love-philtres. The Sacred Basil was also regarded as a magical herb which was able to protect those who cultivated it from all misfortunes, including diseases, and injuries.

In Burma, the *Eugenia* was endowed with similar magical powers. John Weir mentions a plant growing on Mount Lebanon which gives those who take it a condition of visionary ecstasy, corresponding to the effects of the mystic mandrake, which grows in the district. This plant, round which such strange legends and traditions have clustered, has for ages been considered a sleep-producing drug with marvellous powers. Besides its narcotic virtues it was said to produce insanity and awake the passions, and was also regarded as a talisman or charm of infinite value. In early times it was supposed to be the magic herb by which Circe bewitched the companion of Ulysses. It was in general use for its sudo-rific properties, and even the smelling of its fruit was said to induce sleepiness. The leaves, root and fruit were employed to relieve pain and it was used in the treatment of various diseases. Investigation in recent times has shown its properties to be due chiefly to an alkaloid named *Mandragorine*. In 1901, Ahrens found this body to be a mixture of *Hyoscyamine* and Hyoscine in addition to another alkaloid, probably

Scopolamine, a potent drug since employed to produce what has been called "twilight sleep".

Satyrion, a name applied to several species of Orchis, was a favourite herb with magicians and sorcerers, especially for its aphrodisiac properties. The Romans believed that the roots of this plant formed the food of the Satyrs and it is mentioned by two old English botanists. Turner says that all the species have a double root which alters every year "when one waxeth full, the other perisheth and groweth lank". The full root powerfully excites the passions but the lank one has exactly the opposite effect. Gerarde agrees and says that most of the plants were used for exciting the amatory passions. Some of them were called Serapiades because "sundry of them do bring forth flowers resembling flies and such-like fruitful and lascivious insects, as taking their name from Serapias the god of the citizens of Alexandria, who had a most famous temple at Canopus".

Savin (*Juniperus sabina*) is regarded in Italy as a plant of ill-repute, and is known as the "Devil's Tree" and the "Magician's Cypress" on account of the great use made of it in ancient times by sorcerers and witches when working their spells. In later times it had a reputation as an abortifacient.

In Britain the common periwinkle was formerly called the "Sorcerer's Violet" and was frequently used by magicians and practitioners of the Black Art in making charms against the Evil-eye and evil-spirits. In France, it was known as *Violette des Sorciers,* while in Italy it was termed *Centocchii* or *Hundred Eyes.*

A plant with powerful properties, used for producing delirium and intoxication, is Indian Hemp (*Cannabis Indica*) which is mentioned in Chinese herbals of the fifth century and also in the Hindu works of Susruta and Charaka as having anæsthetic virtues. As "hashish" or "bahang" it is used as an intoxicant by some Mahommedan sects in certain rites. It is taken like opium by peoples in the Far East and is smoked or used internally for producing delirium which is often accompanied by hallucinations of an extraordinary character. Opium, most powerful of all narcotics, has been well known from the third century and its effects are described by Dioscorides, Celsus and Pliny, as well as other early writers. It is said to have been introduced into China by the Arabs in the ninth century and afterwards the smoking of opium spread over the Far East. Its action is due to morphine, codeine, narcotine and other powerful alkaloids, all of which are largely employed in modern medicine.

The leaves and seeds of the stramonium plant were long known to have a strong narcotic action, due to the poisonous alkaloid daturine they contain and their smoke was inhaled to relieve asthma. It was largely employed in India, and Bombay thieves are said to have used it to deprive their victims of their power of resistance, while they carried out their nefarious designs.

Henbane, or hyoscyamus, has been used for its sudorific properties from early times and is mentioned by Benedictus Crispus, Archbishop of Milan, A.D. 681. In the Middle Ages its potency as a hypnotic was recognized by the Welsh "physicians of Myddvai." Its action is due largely to the alkaloid hyoscyamine from which is derived Hyoscine, and, like atropine, powerfully dilates the pupil of the eye.

The ancient Greeks held the laurel specially sacred to Apollo and the Pythia who delivered the answer of the gods to those who consulted the famous oracle at Delphi, before becoming inspired, would shake a laurel tree growing close by and sometimes ate the leaves, with which she crowned herself.   A laurel branch was said to impart to prophets the faculty of seeing that which was obscure or hidden, and the tree was supposed to possess the property of inducing sleep and visions.   John Evelyn speaks of "the prophets and soothsayers who, sleeping upon the boughs or beds of the leaves, found the laurel greatly composed the phantasy and did facilitate true visions and that the first was specially efficacious to inspire poetical fury".

The Rowan tree especially, was believed to be endowed with magical properties and was used as a charm against "Evil-eye, witchcraft and wicked spells".   With it may be classed the Elder, the Thorn and the Holly; while the four-leaved clover was said to have the power of indicating the approach of evil-spirits.

Henbane, so-called on account of its evil effect upon poultry, was sought for by sorcerers and witches for use in making their potions, and was also called *Insana*, as it was said to make those who took it light-headed and quarrelsome.   The common hemlock, too, has for ages had the reputation of being an "evil, dangerous and poisonous herb".   In some countries it was looked upon as a Satanic plant, and in England was valued by sorcerers and witches as an ingredient in their hell broths. "Root of hemlock digged in the dark, slips of Yew slivered in the Moon's eclipse" refer to the special time for gathering, when it was said to be most potent in preparing potions and philtres.

The black hellebore, or Christmas Rose, is said to have cured the daughters of Proetus, King of Argos, of insanity and to avert the spells of the wicked.   It was gathered with solemn, mystic rites after a magic circle had been drawn round the plant and a prayer to Apollo and Aesculapius offered for leave to dig it up.

Hellebore accompanied by certain exorcisms, was said to cure deafness caused by witchcraft, and the fumes from it were declared to drive away evil-spirits.   It has always been considered to be a plant of ill-omen, for as the poet Campbell observes:

> By the witches' tower,
> Where Hallebore and Hemlock seem to weave
> Round its dark vaults, a melancholy bower
> For spirits of the dead, at night's enchanted hour.

Sorcerers believed that certain magical formulae, accompanied by fumigations, had the power of raising and causing spirits to appear and to lay and bind them. The fumigations which played an important part in their rites usually contained substances that possessed powerful narcotic properties which they knew, when burnt in a confined space and inhaled, would produce somnolence and sometimes hallucinations. These drugs were usually mixed with aromatic gums or resins, in order to give them a more pleasant odour and be less offensive to the victims. As a writer of the sixteenth century observes:

> There are some perfumes or suffumagations, which make men speak in their sleep, walk and do those things that are done by men that are awake and often, what when awake they cannot do or dare do. Others again make men hear horrid sounds, or delightful sounds, noises and the like.

Among the drugs employed for this purpose were at least five powerful narcotics, the fumes from which when inhaled would affect those in the vicinity. Among the formulae are to be found Cannabis Indica, Opium, Henbane, Hellebore and Mandrake, all of which no doubt contributed to the belief in the visibility of the spiritual beings invoked by the sorcerer.

As examples of the fumigations the following have been taken from a sorcerer's secret formulary:

> A perfume made of hempseede, of the seeds of fleawort, violett roots and parsley maketh men to see things to come and is available for prophesie. A marvellous efficacious fumigation to cause a man to see visions in the air and elsewhere. Take coriander, and henbane and the skin that is within the poundgarnet (pomegranate) and the fumigation is finished as you desire.

Another to cause visions of the earth to appear is, "take of cane-reed and the root of fennell with the skin of pomegranate, henbane, and red-saunders and black poppy". A compound consisting of sperm oil, aloes wood, pepperwort, musk, saffron and red storax, mixed with the blood of a lapwing, it is stated, if fumigated about "tombs and graves of ye dead, causeth spirits and ghosts together".

From other sources it is learnt that "anise and camphor mixed, cause to see secret things, ye clepe spirits. Fumigate with Cardamoms and eat thereof. It causeth gladness and gathers spirits together."

Another method of seeing spirits was by means of a metal mirror, well polished. To use this, take:

Canabis viz. Hemp and Artemesia (wormwood) and stand thee before a steele glasse and ye shall be able, through God's help, to see and bind loose spirits, but if ye anoynt ye glasse with juice of artemesia it is better. To cause apparitions to be visible to ye sight you must take Artemesia, hemp, flax, cardamoms, anise, camphor, coriander, hypericon, aloes-wood, and chicory. To have friendship, or woudst have a Prince of Spirits of the ayre take juice of hypericon, saffron, artemesia, and root of valerian and of these make a fumigation. To see future events fumigate yourself with linseed and seed of Psellium or with violet roots and wild parsley.

In addition to those for causing spirits to appear, there were fumigations to drive them away when necessary. Thus, "to drive away evil-spirits or devils, make a noxious fumigation with sulphur, black myrrh, red sandal, putrid apples, vinegar, wine-galls and arsenic, mixed with dregs of wine".

In these formulae we have the supposed secrets of the sorcerers and the plants and drugs they employed on those who sought their aid. It will be seen that many of them were potent and would produce definite physiological effects.

Chapter XVII

REMEDIES OF ANIMAL ORIGIN EMPLOYED BY THE
ANGLO-SAXONS

We know from various manuscripts written in the early centuries, that the Anglo-Saxon leeches employed many remedies of human and animal origin in the healing of disease. This is evident from the treatise written by Sextus Placitus or Platonicus, who is said to have lived about the fourth century, of which a copy in Anglo-Saxon is now in the British Museum. It is especially interesting on account of the curious drawings in colour with which it is illustrated.

The text deals chiefly with the medicinal properties attributed to various parts, organs and excrements of the animals described, which were believed to possess remedial virtues. These include the hart, fox, hare, goat, ram, boar, wolf, lion, bull, elephant and dog. Very few of them have any rational foundation, and their supposed healing properties are mainly based on legendary superstition. It is thought by some that the use of animals, or their organs, was originally due to totemism, or the belief by virtue of which a tribe traces back its origin and ascribes its continued existence to a selected animal, that is regarded as the god of that particular tribe. The totem animal was killed to preserve and perpetuate the existence of the tribe. Thus, to the Arabs in early times, the camel was sacred and entirely devoured even to its hair, teeth, bones and all parts of the body. Bruce tells us that some of the tribes of Central Africa regard the crocodile as sacred, and when one is killed, the natives rush to the spot and dismember it. Every part of the body, as well as the internal organs, is employed in the cure of some disease. It has been found that nearly all the animal remedies used were traced to magic and religion. The blood was believed to have curative powers as it represented life and the blood of the ox, ass, sow, dog and hart were frequently used in medical treatment in ancient Egypt. The Romans highly esteemed the blood of their gladiators, which was believed to endow them with strength, courage and endurance.

In the work of Sextus Placitus, in case of a sore head, the patient is directed to "drink by weight of five pennies of ashes of hart's horn"; fox grease is recommended for "sore-ears"; a hare's brain for oversleeping; and for dimness of sight, the wood-goat's gall, mingled with a little wine, was prescribed. The use of gall for the eyes, to strengthen and clear the sight, is of great antiquity and is referred to by the Babylonians and Egyptians. In the Leechdoms, the gall of the bull is recommended for obscurity of vision, the gall of the hare mingled with honey was declared to brighten the eyes and the gall of the wild-duck and goat were employed for the same purpose. It is well known that a solution of gall acts as an excellent solvent for foreign bodies and is harmless in its effect on the eyes. Among other interesting Leechdoms are:

Ram's lung carven up small and laid to the sore is good for ulcerous wounds on the face. For devil's sickness (epilepsy) and for ill-sight wolf's flesh should be eaten, well-dressed and sodden. To remove ugly marks from the face, smear with wolf's blood, for it taketh away all marks. For griping also, let the sick drink hound's blood for it healeth wonderfully. For a man who has the falling sickness, work to a drink a boar's coillons in wine or water; the drink will heal him. For sore ears, take fox's loin fat, melt it, drop into the ears; good health will come to him.

There are several Leechdoms for bites from a mad dog and in one the sufferer is recommended to "Take the worms which be under a mad hound's tongue, snip them away, leave them round about a fig tree. Give them to him that hath been rent, he will soon be whole."

In Gothic mythology the disease demons that entered the body of man and caused convulsions were termed dwarfs and in this way the name became associated with epilepsy and convulsive diseases. A curious Leechdom "to do away a dwarf", reads: "Give to the troubled man to eat, thost of a white hound pounded to dust and mingled with meal and baked to a cake, ere the hour of the dwarf's arrival, whether by day or by night it be; his access is terribly strong and after that it diminisheth and departeth away."

That the Anglo-Saxon ladies wished to preserve their beauty is evident from the direction to a woman who desired to clear her complexion from spots or blemishes. To do this she must apply powdered ivory to her face, until it is fair and clear.

The Anglo-Saxon leeches employed splints in cases of fracture of the limbs, and honey was used as a general dressing for wounds. Its use for this purpose goes back to a very early period and a knowledge of its preservative properties was possessed by the Assyrians, centuries before the Christian era. It was also recommended by Hippocrates and several of the early Greek physicians for the treatment of wounds. Cleanliness was enjoined in its preparation, not only of the honey itself but also in the vessel in which it was to be kept. It is directed that the honey should first be warmed before the fire, "then put in a clean vessel with a little salt. Stir until it is the thickness of pottage, smear the wound with it then it cleanseth it."

The actual cautery or "blistering rod" was extensively used by the Anglo-Saxon leeches as a preliminary treatment in a variety of diseases, from gout to headache. Bleeding was practised with the lancet, the cupping-glass or horn and the scarifier, sometimes accompanied by an incantation. Thus, it is directed for paralysis to "Scarify the neck after the setting of the sun, pour in silence the blood into running water. After that, spit three times, then say: 'Have thou this unheal and depart away with it; go again on a clean way to the house and go either way in Silence.' "

A general belief arose later that certain organs of animals and human beings would benefit similar organs in man.   So the application of a dead snake to a bite inflicted by a live one would counteract the effect of the poison, and this led to the idea that snake flesh would cure diseases; and viper's flesh was employed as a remedy for gout, stone, leprosy, scurvy and consumption, down to the eighteenth century.   The fat of the viper was long reputed in this country for healing cuts, sprains and bruises.   A living adder was at one time used in Sussex for the transference of goitre, for which purpose it was drawn nine times across the front of the neck of the sick person.   After the third application, it was allowed to crawl away and afterwards killed, then its skin was sewn up in a piece of silk and hung round the patient's neck.   Sometimes the snake was placed in a bottle alive and then buried and, as it decayed, so the swelling in the neck was said to diminish.   The snake charmers of Egypt are stated to take serpent broth when they go out to catch the live ones and some African natives protect themselves against the bites of snakes by extracting the poison glands, squeezing them into their mouths and drinking the secretion.

The gall of the ox, which had a universal reputation for eye-troubles, was also used by the Anglo-Saxons, who dropped it in their ears to relieve deafness and noises in the head.   The hide, after being buried and dried, was applied to ease the pain of gout and also for hæmorrhoids.   Ants were frequently employed, and in Scotland the eggs, bruised and mixed with water and onion juice, when dropped in the ears, were said to cure deafness.   A spirit of ants was used for apoplexy, giddiness and catarrh, while the winged-ant was a favourite ingredient in love philtres.

Castoreum, prepared from the preputial follicles of the beaver, was used for "cramp, palsies, headache, epilepsy, convulsions and pain in the sinews".   Even the domestic cat was supposed to have its remedial virtues, and in some parts of the country, a black cat's tail was rubbed over a stye on the eye to cure it, while three drops of blood drawn from its tail were used for epilepsy.

Goat's fat was said by the ancient Egyptians to make the limbs supple. There was also a tradition that goats were skilled in the choice of herbs and she-goats were said never to be afflicted with ophthalmia because they browsed on certain plants which other animals refused.   Both the liver and gall of the goat were used in eye-troubles and its brain, drawn through a gold ring, was believed by the Anglo-Saxons to prevent epilepsy.

Many parts of the pig were believed to possess healing virtues.   The fat, blood, gall, teeth and eyes were used by the ancient Egyptians for various remedial purposes.   In this country, pig's fat had a reputation for curing warts.   After being rubbed on the spot it was nailed up in the sun.   It was also used to rub on painful parts for lumbago and pains in the chest, or neck.   For the same ailments a plaster was applied, composed of hog's fat salted and cheese, while the blood was employed as a bath for the feet and legs in cases of gout; the teeth ground to powder were used for indigestion, pleurisy, and quinsy, while the testicles had a reputation for promoting fecundity. The matrix of the pig was regarded as an excellent remedy for epilepsy and the brain as an aphrodisiac. Down to the present day, a powder scraped from a pig's stomach and dried, now known as pepsine, is employed for intestinal indigestion.

Pigeons, when newly split open, were applied to the soles of the feet of persons in extremis and also to snake bites, while wool fat from the sheep, which in a refined form we now call lanoline, was used by the Romans. Pliny enumerates thirty-two remedies prepared from it which were employed for various eye diseases.

From early times it was always regarded as unlucky to kill a spider, and there were many superstitions connected with the insect. The venom attributed to some spiders was supposed to be due to the insect attracting poison from the air, which it sucked up into its body, and so a living spider shut up in a box or walnut shell, was carried or worn round the neck, as a protection against ague. Elias Ashmole in his *Diary* (1681), tells us that he hung "three spiders about his neck to drive away his ague", and the webs, made into pills, were used in Eire for the same complaint. A live spider rolled up in butter was swallowed as a pill, as a cure for jaundice, and an oil, made from the crushed insects, employed for anointing the body, in cases of smallpox and plague.

This does not by any means exhaust the list of animals and other living creatures which from early times man has laid under tribute as remedies for healing, and although many of them have died out, some are still included in the armamentarium of the physician of today.

Chapter XVIII

PRECIOUS AND RARE STONES EMPLOYED IN HEALING

CERTAIN precious and other rare stones have for centuries been believed to possess remedial and healing properties. They were used in magical practises and generally supposed to be the abodes of good spirits, which enabled them to ward off evil influences.

Anselm de Boot, physician to Rudolph II, was of the opinion that "the evil-spirit taking the semblance of an angel of light, taketh up its abode in precious stones and enacts by them prodigies, in order that instead of having recourse to God, we may rest our minds in quiet and peace".

The connection or association of precious stones with the planets no doubt contributed to the faith placed in their mysterious virtues which embraced almost every form of physical or moral ailment. They were carried as talismans about the body, worn as amulets, or taken internally after being crushed and reduced to powder.

Each of the planetary bodies had certain precious stones over which it was believed to rule and exert an influence, and even in the seventeenth century, it was seriously considered whether the power of discrimination between right and wrong, legal or illegal affection, be a natural quality of the stone, or belonged to a spirit residing in it.

The agate was believed to cure the bites of scorpions and snakes, to soothe the mind and drive away contagious air, while amber was used to heal all affections of the throat and in the treatment of dysentery. The amethyst was said to prevent drunkenness and sharpen the wit, while the carbuncle drove away poisonous air and preserved health. The chyrsoprase was believed to strengthen the sight and coral was used to stop hæmorrhage and strengthen the digestion in adults and was given to children in powder, to ward off convulsions. Some of the virtues attributed to stones were no doubt due to the belief in the doctrine of signatures, as in the cases of the carnelian and bloodstone, the former being used to stop bleeding and cure dysentery.

The more valuable precious stones also had their virtues and the diamond was believed to prevent plague, the emerald to promote childbirth, arrest dysentery and act as an antidote to the bites of venomous reptiles. The ruby was said to protect the wearer from plague, to banish sadness, avert evil thoughts, dispel terrible dreams and repress sensuality. It was believed to become darker in colour when danger threatened the wearer, and when the peril had passed, to resume its natural hue.

Many virtues were attributed to the sapphire and it was said to have the magical power of inspiring chaste thoughts. It was believed to preserve the limbs from injury, to cure skin diseases and if held against the forehead to cure "rheumy eyes". St. Jerome asserts in his comments on Isaiah that "the sapphire conciliates the favour of princes, calms the fury of enemies, dispels enchantments, delivers from prison and softens the ire of God". "The sapphire," says another early writer, "banishes melancholy, protects against ague and prevents the eyes from being affected by smallpox." Besides these virtues the stone was said to cure fevers and agues and give strength and energy, when placed on the head. A sapphire worn in a ring was supposed to inspire pure thoughts, and should the wearer be intemperate, it lost its brightness and beauty. Sapphires vary in tint from a deep blue to pale azure, the former being designated by lapidaries as the male and the latter the female stone.

Some remarkable properties were also attributed to the emerald. Worn around the neck it was believed to protect the wearer against evil-spirits and to preserve chastity. It bestowed a knowledge of secrets and future events and gave the wearer eloquence in speech and increased wealth. It was supposed to betray inconstancy by splintering into fragments, when it could not prevent it, and to foretell something evil, should it fall from its setting. At the coronation of King George III, a large emerald is said to have fallen from his crown, which believers in the omen declared to presage the loss of America to Britain. It was believed to possess remarkable medicinal properties and was given internally in powder, for fevers and venomous bites. Hung round the neck of a child, it was said to protect it from epilepsy, and when applied to a wound, to stop hæmorrhage. A Jewish physician of the twelfth century declared that emeralds were the supreme cure for poisonous bites, if nine grains of the powdered stone were taken in wine.

The jacinth or hyacinth, when worn as an amulet, was reputed to prevent infection from the plague. It was believed to strengthen the heart, promote sleep and to increase riches and honours. It was said to give the wearer prudence and wisdom and preserve him from lightning. Medicinally, it was powdered and taken in vinegar to relieve coughs and prevent ruptures.

From time immemorial the amethyst has had a reputation for promoting temperance and preventing drunkenness, and for this reason was frequently used to decorate wine-cups. Camillius Leonardus refers to this property in the words, "bound to the navel it prevents drunkenness, it sharpens the wit, turns away evil thoughts and gives a knowledge of the future in dreams". It became a favourite stone for episcopal rings and is still so used, and was believed to cloud if the wearer was threatened with evil.

The topaz, in ancient times, was believed to possess properties similar to those of the ruby. It became paler in the presence of poisons and was worn on the left hand to "calm anger, banish melancholy, brighten the wit and give courage to the wearer". It was taken in wine to relieve asthma and recover loss of sleep, also to prevent nightmare. As a talisman, if bound to the left arm, it was said to dispel enchantments, calm the mind and cure hæmorrhoids.

For some occult reason that beautiful stone of varied hues, the opal, has acquired a reputation for bringing ill-luck to the wearer, but there appears to be no foundation for the belief. In early times it was called pederos (from *puer* a child) "in so much," says an ancient writer, "it was like a beautiful and innocent child and inspired the love of all". It was highly esteemed by the Romans, and Pliny tells us that "the Senator Monius was exiled by Mark Antony for the sake of the magnificent opal he wore, that was the size of a hazel-nut". Many good virtues were attributed to the opal, and it was reputed to aid the sight, dispel melancholy and sadness and preserve the wearer from contagious diseases.

Beryls were believed to possess many healing properties and were efficacious in relieving hysteria, jaundice, liver troubles and ailments of the mouth and throat. They were given in powder to relieve sore-eyes and stimulate the brain. The most important use of the beryl, however, was for "gazing" by the seers and astrologers as no other stone was believed to be so effective in forecasting the future.

The turquoise, according to ancient Eastern tradition, is a powerful protection against Evil-eye and is employed for this reason by both man and animals. It is worn in rings and in the form of necklaces by many women, and in the East is used to decorate the headbands of horses and the collars of camels. It was further said to possess the property of preventing headache, placating hatred and reconciling lovers. Like other gems, it was believed to change colour should evil threaten the wearer. This virtue is alluded to in the lines by Ben Jonson:

> Observe him as his watch observes his clock
> And time, as turquoise in the dear lord's ring;
> Look well or ill with him.

While Donne wrote:

> As a compassionate turkois that doth tell,
> By looking pale, the wearer is not well.

The aquamarine, so-called on account of its tints being likened to the sea, was said to make the wearer "skilful in navigation and protect him during voyages on the ocean".

The onyx was also associated with magic and was applied to the bites of venomous animals as a protection against the effects of poisonous insects and reptiles, and was worn round the neck to allay pain, stimulate the spleen, dispel melancholy and calm mental disturbance.

The carnelian, probably on account of its colour, was applied to wounds to stop hæmorrhage and prevent infection; the sardonyx was believed to protect the wearer from the bites of scorpions, and the serpentine to cure dropsy and prevent stone in the bladder, while the agate was used as a protection against venomous bites, particularly those given by the scorpion.

Amber, that mysterious concretion washed up by the sea, has long had a reputation for healing and relieving chest-diseases. The oil of amber was used as an embrocation and has been for centuries a favourite remedy for whooping-cough in children. Amber was said to be efficacious for sore-throat and bronchitis and was worn as a necklace in contact with the skin to impart its virtues.

Coral has been highly valued for its occult powers and medicinal properties from early times, and Pliny tells us it was deemed "excellent as an antidote to poisons". Later it was credited with still more marvellous powers, for another writer declares that "witches say this stone withstandeth lightning and putteth it, as well as whirlwindes tempestes and storms, from shippes and houses that it is in". Like turquoise, it was said to alter in colour according to the health of the wearer, and if worn by a person who was ill or in danger of death, it would become livid and pale. In the old play the *Three Ladies of London* (1594), this property is thus referred to: "You may say jet will draw up straw, amber will make one fat, coral will look pale when you are sick and crystal will staunch blood." As an amulet, or charm, it had a universal reputation as a protection against Evil-eye, a belief which is still common in Italy where pieces of coral fashioned in the shape of horns, or hands, are often worn about the person. The belief that it warded off evil-spirits and convulsions in young children led to the custom of placing a necklace of coral round the neck of a child soon after birth, while the "coral and bells" given to the baby, were supposed to drive away the spirits of evil. It was highly valued by the Romans and was believed to be an antidote to all poisons, while Paracelsus, in the sixteenth century, strongly recommended it for epilepsy.

Coral was believed to possess certain healing properties and entered into many medicinal preparations. Six drops of tincture of coral were recommended to be given in pestilential fevers, and ten grains of coral given to an infant in its mother's milk (provided it be a first child), and this be its only food, were said "to preserve it from epilepsy and convulsions throughout life".

In the seventeenth century, Boyle recommended coral to "sweeten the blood and cure acidity". Being chiefly composed of carbonate of lime, it doubtless has the latter property and like pearls, entered into the composition of tinctures, magisteries and syrups down to the eighteenth century.

Pearls continued to be used in medicine until the same period, when it began to be suspected that lime or chalk had the same effect. Seed pearls were ground to powder and taken for their antacid and cordial properties. Pomet says, "this powder was used by ladies of quality to give a lustre and beauty to the face" and thus powdered pearls became one of the first cosmetic powders. It was superseded, however, in the seventeenth century, by the magistery of bismuth, to which the name of "pearl-white" was given. "Pearls," says Jean de Renou in 1607, "are greatly cordial and rejoice the heart. The alchemists consequently make a liquor of pearl which they pretend is a marvellous cure for many maladies." It is recorded that a decoction of pearls and distilled water was one of the medicines administered to Charles VI, in the endeavour to restore him to sanity, and Pope Clement VII when ill, is stated to have taken 40,000 ducats' worth of pearls and other precious stones, within fourteen days.

The widespread belief during the Middle Ages in the healing virtues of precious stones is reflected in the formularies and pharmacopoeias of that period, many of which continued in use down to the close of the eighteenth century, as instanced in the compound called "Hungary Powder" which remained in the Pharmacopoeia of Nuremberg until 1798. This was renowned as a remedy for smallpox and measles and given in doses of from 20 to 30 grains. It was composed of emeralds, rubies, sapphires, hyacinth, pearls, red and white coral, Armenian bole, Terra Lemnia, hartshorn, ivory raspings, cinnamon, cloves, saffron, sorrel seeds, red and white sandal-wood, lemon-peel and gold leaf. All these were to be reduced to powder and carefully mixed together.

Another famous remedy was the Confection of Hyacinth which was regarded as a never-failing cordial for the heart, stomach and brain and was included in most of the old pharmacopoeias. It was said to "resist corruption of the humours and the malignity of the air" and was a favourite remedy with the physicians of the seventeenth century. The original formula consisted of hyacinths (probably amethysts), emeralds, sapphires, topaz, pearls, gold and silver leaves, musk, ambergris, myrrh, camphor, Lemnian earth and coral, made into an electuary with syrup of carnations.

Still another precious compound was that devised by the famous doctor Sennertus and called "Powder of Bezoar". It consisted of sapphires, rubies, hyacinths, red coral, Oriental bezoar, pearls, crabs' eyes, amber, white bole, bone of a stag's heart, and gold leaves, reduced to powder and well mixed. Given in doses of from 20 to 30 grains in wine, it was used as a remedy in cases of malignant fevers, smallpox and measles.

The Emperor Ferdinand devised a medicine as a protection against plague which consisted of 20 drugs and 20 grains each of sapphires, hyacinths, emeralds, rubies and garnets, reduced to powder and taken in doses of from ten to 40 grains.

William Bulleyn, author of the *Breviary of Health* and famous as a physician in the time of Henry VIII, advocated the use of an "Electuary of Gems" which, according to his prescription consisted of:

pearls, two little pieces of sapphire, jacinthe, cornelian, emeraldes, garnettes, of each one ounce; with mace, basil-seeds, ginger, cinnamon, spikenard, gold and silver leaves, redde coral, amber and shavings of ivory, made into an electuary with honey of roses.

He tells us, "it healed colds, disease of the brain, heart and stomach" and says, "Kings and Noble men have used it for their comfort. It causeth them to be bold spirited, the body to smell well and engendereth to the face good colour."

Even Galen, one of the "Fathers of Medicine", recommended jasper to benefit the chest when laid on the stomach, and says, "a necklace of jaspers hung round the neck should reach down to the affected part".

It was chiefly owing to the ancient tradition that nearly all precious stones were antagonistic to poisons that led to them being so frequently used to decorate wine-cups, to which a piece of unicorn's horn was often added as an antidote.

When Louis XI became reconciled to his brother the Duc de Guienne after their quarrel, the king sent him as a token of renewed friendship, a beautiful gold cup encrusted with precious stones which were said to have the power of protecting from poison anyone who used it. Among them was a fine ruby, which was regarded as an antidote to poison and a protection from plague.

There was a general belief among the Greeks and Romans that the engraving of a figure or design on the stones worn increased their medicinal virtues. This idea was ultimately reduced to a system, for many purposes. Thus we find that a dog and a lion engraved on a stone, worn in a ring, was regarded as a protection against dropsy and pestilence. Jupiter, with a ram's head, secured confidence and plausibility; the figure of Orion gave victory in battle and Perseus, holding in one hand a sword and in the other the Gorgon's head, preserved the wearer against lightning and assaults of the devil.

Camillius Leonardus, physician to Caesar Borgia, declared that "if precious stones were engraved by a skilful person under a particular influence that influence would be transmitted to the stone and the virtue of the figure and of the stone would be doubled".

Such were some of the curious beliefs in precious stones in the Middle Ages and later, when Jerome Cardan and other writers on medicine gave great prominence in their works to their marvellous healing virtues. The great cost of the gems employed in compounding these recipes and prescriptions in the seventeenth and eighteenth centuries, however, often led the apothecaries to substitute artificial in place of genuine stones which, while it increased their profits, apparently did no harm to the patients. So these costly ingredients gradually went out of use.

Chapter XIX

MAN'S BODY AND ITS USE IN HEALING

ORGANOTHERAPY, or the employment of the organs of man and animals as remedial agents in healing the body, is by no means a modern development in medicine, as it goes back over 2000 years. Charas, the famous physician and chemist, writing in the seventeenth century says:

The creator has given to man a peculiar knowledge of many medicines contained in his own body in his lifetime and in the body of other men after their deaths, far superior to those that are comprehended in the bodies of any other creature whatsoever; so that chemistry need not want work, while busied in those copious preparations, which include not only the skull and other bones of men, the blood, the fat, the flesh and mummy which is the body embalmed and dried, but also the nails, the hair, the urine and other excrements even to the secundines of women; so that it may be said there is not any part, no superfluity in man or woman which chemistry cannot prepare for the cure and ease of the most diseases and pains to which they both are subject.

This is to a large extent true today, for we get adrenalin from the suprarenal and iodothyrin from the thyroid gland ; and epinephrin, insulin, and many other substances now regarded as of the utmost value in healing, from the organs of animals.

The fundamental idea underlying the belief in the remedial virtues of animal substances in ancient times was that the principal parts and organs of the human body were furnished with a volatile salt which, when separated out by distillation, possessed medicinal properties capable of healing many diseases to which man was liable. Thus we find that portions of the skull, before being employed, were first subject to distillation and broken pieces, or filings, were placed with sufficient spirit of wine and sage and digested for twenty days in a retort. The residue was again digested with more spirit and redistilled thrice; then after seven days, the spirit was partly driven off over a Balneo Marie and the concentrated essence was ready for use. From two to twenty drops of this were administered in cases of epilepsy. This spirit of skull had a great vogue and Charles II, whose interest in chemistry is well known, was accustomed to amuse himself by preparing it in his private laboratory at Whitehall. He is said to have purchased the secret of its preparation for the sum of £1,500, from a Dr. Goddard, the inventor of "Goddard's Drops," which he introduced in the time of the Commonwealth. Goddard afterwards became professor of physic at Gresham College and, says Monk, "He was a good practical chemist and his drops were recommended by Sydenham." This preparation, which obtained a wide reputation, was afterwards known as the "King's Drops" or the "English Drops".

Dr. Martin Lister when in Paris in 1698, was summoned by the Prince de Conti to see his son, who was suffering from this disease and was requested to bring with him some of "King Charles's Drops", as it was believed to be a specific in epilepsy. The formula as published in *Bate's Dispensary* contained opium, which was to be distilled with the spirit of wine and pieces of skull.

Human skulls are quoted in a price list of drugs, printed in London in 1685, at eight shillings, nine shillings and ten shillings each, and like other human bones used in medicine, were sometimes calcined and when powdered given for dysentery, the marrow and oil, after being extracted from the bones, being employed for rheumatism. Curiously enough, the last remedy administered to Charles II in his fatal illness was the Spirit of Skull in which he was so much interested, for it was believed to possess powerful stimulating properties.

Paracelsus was the originator of a confection which he called "Confection Anti-Epileptica" which was prepared from three human skulls taken from men who had died a violent death and had not been buried. When broken up, the skulls were distilled with musk, castoreum and honey after which liquor of pearls and a few drops of oil of vitriol were added. Berlu says the skull of a man ought to be "such as one which dieth of a violent death as in war, or criminal execution and never buried".

In connection with the skull, another curious remedy was the moss found growing on skulls of the dead, called *Usnea*. "English druggists," says Pomet, "especially those in London, sell skulls of the dead upon which there is a little greenish moss called *Usnea*, because of its near resemblance to the moss which grows on the oak. These skulls mostly come from Ireland where they frequently let the bodies of criminals hang on the gibbet till they fall to pieces." Another writer says, "the skulls from Ireland are best esteemed, being very clean and white and often covered with moss, which possesses great astringent properties and when applied to a wound will stop hæmorrhage". *Usnea* was exported to Germany where there was a considerable demand for it for making the Sympathic Ointments and Powders then in vogue.

The human brain was employed as a remedial agent by the ancient Egyptians at least 3000 years ago and is mentioned in the *Papyrus Ebers*, in a recipe given as an application for the eyes. It reads: "Take the brain of a man and divide it into two parts. Mix one part with honey and with it anoint the eyes each evening. The other half dry and powder it finely and with it anoint the eyes in the morning."

The brain was also used in the form of spirit and oil, one recipe for the former being as follows:

Take the brain of a young man under twenty-four, that died violently, with all its membranes, arteries, veins and nerves, with all spinal marrow. Beat it and add Cephalick Water as of Tile flowers, Peony, Betony, Black cherries, Lavander, Lilly. Let them stand a while then distill by cohobation.

Make a salt from the residue and join to the spirit. It is a brave anteplepticat given from half to four scruples a dose.

The spirit of the brain of man called "Golden Water" was also given in cases of epilepsy.

Human blood has been employed as a healing agent from times of antiquity. The Romans believed the blood of the gladiators gave strength and courage and Celsus alludes to it and says: "Some persons have been freed from this disease (epilepsy) by drinking hot blood, taken from a gladiator who had just been slain." It continued to be used by the physicians in the Middle Ages to prevent convulsive attacks, and when dried and powdered, as a styptic to stop hæmorrhage. Several writers on medicine in the sixteenth and seventeenth centuries comment on its value. "Blood," says Renodaeus, "is Nature's treasury. The blood of a diseased or intemperate man must not be collected and kept in the shops but only that from sound and temperate men", while Charas observes: "All writers extol the volatile salt of man's blood for the cure of epilepsy. It is also effectual in dropsy, in gout and as a scorbutick to help eruptions of the skin." In connection with the last statement, it is interesting to note that fresh human blood, taken from a patient suffering from eczema, has been recommended by leading French dermatologists to be administered subcutaneously in obstinate cases of dermatitis and skin troubles. A spirit of human blood which consisted of the liquid distilled from it mixed with angelica water and tincture of peony flowers, was highly esteemed as a remedy in cases of asthma, palsy, apoplexy and epilepsy in the seventeenth century.

The employment of human blood drawn from living persons for the purpose of transfusion is now recognized as being of the greatest possible value in saving life and its collection is regarded as of national importance in wartime.

During the Middle Ages, even menstrual blood was used and recommended as an application for gout by Paracelsus who called it, "Maid's Zenish". Etmuller says, "it should first be mixed with crow's fat and was then a good application for abcesses and carbuncles". Urine, as might be expected on account of its colour, was given internally in cases of jaundice and dropsy, while it was also said to cause easy delivery, if taken by women in labour. It was further employed to cleanse wounds, and the urine of a boy was dropped into the ears to relieve soreness. Of the many preparations made from urine the best known was the spirit which was given for stone, gout and asthma, while the volatile salt and the magistery were said to possess anodyne and sudorific properties. To prevent the formation of calculi, the magistery was given in doses of ten grains to be taken once a month before the new moon, when it was said "to cure consumption wonderfully".

With reference to its reputed anodyne property, there is the evidence given by Madame de Sévigné who, writing to her daughter on June 13,

1685, remarks: "For my vapours I take eight drops of essence of urine and contrary to its usual action, it has prevented me from sleeping."

Human fat also had its uses and was greatly esteemed as an embrocation for rheumatism and pains in the joints. "The fat of man," writes Berlu, "gathered from those parts, as suet is made from other creatures," was highly valued. Pomet declares that "Everybody in Paris knows the public executioner sells it; the druggists and apothecaries a little; nevertheless they vend a sort of it, prepared with aromatic herbs and which is without comparison much better than comes from the hangman".

A liquor distilled from human hair, mixed with honey, is recommended by Lovell as "a stimulating application for a bald head" and when finely chopped up was given internally for jaundice.

It is well known that burning hair, like feathers, has been used as a restorative in fainting attacks from an early period, and nail-parings from the fingers and toes when put into wine, were given as an emetic. A cure for consumption was carried out by taking portions of hair and nails from a suffering patient and, after being cut up in small pieces, inserting them in a hole made in the root of a cherry tree; or they were mixed with wax and attached to a live crab and thrown into the sea.

Pliny says that Marcellus employed human gall in the treatment of cataract and it was also utilized for all affections of the eyes. An extract made from the spirit was dropped into the ear for deafness and the Chinese still employ it to clear the sight, in all eye troubles.

Frequent mention is made by many early writers of human milk as a remedial agent, and in the *Papyrus Ebers* it is given as an ingredient in several recipes for diseases of the eyes. The Hindus and Arabs also believed in its efficacy for the same purpose, and down to the seventeenth century it was used to allay irritation of the eyelids.

The use of human saliva in healing has been recognized from time immemorial and is frequently mentioned in the Bible and the Talmud. In the latter, it is affirmed that while the saliva of a newborn male child is effective, that of a female is useless for healing purposes. The Romans believed that Imperial saliva had special curative virtues and Pliny states that ophthalmia may be cured by the application of a woman's saliva to the eyes every morning. The Arab physicians were firm believers in its efficacy and Rhazes recommends it to be dropped into the eyes after an operation, and as a cure for white specks in the eye. It was also used as an antidote for the bites of snakes, venomous reptiles and mad dogs, while it was declared to act with magical effect in the removal of warts, a common belief at the present day.

Finally, we have mention of the human heart, after being dried and powdered, as a curative agent in the treatment of epilepsy, while a valued remedy for consumption consisted in a decoction prepared from the heart, liver and lungs taken from a freshly slaughtered young black calf. This preparation remained as an official agent in the pharmaceutics for the treatment of persons suffering with paralysis of the extremities and emaciation down to the eighteenth century, and the formula for making it was included in the Prussian Dispensatory, as late as 1744.

Having dealt with the various organs of the human body which were believed to possess remedial and healing virtues, mention must be made of the mummified remains of man's frame which were extensively employed in medicine from the twelfth to the seventeenth century. The name of the person who first introduced mummy into medicine has not been handed down to posterity, but we know from the works of Avicenna, the Arab physician, who flourished between A.D. 980 and 1037, that it was used in his time in the treatment of paralysis, skin eruptions, abcesses and disorders of the liver and spleen.

Its healing properties were believed to be due to the bitumen obtained from the Dead Sea, which was said to be employed in embalming. Diodorus Siculus refers to the medicinal value of bitumen from Babylonia and the Dead Sea and declares that the Barbarians exported it to Egypt, where it was sold for embalming the dead; while Strabo alludes to asphaltum used by the Egyptians for embalming. There seems little doubt that bitumen was largely used as a remedial agent. Recent investigators, however, deny that it was used in embalming, and hold that the tradition arose from the statements of the early classical authors, owing to the resins and other substances which are black and lustrous simulating bitumen. Analysis shows it was not employed in embalming in Egypt, or else it has eluded modern scientific research made by well-known chemists.

From the works of the classical writers, the use of mummy for medicinal purposes passed into the Middle Ages, from which period to the end of the seventeenth century it is frequently mentioned. Guy de la Fontsine, physician to the king of Navarre, made a journey to Egypt to investigate the source of supply as the demand increased. He states that while in Alexandria, he visited a Jew who showed him his stock, which consisted of some forty mummies which he owned that he himself prepared in four years. He admitted having collected the bodies of slaves and other persons which he opened and filled with bitumen. He then bandaged them and dried them in the sun, until they assumed the appearance of true Egyptian mummies. The increased demand for mummy led to the manufacture of substitutes and fraudulent commerce. Pomet, writing in the seventeenth century says:

We may daily see the Jews carrying on their rogueries as to these mummies and after them the Christians, for the mummies which were brought from Alexandria, Venice and Lyons are nothing else but the bodies of people who have died various ways. I am not able to stop the abuses committed by those who use this commodity. I shall only advise such as buy, to choose what is of fine shining black, not full of bones and dirt, of good smell and which being burnt does not stink of pitch. Such is proper for contusions and to hinder blood from coagulating in the body.

Sir Thomas Brown aptly remarks in his *Hydriotaphia*: "The Egyptian mummies which Cambyses or time hath spared, avarice now consumes.

Mummy has become merchandise. Mizraim cures wounds and Pharaoh is sold for balsams." And so the Jew eventually had his revenge on his ancient oppressors.

Ambroise Paré (1509–1590), the famous French military surgeon, strongly deprecated the use of mummy as a remedial agent but he did not convince many other physicians of his time, for even the renowned Paracelsus (1492–1541) recommended it and devised a Balsam of Mummy and a Treacle of Mummy, both of which had a considerable vogue.

In the Middle Ages magic still played a considerable part in rational medicine. The bitumen employed as a remedial agent was no doubt derived from natural sources in early times; it was succeeded by the pitch-like resinous substances obtained from mummified human bodies, and its virtue was so believed to be transferred to the bodies themselves by some magical power. Thus we find that Parkinson in his *Theatre of Plants* (1640), in his account of the Virtues of Mummies, remarks: "It is the very body of a man or woman, brought chiefly from Egypt or Syria (no other part of the world so good). True mummy must be embalmed in the Egyptian fashion and not after the manner of the Jews." The chief preparations of mummy in the pharmacopoeias of the fifteenth and sixteenth centuries were a tincture, a treacle, an elixir and a balsam. The substance was rarely given alone. The balsam was prepared by mixing and digesting for a month, half a pound of the tincture, with Venice treacle 4 ounces, Salt of Pearl 2 drachms, Coral 2 drachms, Terra Sigillata 2 ounces and Musk 1 drachm. This mixture was declared to possess such a "piercing quality that it pierceth all parts, restores wasted limbs, hecticks, and cures all ulcers and corruptions".

Mummy itself was administered in the form of powder, or as a bolus, in doses of two drachms for epilepsy, vertigo and palsy and was also applied externally to wounds, to prevent mortification. It is quoted in a price-list of drugs in 1685, at 5s. 4d. a pound. It is still sold in the Turkish drug shops in the Grand Bazaar at Istanbul but is very costly. A few grains in wine is said to be taken by Turkish women to relieve headache. As late as 1750 it was included in the *Pharmacopoeia Universalis*, although by that time it had lost favour among the practitioners of medicine.

Its popularity in earlier years may be judged from the many allusions made to it by Shakespeare and other playwrights of the period. Thus, in *Macbeth* (Act IV, Scene I), tooth of witches' mummy is mentioned as one of the ingredients in the cauldron. And in the *Merry Wives of Windsor* Falstaff declares: "Water swells a man and what a thing I should have been when I had been swelled! I should have been a mountain of mummy." Again in *Othello* (Act III, Scene V) his handkerchief, which had great virtues, "was dy'd in mummy which the skilful conserved of maiden's hearts".

James Shirley (1596–1666) in his *Honest Lawyer* observes: "That I might tear their flesh in mammocks, raise my losses from their carcasses turn'd mummy"; and in the *Bird in a Cage* we have the lines: "Make mummy of my flesh and sell me to the apothecaries."

Chapter XX

MAGICAL GIRDLES USED IN HEALING

CHARMS and incantations have been associated with childbirth, particularly in connection with girdles and belts, from early times. Women, no doubt almost by instinct, found relief in pressure in difficult labours and the employment of a girdle for the purpose, especially one supposed to be endowed with magical virtues which would bring about a successful and safe delivery, was eagerly sought.

Henry, in his *History of Britain*, tells us that among the ancient Britons, when a birth was attended with any difficulty, they put certain girdles made for that purpose about the women in labour, which they imagined gave immediate and effectual relief.

Girdles of this description were, until recent times, preserved with care by many families in the Highlands of Scotland. Some of these were imprinted with mystical figures and the ceremony of binding about the woman's waist was accompanied by words and gestures, which showed the custom to have been one of great antiquity.

We know from the "Injunctions at the Visitation of Edmundes, Bishop of London", between 1555 and 1559, that the midwives in that period used charms and magical invocations during childbirth. Thus, in the article to be enquired in the "Visitacyon in the fyrst yeare of Queen Elizabeth" it is stated: "Item, whether you know anye that doe use Charms, Sorcery, Enchauntments or Invocations, Circles, witchecrafts, southsayinge or any lyke craftes or Imaginacions invented by the Devyl and especially in the tyme of Womens travayle."

A written charm to be bound to the wrist to promote easy delivery, is inscribed in a manuscript dated 1475.

The girdle also played a part in the religious ceremonials of ancient races, including the Hindus and Mexicans. In the Zorastrian ritual, the sacred Kusthior girdle with which all children were invested at the age of fifteen, had to be made according to a definite numerical design and was passed three times round the waist and knotted twice. The oldest charms connected with the girdle are to be found in the *Atharva-Veda*. It assumed its healing significance on the birth of the Buddha, the Sun-physician, who was believed to have come into the world with a branch of sandalwood in his hand, symbolic of medicine, and among his other possessions was the "girdle of the circling sun, who bound day and night into a perfect whole".

The function of the girdle as used for the suspension of amulets is commented upon by the late Sir Grafton Elliot-Smith, the Egyptologist, who attributed its employment for this purpose to its use as a precaution against danger to life. And also as a means of conferring fecundity on girls by providing the circumstances which enabled men to discover that the sexual attractiveness of maidens—in a state of nature originally associated with modesty and coyness—was profoundly intensified by the artifices of clothing and adornment.

From the love-compelling girdle of Aphrodite to the Teuton Brunhilde's belt which promoted great strength, the girdle has been associated with magic, and from the protection given by the magic girdle originated the amulets used in ancient times as a protection against evil-spirits, especially those which were believed to bring disease. Pliny the elder asserts that if the girdle worn by the Romans every day was tied very hard with a Hercules knot in which no ends were visible, it would have a good effect and that Hercules himself was the first to discover it. From this it may be inferred that the value of the girdle in giving support to the muscles of the abdomen was recognized in classical times.

It was customary in Macedonia, in order to cure a woman of hæmorrhage, to write the following prayer on a piece of paper and tie it to her belly with a single thread saying: "Our Father the God of Abraham; the God of Jacob; the God of Isaac; the God who stayed the river Martham on the sixth day; stay also the flowing of the blood of thy servant . . . and the seal of our Lord Jesus Christ. Stand we fairly; stand we with fear of God. Amen. And may the evangelists Matthew, Mark, Luke and John cure the patient."

In early times both the Scottish and the Irish placed the greatest faith in the power of magic belts or girdles to protect them from danger. Thus, MacCuaric, or Kennedy of Lianachan in Lochabar, bound the captured Glaistig to his horse with "the Wizard Belt of Fillan"; while a charm attributed to an Irish monk found in the library of the monastery at Klosterneuburg ran as follows: "The girdle of Finnan is round about me that I walk not the way which encudeth the people . . . against disease, against anxiety, against the charms of foolish women. The girdle of St. John is my girdle, the serpent is about me that men may not wound me, that women may not destroy me; to the stars that it hath exalted me; at my hour it is about me." In Norse folk-lore the magical blue belt of the elfin had the power of increasing the wearer's strength, and in the Island of Harris and the neighbouring country, the crofters used to wear a girdle of sealskin below the waist as a protection against sciatica, while in Aberdeen it was said also to cure "Chin-cough". The faith in the healing belt persists in the northern counties of England today, where a broad belt of red flannel is often worn as a protection against rheumatism, or sciatica.

In Ardnamurchan, when a child was born, it was customary to wind a rope of grass round it, which was believed to act as a protection against many diseases. To make it effective, however, it was necessary that the grass should be pulled and not cut, while its power was said to be increased if it was also put round the neck and chest of the child, in the form of a cross.

De Plancy, writing on *Ceintures Magique*, says that "in France many secret books teach you that all sorts of internal maladies are cured in sick persons, by wearing a girdle of ferns plucked at noon, on the eve of St. John's day and then woven, so as to form the magical characters HUTY".

In some Roman Catholic countries, belief in the efficacy of the girdle in difficult labours still persists ; Lupton especially mentions the skin of the snake for the purpose and says: "Let the woman that travails with her child be girded with the skin that a serpent, or snake, casts off and then she will quickly be delivered."

In France these girdles were usually associated with the name of some saint, as in the case of the famous girdle of St. Oyan, while a more modern survival is perpetuated in Brittany, where the nuns of St. Ursula of Quinton, when any of their pupils marry and become pregnant, send a ribbon of white silk embroidered in blue with the words *Notre Dame de Deliverance Protegez-vous*. Before being sent, the ribbon is touched with the reliquary preserved in the Church in which is kept the precious relic of a girdle believed to have been worn by the Virgin Mary.

The Serbian and Bosnian gipsies wear a girdle, five fingers in breadth, worked from the hair of an ass's tail, in which is sewn successively with red cotton a star, a waxing moon and a waning moon. It is believed to diminish the pains of labour and keep away from the body the demons of disease. The Danes were accustomed to wear girdles of human skin to promote easy childbirth. Down to the close of the eighteenth century the strips of skin employed are said to have been obtained from condemned criminals, while living, by the public executioners.

Macpherson tells us that, according to his knowledge, sanctified girdles were kept in many families in the north of Scotland, to bind about women in time of travail. They were inscribed with mystic symbols and on putting them on, certain invocations were muttered.

Belief in the magic girdle has not yet died out in some parts of Britain and only a few years ago, a doctor on proceeding to examine the chest of a woman patient at Keith, discovered a leather belt around the part and on inquiring why she wore it, was told that it helped her trouble which she believed was heart disease.

Before leaving the subject of girdles, mention should be made of the chastity-belts or girdles worn in the Middle Ages by the women in Continental countries.

It is stated that Roman maidens wore them as emblems of chastity, but from the fourteenth to the sixteenth century there is evidence that jealous husbands used to gird their wives and securely lock the belt before leaving them, when setting out for the Wars. These girdles were made of thin metal, hinged, and covered with velvet, and were secured by a small padlock, the key of which was kept by the husbands. Specimens of these curious relics are still to be found in museums, and two authentic girdles of this description are preserved in the Museum of the Royal College of Surgeons of England, in London.

Chapter XXI

MAGICAL AND MEDICINAL RINGS OF HEALING

THE connection of rings and certain curious stones with magic and healing is of great antiquity, and was probably of similar origin to the circle that played such an important part in magical ceremonies in giving protection and warding off the spirits of evil.

There are many early traditions concerning the famous ring of King Solomon that was said to have been inscribed with the mystic word "SCHEMHAPHORASCH", and which gave the King the command of spirits and procured for him the wonderful "SHAMIR" that enabled him to build the Temple. Every day at noon, it was said to transport him into the firmament where he heard the secrets of the Universe. This continued until he was persuaded by the Devil to grant him his liberty and to take the ring from his finger. The demon then assumed his shape as King of Israel and reigned three years, while Solomon became a wanderer in foreign lands.

There is another story that when Solomon looked on his ring, he beheld whatsoever he desired to know in heaven and upon earth. One day, when about to enter his bath, he took it off, when it was snatched up by a fury and thrown into the sea. Greatly disturbed by his loss which not only deprived him of power over the spirits of the air, earth and sea, but also his wisdom to rule, he resolved never to reseat himself on his throne until he recovered it. This he miraculously did for the ring was found in the belly of a fish that was brought to the King's table.

The earliest magical rings were probably those bearing mystic symbols. The metals of which they were composed also had a bearing on their power, and in an early Hebrew manuscript there is mention of a ring of copper and iron which was said to make the wearer invisible.

The ancient Greeks favoured rings on the stones of which were engraved the heads or figures of certain deities whom they believed had the power of warding off evil and promoting health. In the Scholiast of Aristophanes of Plutus (408 B.C.) allusion is made to magical or healing rings which were sold at Athens and in the play the Just Man observes: "Here's a charmed ring I am wearing that I bought for a drachma from Eudemos." Such rings are said to have been sold by the drug vendors for their curative properties.

Rings bearing Runic characters, believed to possess remedial virtues, were worn in Anglo-Saxon times, and one is described in the *Archaeological Journal*, bearing the words: "Whether in fever or leprosy let the patient be happy and confident in the hope of recovery." Others were worn to

135

prevent plague, as instanced in a Dano-Saxon ring excavated a few years ago, inscribed:

> Raise us from dust we pray thee,
> From pestilence, Oh set us free,
> Although the grave unwilling be.

Many examples of mystical formula came through Alexandria from Egypt and the countries of the Far East and these continued to be used on rings throughout the Middle Ages.

The Roman physician Marcellus, who flourished in the second century, advised those who were afflicted with a pain in the side to wear a ring of pure gold, engraved with Greek letters, each Thursday, on the wane of the moon. It was to be worn on the right hand if the pain was in the left side and vice versa. Alexander of Tralles, another famous physician of the sixth century, recommended an octagonal ring of iron on which eight words were engraved that commanded the bile which caused colic and bilious ailments to enter the body of a lark. He was a firm believer in amulets and talismans as remedial agents and mentions a copper ring bearing the figure of a lion, a crescent and a star, to cure stone when worn on the fourth finger of the right hand. For colic alone, he preferred a ring bearing a representation of Hercules strangling a lion.

During the Christian era, rings engraved with sacred symbols or the figures of saints and invocations, came into vogue for healing purposes. Although the Church disapproved of the custom it added to the stock of magical formulae with words taken from scripture, or the angelic salutation. Some bore an invocation to the Saints Cosmas and Damian, the patrons of medicine and pharmacy, while others were inscribed with the names of the three Magi, Caspar, Melchior and Balthazar who were supposed to give protection against attacks of epilepsy. John of Arderne, the English physician (1307), recommended these names to be written with blood drawn from the little finger of an epileptic person, to be worn as a charm to ward off the disease. The "Three Kings of Cologne" appear to have had a close connection with epilepsy and sufferers were recommended to carry about with them the following lines, written on parchment:

> Caspar with his myrrh beganne
> These presents to unfold,
> Then Melchior brought frankincense
> And Balthazar brought gold.
> Now he that of these Holie Kings
> The names about shall beare,
> The falling yll by grace of Christ
> Shall never need to feare.

The words *Ave Maria* seem to have been the words most frequently used on prophylactic rings. One recently examined, which is set with a large cabochon sapphire held in three lion's mouths, is inscribed, "AVE MARIA GRACIA PLENA" and another, set with an uncut sapphire, bears the words "AVEMARIAGI".

The sacred names "Jesu" and "Maria" were also sometimes inscribed on rings of healing, and Joan of Arc is said to have always worn a ring bearing the words "JESU MARIA" on her finger, a gift from a member of her family. Another inscribed "JESUS AUTEN TRANSI" is referred to by Mandeville as being a charm against enemies and thieves. A carved figure of the Virgin and Child has also been found, bearing the words "AVE VIRGO MARIA MATRE" and "DE PIETATE MARIE."

In early times, it is well known there was a belief that the planetd were closely connected with certain metals, as well as precious stones ane herbs, and John Gower gives some account of this. He says: "Rings made of lead should be set with black onyx and have a piece of root of yew, cypree, willow, or black hellebore. Of tin, set with a sapphire, amethyst or emerald, hyacinth or topaz and root of oak, cherry-tree, almond, chestnut, clove, mulberry or barberry trees. When made of copper, they should be set with jasper and the root of olive, sycamore tree, or of silver set with sardis or crystal and root of the linden tree." The practising magician's ring which usually formed part of his equipment was made of copper or lead, was three inches in breadth and inscribed with the word "TETRAGRAMMATON". A hole was made through the middle of it so it could be secured to the finger; and before being worn, it had to be consecrated and anointed with Holy Oil, then placed on a finger of the left hand.

Magic rings of gold are not common but one is known set with a crescent-shaped turquoise, bearing the inscription: "ET VERBVM CARO FACTUM EST ET ABABITABIS INOBIS ETVDIMUS GROLIAM". Anrold de Villanova in the sixteenth century states that these words were used as a talisman and worn as an amulet against disease.

Rings worn as a protection against attacks of cramp and epilepsy have been used in England since the time of Edward the Confessor, to whose famous ring their origin is said to be due. The story of the miracles performed by it are told in Caxton's *Golden Legend*. Cramp, the name commonly applied to that painful muscular contraction in limb, finger or stomach, the cause of which was regarded as a mystery, was a frequent ailment among the people of England in the Middle Ages, when the dwelling-places were both damp and cold. So it is little to be wondered at that sufferers turned to magic for its cure.

There is a tradition that the sapphire now set in the British Crown came from the ring of Edward the Confessor, the possession of which gave English sovereigns not only the power of "Healing by Touch" but also of transmitting that virtue to rings "hallowed" or "blessed" by them. Others state that the healing power was acquired by the monarchs from the anointing with Holy Oil, used at the Coronation.

Although the kings of France participated in the "Healing by Touch" the blessing, or hallowing of the Cramp-rings was the exclusive prerogative of the kings and queens of England. These rings, we are told, were much sought after by sufferers from cramp and epilepsy and were even sent to foreign countries as special gifts. There is authentic record that from the early part of the fourteenth century, the kings of England took part in the ceremony of "Hallowing the Rings" in a special service, at which the following prayer was said: "Sanctify O Lord these rings and graciously bedew them with the dew of Thy benediction and consecrate them by the rubbing of our hands, which Thou hast been pleased according to our ministery to sanctify with an external diffusion of holy oyle upon them; to the end that what the nature of the mettal is not able to perform, may be wrought by the greatness of Thy grace."

The Royal Cramp-rings were of gold or silver and made from the royal offerings to the Cross on Good Friday, after being touched or handled by the monarchs. Other rings were made of the baser metals such as iron, lead or bronze, while the nails and metal furniture from coffins that had been buried were supposed to possess special remedial virtues. It is probable that these rings were hallowed by dignitaries of the Church and distributed to those who needed them. There are very few authentic Cramp-rings now known to exist.

Through the kindness of Her Majesty Queen Mary a search was made among the relics at Windsor Castle a few years ago, for a specimen of the Royal Cramp-rings of gold but nothing of the kind was discovered. Waterton surmised that Cramp-rings were plain hoops like a wedding-ring, although he had never met with a specimen. It is probable that the style of the rings varied according to the period in which they were made, but there is evidence also that people were allowed to bring their own personal rings to be "blessed" by the monarchs.

The most authentic Cramp-ring known was discovered some years ago, when excavating on the site of a monastery of the Black Friars, near Perth in Scotland. It was found, together with some surgical instruments, coins and other dateable objects of the sixteenth century, although the ring itself is at least a century earlier. It is a hoop of bronze, or brass, with a slightly flattened bezel on which is inscribed the sacred symbol "I.H.S." and is much worn.

The earliest record concerning the Royal Cramp-rings occurs in the Constitutions of the Household of Edward II, 1307–1327, where it is stated: "Likewise the King must for certain offer on Good Friday, 5 shillings which he is accustomed to receive in person from the hand of the chaplain, to make rings of them to give for medicine to divers persons."

Further references to the Royal Cramp-rings are made in the Account Rolls of Edward III, Richard II and Edward IV.

In a manuscript now in the British Museum, written in 1422 during the reign of Henry VI, an interesting reference is made to the "Kings of England and their endowment with certain powers by special grace from heaven, whereby they cure the disease known as the King's Evil". It is also recorded that:

Epileptics too and persons subject to the falling-sickness are cured by means of gold and silver, devoutly touched and offered by the sacred anointed hands of the Kings of England, upon Good Friday during Divine Service, according to the ancient custom of the Kings of England, as has been proved by frequent trials of rings made of the said gold and silver and placed on the fingers of the sick persons, in many parts of the world.

Henry VIII appears to have hallowed Cramp-rings both before and after his breach with the Roman Church, and Brewer, in his reference to the amusements of the Court in 1516–1518 says "they were diversified by hunting and outdoor sports in the morning and in the afternoon by Memi's music and by the consecration of cramp-rings". Writing to Bishop Gardner on April 4, 1529, Anne Boleyn, who was then in Rome, says: "Mr. Stevens . . . I send you here Cramp-rings for you and Mrs. Gregory and Mr. Peters. Pray you distribute them. . . ." These rings Gardner appears to have distributed among the English Embassy to the Pope, then in Rome on a mission concerning the proposed divorce of the King and later he writes of "The Royal fingers pouring such virtue into the metal that no disorder could resist it". The making of Cramp-rings increased considerably about this time and the "English Rings", as they came to be called, were in great demand in many countries in Europe, where they were highly valued.

Some idea of the number made may be gathered from the Account Book kept by Bryan Tuke, Treasurer of the Chamber to Henry VIII, in which "40 ounces of gold of the fynest at 41s. 4d. per ounce and 130 ounces of silver rings at 4s. 4d. per ounce" is charged for Cramp-Rings. Robert Amadas, "Maister of the Kingis Juelles" also received "£118 16s. 8d. in December 1532 for Cramp-Rings, namely £8 more than is warranted if gold of the fynest be reckoned at 41s. 4d. per ounce."

In the exchequer accounts of Henry VIII in the year following 1533, mention is made that he gave sixty specially blessed golden rings to Hubertus, the Envoy of the Palgrave Frederick II, Elector Palatine.

Another item reads:

To the Kynge's offerings to the Crosse on Good Friday, from the countyng house for medcynable rings of gold and sylver delyveryed to the jewell house.

Healing and medicinal rings to relieve gout and rheumatism were also made as early as the sixteenth century and a favourite one for the last-named malady was composed of zinc and copper, similar to the so-called rheumatic rings sold in Britain in recent years.

There is an interesting letter among the historical MSS. in the British Museum, addressed to the Earl of Lauderdale, requesting him to send the

Duke of Hamilton a "gout-ring". The letter is partly in cypher and signed M.L. 8 of Feby. 15—. It reads:

> This is only to demonstrate that I doe willingly neglect occasion of writing, when I shall only say none knew you were in Scotland, Lord save my lady Duchess, for my Lord Duke is gone away to day. . . . Speaking of the Duke puts me in mind to bid you send him such a *gout-ring* as you gave me to send to my father when you were last at home, for the Duke hath that wearing now and your old servant Kennedy hath got loan of it from my father and he wanted it, for he is undone with the gout, which was a means to keep him from any trouble of it while he wore it.

The Earl of Peterborough possessed a magical seal of silver in 1671, which was engraved with symbols. The centre was a square in which was enclosed a diamond-shaped diagram, surrounded by crosses and stars. Around it, engraved in a circle, were the words:

Agla + Barachiel + On + Astasteel + Alemaeto + Raphael + Algar + Uriel. Michael + Jehova + Gabriel + Adonai + Haka + Jan Tetragrama-ton + Uvsio + Vacactra + Jenifra + Mene + Jana + Ibam Femifra + Medchaet + Melcham +.

The notorious Simon Forman, astrologer, alchemist and magician, had a magical ring of silver, dated 1598, inscribed with the words "ARIEL VANAEL".

Yet another interesting ring was a thick hoop formed from an ass's hoof, bound on the inner and outer edges with silver. The oval silver-covered bezel was incised with the figure of St. George carrying a sword with a dragon at his feet. Ass's hoof had a reputation in ancient times as a prophylactic against epilepsy and is mentioned by Sir Thomas Browne and also by Robert Burton in his *Anatomy of Melancholy* in 1621.

Several ancient Scottish families possess interesting rings which were held in high esteem in former days for their magical properties. Among these the Graemes have one known as "Inchbraikie's ring", which is set with an uncut bluish sapphire. It was formerly known as the "Witch's ring", as according to a local tradition, it originally belonged to the famous witch of Monzie, Kate McNiven.

A silver ring in the Pichon collection has an oval pebble set in the bezel, roughly carved with a human head inscribed, *Agios Oteos Atanatos*, an abbreviation of the Greek "God is Holy". Such words and phrases, often found on rings, were believed to have magical power and probably came from Eastern sources, or books on magic. Although the Church disapproved of such symbols, it added to the stock of magical formulae from the Bible and in the service of the Mass.

That the Cramp-rings, hallowed by the monarchs of England, had a special significance and were held in high esteem throughout Europe, may be judged from a letter from Saragossa written by Lord Berners, Ambassador to King Charles V and dated June 21, 1510. He says, writing to

"My Lord Cardinal's grace: If your Grace remember me with some Crampe Rings ye shall do a thing mushe looked for and I trust to bestow thayme well with Godd's grace, who ever more preserve thayme and increase your moste reverent estate."

"The Emperor's jewel case contained among other charms," says Stirling in *Cloister life of Charles V*, "bezoar stone against the plague and *gold rings against the cramp*."

A letter from Dr. Thomas Magnus, Warden of Sibthorpe College, Nottinghamshire, to Cardinal Wolsey, written in 1526, contains the following allusion to Cramp-rings:

Pleas it your Grace to wete that M. Wyat of his goodness sent unto me for a present, certaine cramp-ringges, which I distributed and gave to sondery myne acquaintance at Edinburghe, amonges other to M. Adame Otterboarne who with oone of thayne, releved a mann lying in the falling sekenes in the sight of myche people, sethenne whiche tyme many requestes have been made unto me for cramp-ringges at my departing there and also sethenne my comyng frome thennes. May it pleas yur Grace therefore to show your gracious pleasure to the said M. Wyat that some ringges may be kept and sent unto Scottelande, which after my poore oppyunyoun shulde be a good dede, remembering the power and operacion of thaym is knowne and proved in Edinburgh and that they be gretly required for the same cause, both by grete personages and others.

Andrew Boorde, a physician who lived in the time of Henry VIII, writing on the treatment for cramp states "The King's Majesty hath a great help in this matter in hallowynge crampe rings and so geven without money or petition".

Burnet later notes that use of the rings "had been discontinued in King Edward VI's time but that under Queen Mary it was designed to be revived."

The ceremony of "Blessing the rings" which was held on Good Friday, was regarded as a very solemn and important function. The Sovereign came in State to the Chapel, where a crucifix was laid upon a cushion and a carpet spread on the ground before it. The King crept along the carpet to the crucifix, as a token of his humility. The quaint and full text of the liturgy used at the service in the time of Queen Mary, was as follows:

THE
CEREMONIES
of blessing
CRAMP-RINGS
on Good Friday
used by the
CATHOLICK KINGS
of England.

The psalm *Deus misereatur nostri*, etc., with the *Gloria Patri*.

Then the King reads this prayer:

Almighty eternal God who by the most copious gifts of Thy Grace flowing from the unexhausted fountain of Thy bounty, hast been graciously pleased for the comfort of mankind, continually to grant us many and various means to relieve us in our miseries, and art willing to make those the instruments and channels of Thy gifts and to grace those persons with more excellent favours whom Thou hast raised to the Royal dignity, to the end that as by Thee they reign and govern others, so by Thee they may prove beneficial to them and bestow Thy favours on the people; graciously hear our prayers and favourably receive those vows we poure forth with humility, that Thou mayst grant to us who beg with the same confidence the favour which our ancestours by their hopes in Thy mercy have obtained, through Christ our Lord. Amen.

The rings lying in one bason or more this prayer is to be said over the m.

O God, the Maker of Heavenly and earthly creatures and the most gracious restorer of mankind, the dispenser of spiritual grace and the origin of all blessings; sende downe from Heaven Thy holy Spirit the Comforter upon these Rings, artificially framed by the workman and by Thy greate power purify them, so that all the malice of the soule and venomous serpent be driven out, and so the mortal which by Thee was created, may remain pure and free from all dregs of the enemy. Through Christ our Lord. Amen.

The blessing of the King.

O God of Abraham, God of Isaac, God of Jacob, heare mercifully our prayers. Spare those who feare Thee. Be propitious to Thy suppliants and graciously be pleased to sende downe from Heaven Thy holy Angel that he may sanctify and bless these rings to the end they may prove a healthy remedy to such as implore Thy name with humility and accuse themselves of the sins which ly upon their conscience, who deplore and beseech with earnestness and humility Thy most serene pity. May they in time by the invocation of Thy holy name become profitable to all such as weare them for the health of their soule and body through Christ our Lord. Amen.

A blessing.

O God, who hast manifested the greatest wonders of Thy power by the cure of diseases and who were pleased that Rings should be a pledge of fidelity in the patriak Judah, a priestly ornament in Aaron, the mark of a faithful guardian in Darius and in this Kingdom a remedy for divers diseases; Graciously be pleased to bless † and sanctify † these Rings to the end that all such who weare them may be free from all snares of the devil, may be defended by the power of celestial armour and that no contraction of the nerves to any danger of the falling-sickness may infest them, but that in all sort of diseases by Thy help, they may find relief. In the name of the Father † and of the Son † and of the Holy Ghost † Amen.

Then follows the Psalm beginning:

Bless O my soule the Lord and let all things which are within me praise His holy name. We humbly implore O merciful God Thy infinit clemency that as we come to Thee with a confident soule and sincere faith and a pious assurance of mind, with the like devotion Thy believers may follow on these tokens of Thy grace. May all superstition be banished hence, far be all suspicion of any diabolical fraud and to the glory of Thy name let all things succeede; to the end Thy believers may understand Thee to be the dispenser of all good and may be sensible and publish that whatsoever is profitable to soule or body, is derived from Thee through Christ our Lord. Amen.

These prayers being said, the Kings highnes rubbeth the Rings between his hands saying:
Sanctify O Lord these Rings and graciously bedew them with the dew of Thy benediction and consecrate them by the rubbing of our hands, which Thou hast been pleased according to our ministry to sanctify, by an external effusion of holy oyle upon them; to the end that what the nature of the mettal is not able to performe may be wrought by the greatnes of Thy grace, through Christ our Lord. Amen.

Then must holy water be cast on the rings saying:
In the name of the Father and of the Son and of the Holy Ghost. Amen.
O Lord, the only begotten Son of God, Mediatour of God and men, Jesus Christ, in whose name alone salvation is sought for and to such as hope in Thee givest an easy access to the Father who when conversing among men, Thyself a man, dost promise by an assured oracle flowing from Thy sacred mouth, that Thy Father should grant whatever was asked him in Thy name, lend a gracious ear of pity to these prayers of ours, to the end that approaching with confidence to the throne of Thy Grace, the believers may find by the benefits conferr'd upon them, that by Thy mediation we have obtained what we have most humbly beg'd in Thy name, who livest and reignest with God the Father in the unity of the Holy Ghost, one God, ever and ever. Amen.
Wee beseech Thee O Lord that the spirit which proceedes from Thee may prevent and follow on our desires, to the end that what we beg with confidence for the good of the faithful, we may efficaciously obtaine by Thy gracious gift, through Christ our Lord. Amen.
O most clement God, Father Son and Holy Ghost, wee supplicate and beseech Thee that what is here performed by pious ceremonies to the sanctifying of Thy name, may be prevalent to the defence of our soule and body on earth and profitable to a more ample felicity in Heaven, who livest and reignest God, world without end. Amen.

Henry VIII is said to have ceased the practice of blessing the rings after he was declared to be the head of the church, by law established. The office was, however, revived by Queen Mary and her illuminated manual, which she used on these occasions, was formerly in the possession of the late Cardinal Wiseman. It is still preserved in the Roman Catholic Cathedral at Westminster. At the beginning of the manuscript are emblazoned the arms of Philip and Mary. On the second leaf is the heading, "Certeyne Prayers to be used by the Quenes Heighness in the Consecracion of the Cramperings", which is accompanied by an illuminated miniature representing the Queen kneeling, with a dish containing the rings on each side of her.
Burnet, alluding to the ceremony, states, "the Queen's highness rubbeth the rings between her hands, saying: *Sanctifice, Domine, annulos istos,*

rubbing the virtue of the holy oil with which her hands were anointed at her coronation, that it might be infused with their metal and by grace of God be efficacious".

It is also recorded in the Household Books of Henry IV and Edward IV, that "the cramp-rings were made from the metal derived from the King's offering, called 'Creeping Silver', which he was wont to make on Good Friday, when he with all his household venerated the Cross, by creeping to it on his knees".

This is confirmed in a manuscript, now in the College of Arms, which consists of a collection of Royal Ceremonies of the sixteenth century. It shows that the service for the blessing of the Cramp-rings was not an integral part of "the worthy of the Cross", a ritual in which the entire Court took part, and which is still, in a modified form, included in the Good Friday ritual in the Roman Catholic Church. After "Creeping to the Cross," it was the King's practice to consecrate the rings, before the Queen and the rest of the congregation knelt in turn before the Crucifix.

An eye-witness account of the ceremony is given in an interesting letter in the Venetian Calendar, written by Mari Antonia Faitta, secretary to Cardinal Pole, dated May 3, 1556, to Ippolito Chizzola. It states:

On Good Friday her Majesty next gave her benediction to the rings, the mode of doing so being as follows: an enclosure was formed for her Majesty to the right of the High Altar, by means of four benches to form a square, into the centre of which she again came down from her oratory and placing herself on her knees, two large covered basins were brought to her, filled with rings of gold and silver. One of these basins contained rings of her own, whilst the other had those of private individuals (particolari), labelled with their owners' names. On being uncovered she commenced reciting a certain prayer and psalms and then taking them in her two hands, she passed them again and again from one hand to the other, saying another prayer which commences, *Sanctifica, Domine, annulos istos.*

It is evident from this account that private individuals could send their own rings to be blessed, as one found is said to have been set with an agate. On the other hand, their plain appearance is inferred from a allusion made by Gordon, in his *Cordial Low Spirits*, in 1750, in which the question is asked, "Is not a brilliant more attractive than a Cramp-ring?"

The playwrights of the seventeenth century also make several allusions to the rings, as in Cartwright's *Ordinary*, in 1634, where Moth, the antiquary, betrothes the widow Potluck with his "Biggest Cramp-ring" and Middleton, in his play *Roaring Girl* (1611), describes one of the characters as having a face "which shone like an agate, set in a Cramp-ring".

The great esteem in which Royal Cramp-rings were held in the sixteenth and seventeenth centuries is shown by the demands made for them from other countries. Mrs. Cust, in her *Gentleman Errant*, mentions a request from Germany, in the sixteenth century, for the English rings or, "those blessed by the King and given to epileptics", and Benvenuto in his Life (1500–1571) states that Cramp-rings were sent from England into Italy and cost ten shillings. They were known as *Anellidel Granchio* (Cramp-rings) but they now term them *Anelli di Salute* (Health-rings).

Judging from the following charm taken from a manuscript of the sixteenth century Cramp-rings were sometimes put to uses other than warding off that ailment. As love tokens, it is directed to "Take two Cramp-rings of gold or silver and lay them both in a swallow's nest that buildeth in the summer. Let them be there nine days, then take them and deliver the one to thy love and keep the other."

Belief in the healing power of the Royal touch had not died out in Scotland in the eighteenth century and it is said that in the Shetland Islands, crown or half-crown pieces of the Stuart period were carefully treasured and handed down, with the object of "touching" a person afflicted with King's Evil, and in the hope of healing the sufferer.

Within recent years, a Sussex clergyman stated that an application had been made to him by a parishioner for a "Sacrament Shilling", or a piece of silver given during the offertory at Holy Communion, in order to buy a ring to cure a girl who suffered from epileptic fits. The shilling was to be paid for in coppers, or in exchange for another. It was to be hung round the neck of the girl, for epilepsy, or could be used to rub on a limb affected with cramp.

Like other amulets of healing, there is little doubt that the efficacy attributed to the Cramp-ring depended on the faith of the wearer and was the effect of the power of the mind or the imagination, brought into activity through some chosen symbol, of which we may find many instances among the credulous of the present day.

The source of the belief in the efficacy of the Royal rings of healing, or Cramp-rings, is not difficult to trace, and was in all probability a survival of the ancient talismanic theory that certain occult virtues could be imparted to an inanimate object by a king or priest who had been divinely anointed. The form of the talisman was sometimes supposed to have an intimate connection with its use, and so to relieve cramp, an ailment which at once suggests constriction, a ring or bandage to constrict a member of the body came to be employed.

It is well known that garters of eelskins, leather, or rings placed tightly round the leg were used as a common cure for cramp in the Middle Ages and are, indeed, employed in folk-medicine in some country districts in Britain at the present day.

Chapter XXII

MAGICAL STONES OF HEALING

IN various parts of Britain, certain strange stones and pebbles are still preserved which from time immemorial have been endowed with traditionary powers of a magical character, in the healing of disease. Wales in particular, where superstition still lingers in some districts, has several of these interesting relics of a remote age. One of them, known as the "Gilfach Wen" Hydrophobia Stone is called *Llaethfaen*, and until 1924 was in the possession of the Lloyd family of Gilfach Wen. In this instance the stone itself was not used as a talisman, but portions were scraped off and administered to the patient in milk.

The owner of the stone states that it came into the possession of his father in about 1847.

In those days and for many years afterwards, mad dogs were very "fashionable", a summer never passing without one hearing of a great many people having been bitten and consequently a great many people called at Gilfach Wen, for a dose of the *Llaethfaen*. People who had been bitten would travel immense distances in order to get the stone. One day, a whole family who had been bitten by the same dog, arrived early one summer morning, having travelled all night in order to be treated with the stone cure. They went away very happy and relieved in mind, after each had received a dose.

Another hydrophobia stone or *Llaethfaen*, as they generally seem to have been called, was known at Henllan, Cardiganshire. The owner relates an account of a case in which it was used, as follows:

Two men employed in a brewery at Llanon, who had been bitten by the same dog, supposed to be mad, came here after they had spent nearly a week enquiring for the stone. They arrived in a terrible plight and after giving each of them a dose of the *Llaethfaen* and a good meal, they went away happy.

Two stones, the scrapings of which had a widespread reputation as a specific against hydrophobia in the coastal districts between Tregaron and Aberystwyth, were in the possession of Mr. William Jones, of Lledrod, in Cardiganshire. They are said to have been in his family for countless years. The scrapings were administered to the patient in milk and the amount of the powder given was as much as could be placed on a sixpence.

A stone, known as the *Carreg Cynddaredd*, was kept also at Henllan, of which the following is related by the owner:

An old gentleman who had lived to the age of ninety-six told me that years before, when he was a young man, a cat either scratched or bit his hand badly one day and that soon after he felt an almost irresistible inclination to mew like a cat and he made at once to get a dose of the *Carreg Cynddaredd*. After he had got it he at once lost any desire to mew. Sufficient of the stone was grated off and given to the patient, mixed with as much white Alabar in fresh milk.

Dr. F. J. North, who investigated some of the stories, says the "Gilfach Wen" stone is of white alabaster, of the type that occurs in Derbyshire. The "Henllan" stone is a small nodule of pink alabaster, such as occurs in the triassic marls of Penarth. Certain water-worn stones, or flints, having a natural hole in them, have a wide reputation in the north of England as a protection against evil-spirits, to avert disease, to charm away warts and also as a sovereign remedy against nightmare. In Lancashire, these stones are hung up in stables and shippons to prevent the horses and cattle from sweating when in a state of fear from the evil influence of witches.

Sir Thomas Browne alludes to the custom in his *Vulgar Errors* when he asks: "What natural effects can reasonably be expected when, to prevent the ephialtes, or night-mare, they hang on a string, a flint with a hole in it," and Aubrey mentions the use to "hinder nightmare viz: the hag from riding their horses who will sometimes sweat at night. The flint thus hung, does hinder it". In Bavaria, the *Druten-stein*, a natural pebble with a hole through it, is used as a charm against witches; while in Scotland these witch-stones, as they are called, are hung up in the byres as a protection for the cattle.

In some of the Welsh churches of Penmynydd, scrapings from ancient tombs are said to have healing virtues, and at Clynnog a stone column has been damaged by visitors who have scraped portions away to use as a remedy for sore eyes.

Creeping through Dolmens or perforated stones was a Druidical ceremony and is still practised in the East Indies. Borlase tells of a stone in the parish of Marden through which many persons crept, to cure pains in their backs and limbs; and in some parts of the country, children suffering from rickets are pushed through similar stones, or hollows in old trees, in the hope of healing them.

In some districts of Scotland and Eire, certain small stones, or pebbles, are believed to have the property of imparting remarkable curative properties to water in which they have been placed. Such stones, commonly known as "Murrain Stones", are believed to be specially effective in cattle diseases. After they have been immersed in the water, it is sprinkled on the animals suffering from, or likely to be attacked by, the disease.

The most celebrated of these healing-stones, however, is the "Lee Penny", which for centuries has been an heirloom in the Lockhart family. Its story is related in *The Talisman*, by Sir Walter Scott, who tells how

Saladin, the Saracen King, disguised as a physician, cured Richard Coeur-de-Lion of a dangerous fever, by its agency. He states that its virtues are still employed for stopping blood and against hydrophobia.

The stone itself is heart-shaped and is set in the reverse of a silver groat piece of Edward IV, of the London Mint, hence the name "Penny". The method of using it was to draw it once round a vessel filled with water and then dip it in three times, or as they say, "three dips and a sweil" and in this way the water received its power of healing.

Sir James Y. Simpson, who was interested in healing stones, says he was once told by an old Scottish farmer that in his young days no byre was considered safe, unless it had a bottle of "Lee Penny Water" suspended from the rafters. So great was the faith in the healing properties of the stone, at one time, that people and animals who were ailing were brought to Lee from all parts of the country.

In former times, when a town in the North was visited by plague which proved intractable to ordinary measures, application was made for the loan of the "Lee Penny". Thus, during the outbreak of plague in the time of Charles I, when Newcastle was being ravaged by the pestilence, the Corporation of the town borrowed the "Penny" under the heavy bond of £6,600. As late as the early part of the eighteenth century, it was lent to the Baird of Saughtonhall, near Edinburgh, to cure his lady, who was believed to be suffering from hydrophobia. According to the account given at the time, Lady Baird was actually in the horrors of rabies when the "Penny" arrived, but by drinking the water impregnated by the stone and bathing in it, she was soon restored to health. Towards the end of the century, however, belief in the efficacy of the "Penny" in healing human diseases seems to have almost vanished, but it was still supposed to be of value to cattle. In his account of the "Lee Penny" given by Hunter in 1782, he says: "It being taken and put into the end of a cloven stick and washed in a tub full of water and given to cattell to drink, infallibly cures all manner of diseases. The people come all airts of the Kingdom with diseased beasts."

Among other stones with which curious traditions and magical properties have been associated from early times, is the "Toad Stone". It was believed to be an antidote to all poisons and also to give warning of their presence, by changing colour.

Varying in size from about half an inch to an inch, toad-stones which were of a brownish or grey colour were usually worn as rings, or set in silver. Their origin was wrapped in mystery but they were generally believed to be found in the heads of old toads which when caught, were placed on a red cloth and the stone extracted through the mouth. They were considered of great value on account of their rarity, and when set in rings were usually mounted so that the back of the stone could touch the wearer's skin. The stone was said to notify the presence of a poison by producing a sensation of heat in the finger, at the point of contact.

Fenton, writing in 1569, says: "They are found in the heads of old

and great toads and most commonly found in the heads of a he-toad".
"To know whether the toad-stone called *crapavdina* be the right and
perfect stone or not, hold it before a toad so he may see it," and,
declares Lupton, "if it be a true stone the toad will leap towards it and
make as though he would snatch it from you."

Ben Jonson refers to the stone in *Fox* where he remarks:

> Were you enamoured on his copper rings,
> His saffron jewel, with the toadstone in it.

Shakespeare alludes to it also in the lines:

> Sweet are the uses of adversity
> Which like the toad, ugly and venomous
> Yet wears a precious jewel in his head.

Pomet, who wrote in the seventeenth century, casts a doubt on their
source of origin and says that "toad stones are found in the mountains or
plains". He describes two kinds, viz: the long and the round, the latter
being of a deep grey, inclining to blue and the long being of a redder grey
with reddish spots. Lemery, another French writer, says that when
applied to the sting or bite of venomous beasts, they draw out the poison.

Other writers of the seventeenth century give various methods said
to have been used for obtaining the stone from the toad. Lupton directs
that "a great or overgrown toad (first bruised in divers places) should be
put into an earthen pot; put the pot into an ant's hillock and cover the
same with earth, which toad at length the ants will eat so that the bones
of the toad and the stone will be left in the pot". Another states that
the stone should be obtained while the toad is living, and gives directions
how this should be carried out. "The stone," he says, "is recovered, by
simply placing him upon a piece of scarlet cloth, wherewithal they are
much delighted so that while they stretch out themselves, as it were in
sport upon that cloth, they cast out the stone of their head but instantly
sup it up again unless it be taken from them, through some secret hole
in the cloth." But the scarlet cloth operation did not always prove
successful according to Boetius, for he records how he watched for a whole
night an old toad he had laid on a red cloth, but the toad was stubborn
and "left him nothing to gratify the great pangs of his whole night's
restlessness".

Investigations have shown that the mystic toad-stone around which
so many peculiar traditions have gathered for over 1000 years, is nothing
more than the palatal tooth from the fossil of a fish (Lepidotus). It is
first mentioned in the Kyranides by a late Greek lapidary, probably about
200 B.C.

Another mysterious stone greatly valued in early times was the
Aetites, or Eagle stone. It was regarded as a rare charm in the Middle

Ages and much sought after by women, who believed that if worn during pregnancy, it would prevent miscarriage.

According to ancient tradition, it was only to be found in eagles' nests. This arose from a belief that the bird could not hatch her eggs without its assistance.

Lemnius, writing in 1658, declares that "being bound round the wrist of the left arm by which from the heart the ring finger next to the little finger an artery runs, and if all the time the woman is great with child, this jewel be worn on those parts, it strengthens the child and there is no fear of abortion".

Lupton tells another story and says, "It brings love between man and wife, and if a woman have a painful travail in the birth of her child, the stone tyed to her thigh brings an easy and a light birth."

These stones vary in size from one to two inches and are of a light brown colour. They are found to be composed of an argillaceous oxide of iron, deposited round a nucleus of some other material of unknown origin.

Relig Healing Stone,
near Bruckless,
Donegal.

Chapter XXIII

HORNS OF HEALING

THE horns of certain animals and other creatures have been credited with mystic and healing virtues from a very early period, as instanced in the horn of the unicorn which was believed to possess the property of being an infallible antidote to all poisons. The horn was not only believed to counteract the effects of poisons, but also to give an indication of their presence. As far back as the fourth century before the Christian era, Ctesias referred to drinking vessels made from the horn and those who used them being protected against poisons, convulsions and epilepsy. Other writers claimed that even poisoned wounds could be healed by merely holding the horn close to the injured part.

Many early travellers endeavoured to describe the unicorn and some, like Vartomannus, even claimed to have seen it. He says:

it was of the size of a horse, thirty months old. It had a fairly long horn in the centre of its forehead. Its colour was like that of a chestnut horse, the head like that of a deer; the neck was not particularly long, being covered by a short mane, while the legs were slender and the feet cloven like those of a goat.

Marco Polo, on the other hand, declares that the animal he saw was a little smaller than an elephant, with the head of a boar which was bent towards the ground.

Ambroise Paré, who wrote a treatise on the unicorn, says "it is of the size of a large grey-hound and of a beaver grey". He, however, doubted its value as an antidote to poisons, for which purpose it was so largely sought.

Until the seventeenth century it was not generally agreed what the genuine horn looked like. By some, the *black* horn was said to be the true variety, no doubt based on Pliny's observations, but Boetius de Boott, who saw a horn in Venice at the close of the sixteenth century which was claimed to be a genuine unicorn's horn, says, "it was like a gazelle's horn similar to the one he saw at Prague". Later writers, however, agree that the genuine horns are long, like bone or ivory, and twisted into slender cones. Several of this kind are preserved in churches, monasteries and museums in Europe, one of the most renowned being that kept at the monastery of St. Denis, near Paris.

Cardanus, who saw it when he visited that Institution in the sixteenth century, says "it was so long that he could not reach the tip when he placed it at his side. It was not particularly thick, becoming gradually thinner towards the tip and curling like a snail's shell." The colour was that of hartshorn. This horn was held in great veneration and was included in the inventory of gold, precious stones and holy relics. It was regarded as genuine, until Olaus Worm established the fact that this specimen, like the two preserved at St. Mark's in Venice which were exhibited to the people on Ascension Day, was in reality the tusk of the narwhal.

How the belief in its extraordinary virtues arose it is impossible to state, since the animal itself is fabulous. Nevertheless the horn of the unicorn continued to be eagerly sought for and the value placed upon it was so great that it is no wonder that other horns came to be substituted for it, by apothecaries and others. Among these were the fossil bones of the elephant, rhinoceros, tiger, and the bones of other large animals.

The horns came to be highly esteemed in all the countries of Europe for their cordial, astringent and diaphoretic properties, and were considered valuable in cases of epilepsy and malarial fevers. The horn of the narwhal, or sea-unicorn as it was called, continued to be regarded as the genuine horn and was made into cups, with the idea of counteracting the effects of any poisonous liquid that might be placed in them.

Ducal cups, often richly encrusted with precious stones, were used as drinking vessels by those of high birth whose lives might be sought by poisoners. Gesner says, "that the rich put a piece of the horn in their cups to protect and cure themselves".

A fabulous value was placed on the horns, and in 1553, a unicorn's horn which was brought to the king of France was valued at £20,000 sterling, while one presented to Charles I, said to be the largest known, weighed 13 pounds and was seven feet long. Edward IV gave the Duke of Burgundy a gold cup set with jewels, which had a piece of unicorn's horn worked into the metal and it is recorded by Dr. Racq of Florence, that a German merchant sold one to the Pope for 4,000 livres.

From early times, all kinds of horns were used as natural drinking vessels, not only on account of their shape, but also because of the idea that they had health-giving properties which they imparted to liquids placed in them. In the Far East, this belief in their virtues was associated with the horns of several animals and until recent years a considerable traffic was carried on in the bones of the *tahr*, the native name of the wild goat which frequents the slopes of the Himalayan range, which had a ready market in India, as a remedy for rheumatism. Wapiti horn is still said to be extensively used in China and the wapiti, the species of deer from which it is derived, are found wild in the upper basins of the Yenesei River. The people of the primitive tribes inhabiting that part of Siberia, who live largely on reindeer, trade with outsiders in the skins and horns of the wapiti. The animals are collected at Sabie and kept alive in enclosures, their horns being sawn off yearly, while still soft. They are then boiled in weak tea to preserve them, and when ready are sent down the river to Chakut where they are sold at very high prices, the average being about ten shillings a pound. The Chinese declare that they possess tonic properties and they are to be found for sale in most of the Chinese drug shops.

Next in value to unicorn's horn came that of the rhinoceros which has been highly esteemed in the East from very early times, and later, during the Middle Ages, was much in demand in European countries. In China, Japan and India, it was given in the form of powder as a life-giving tonic, while cups made from the horn were declared to give warning by sweating, should any poisonous liquid be placed in them. Rudolph II of Germany (1576–1612) the patron of Tycho Brahe, possessed such a cup, which was preserved in the National Museum at Copenhagen. In China, the horns are often rendered more valuable by exquisite carving and other decoration, which makes them much sought after by collectors and they sell for high prices. In Denmark, in the seventeenth century, a drink from a cup of rhinoceros horn was accounted as being excellent for the health; and the powdered horn, for medicinal purposes, was commonly found in the apothecaries' shops.

In some of the northern countries of Europe the horns of the elk were esteemed as an astringent and like the hoofs, were believed to be a cure for epilepsy and "hysteric passions". Rings made from the horn and worn on the finger were also believed to protect the wearer from con-vulsive fits.

Several small bones and teeth derived from certain fish were credited with healing virtues. Thus, the little bones found in the heads of large whiting and haddocks, which appear to have teeth on each side, were dried, and after being reduced to powder, were taken for indigestion; while a white bone from the manatea, a fish plentiful in the West Indies, was employed for the same purpose.

The bone of a stag's heart (*Os de Corde Cervi*) which hunter's call the "hart's cross", after being dried and powdered, was given in affections of the heart.

Perhaps the best-known preparation from horn, the use of which has survived today, is the hartshorn, which was highly esteemed as an astringent, absorbent and for its antacid properties. When subjected to destructive distillation it yields ammonia, and hartshorn and oil is still largely employed as a domestic remedy for sprains and rheumatic pains. The hartshorn shavings, when boiled in water and flavoured with orange or lemon juice and sugar, were also regarded as a highly nutritious jelly. Powdered hartshorn had formerly a wide reputation as a remedy for diarrhoea and intestinal worms, and filings of the horn were employed to cure impotence. Spoons made from the horn of a living cow were said to enhance the virtues of medicines placed in them and the dried horn crushed was highly valued in cases of epilepsy.

In connection with this it is interesting to note that powdered bone from a human skull was one of the earliest known remedies for the same disease. The first neck-bone of the spine of the codfish was powdered and taken in milk for stomach troubles, while goat's horn when laid under the pillow at night, was credited with the power of inducing sleep. Shavings of the horn were given in goat's milk in cases of snake-bite.

Chapter XXIV

MIRACULOUS BEDS OF HEALING

BEDS play such an important part in human life, both in sickness and health, that it is little wonder they became associated with magic and healing. Among others which became famous was the "Miraculous Bed" of Pistoja, still preserved and venerated in that ancient city which lies in a luxuriant valley in the heart of the Tuscan Hills. This famous relic has for centuries been carefully preserved in the little church of St. Marie della Grazie and is yet believed by the Tuscan peasants to possess marvellous healing virtues. To the church are brought the sick and suffering from far and near, to be laid on the bed, from which they are said to rise completely cured of their maladies.

For over six centuries the bed has remained in the possession of the Augustinian monks, who guard it jealously as a sacred relic and believe in its power to restore the sick to robust health. The church of St. Marie della Grazie where it is kept, stands on the outskirts of the city and was built on the site of an ancient hospital founded in the year 1333.

According to an ancient chronicle still extant:

a little hospital was erected on the piazza of St. Lorenzo, not far from the glorious church which in 1278, the Municipality and charity of many had erected to the glorious martyr by a will of Giovanni di Matteo Gualdinari, a citizen of Pistoja, dated July 5th, 1330 and signed by the notary Se Schiatta di Pisano.

The chronicler goes on to state:

the bequeather in fact, left for the salvation of his soul and those of his parents, to the executors of his will, 1,700 lira of small Florentine denari, ordered to find and buy a small house or some land in Pistoja and institute a hospital to receive and lodge in it the poor and pilgrims under the title of the beautiful apostle Saint Jacopo and the Martyr Lorenzo, and the management of the hospital to be under our municipality, by right of patronage. The executors, together with the workmen of Jacopo, fulfilled the will of the testator and in 1333 they opened the modest asylum to which in the year 1350 was added perpetually with its rents, that of St. Domenico di Abaia, which at that time belonged to the diocese of Lucca, as testified in the ancient book of the hospital of St. Jacopo and Lorenzo which exists in the archives of the Opera di St. Jacopo. But of this place at the present day there would be no recollection were it not for the great fact so dear to many of Pistoja.

Thus the chronicle records the foundation of the little hospital in which the miracle of the bed took place. The story of this event is recorded by several contemporary writers and is, perhaps, best given in the quaint language of the time. It is thus quoted from a manuscript of the fifteenth century:

Now this is the fact as given in an ancient chronicle kept in the church of Beati Virgini della Grazie:

"In the year 1336 there was for a while in this place which was anciently a hospital, a poor young woman, twenty-five years old, bedridden for seven years on account of an incurable disease, when one day there appeared to her and sitting on the bed, the Holy Virgin in the likeness of a very brilliant sun, surrounded by celestial splendour, so that she rendered all the room luminous and resplendent. From the moment of seeing the apparition, the suffering woman was at once healed and restored to robust health.

"The great Mother of God, the Virgin Mary of Graces (now known as the Madonna of the Bed), then ordered certain children, who were also in the hospital to go and call Father Fra Jacopo of the Augustinian Cappa, who was at that moment confessing in the St. Lorenzo and the said children, with ready obedience, ran to the confessional of the Father, telling him what the Virgin had told them; but the same having thought it was not well to leave the confession unfinished, for the sole object of believing what the children said, did not come at once.

"The children having returned without the said Father, the Virgin with a renewed command, said to them emphatically, 'Return and tell him to come at once, because I want him to preach the plague and tell him that within a month he will surely die.'

"On hearing this the good servant of God arose from the confessional and quickly ran to the hospital where, having arrived, he found the Virgin had disappeared but leaving on the wall a picture, or image, of herself, with a child in her arms in the act of leaving as by flight and adored up to the present day.

"The people of Pistoja were further surprised when the prediction of the Virgin became completely accomplished in the death of the Father Fra Jacopo and in the coming of the menaced punishment of the plague. The former with true apostolic zeal preached during the few days that remained to his life and in the year 1340, by the arm of the omnipotent God on account of the sins of the world, humanity was afflicted with the terrible scourge of the plague. This can be seen in the remembrance that is kept of the glorious apostle St. Jacopo, patron of the city. One also reads in the works of other notable authors, distinct mention of the miracle of the Holy Virgin, which was antecedent to the plague, to whom always as is due glory, praise and honour."

Another account of the miracle of the bed of the Madonna of the Graces is recorded in a manuscript of the fourteenth century, still preserved in the city archives, of which the following is a translation :

"This year, took place the miracle of the Madonna of the Graces and the Bed in the hospital of St. Jacob and St. Laurence at the bridge of the Brana, erected in the year 1331 by a certain Giovanni Matteo.

"It is said in this way, the Holy Virgin Mother of our Saviour in the act of sitting on the bed in the said hospital, appeared to certain children and said to them, 'Go and call a certain Fra Jacopo, Cappa of St. Laurence, who was confessing in his church'.

"And so they did, but the friar attending to his ministry took no heed and did not believe the children. They returned, saying he did not want to leave the confession unfinished.

"The children were again commanded by the Virgin to return to the said friar and tell him again that she wanted him that he should preach the great mortality that should follow in the same year and that he would die within a month. The friar, at the second injunction went to the hospital.

"Then the Madonna had disappeared from the bed and appeared on the wall, where even now, one may see the Holy image in the act of disappearing, with her Son in her arms, which image is kept in such devotion and reverence in our city and where the people erected a church, which is to be seen today, leaving the Madonna intact on the wall on which she deigned to leave her image.

"The design of the church is of Venturi Vitoni, a famous architect of Pistoja."

A still more vivid description of the "miracle" is given in a letter written by one, Andrea di Rossi, which is also still preserved among the archives of the Municipality of Pistoja. The letter was written by Rossi to the Pope of the time, to inform him of the "miracle", and asking him for spiritual favours for the oratory. He says:

tell the Holy Father how in Pistoja is a hospital of the Virgin, in which for many years are gathered in the poor and pilgrims and how one day at noon, our Lady appeared in the hospital and sat on one of the beds, where a poor girl slept and here rested for some time; and how she was seen by many pure virgin youths, and they called several persons and told them that a beautiful woman dressed in gold with great splendour was sitting on one of the beds in the hospital, and that as they looked through a grid that was on the door of the hospital, they constantly saw the Virgin on the bed and no one else was able to see her, but the said virgin youth who after a certain time said, "Look,! that beautiful woman goes away", and then departing, she left her image on one of the walls of the said hospital, which is very worthy and devout and makes miracles of which we have the image and proofs and where the hospital was, is now made an oratory, with an altar at the foot of that image which remained when the Virgin departed.

Of the wonderful picture on the wall, referred to in the chronicle, nothing now remains, as it is supposed to have been destroyed with the original church in the sixteenth century, but Dondori, who claims to have seen it, has left the following description of it in his work; and observes:

On examining the picture on the wall, one clearly sees that it cannot be held to have been drawn by hand but left by the Virgin herself, in her prodigious apparition. It is not possible for it to have been painted in that attitude and position, especially in those days which were scarce of invention and when figures were painted standing and with rude contours. This one has drawing, beauty and movement in the folds of the draperies as if floating in the air.

"But," said an aged monk to the present writer, when he visited the
church a few years ago, "one of the greatest proofs of the miracle is *the
bed* on which the Virgin sat, which still remains preserved to this day,
intact in all its parts as in the fourteenth century."

The little church was almost in darkness when we entered it one
afternoon in winter, but from the glow of many candles it could be seen
that it was full of worshippers, mostly devout women who had remained
to pray after mass had been celebrated.

"You want to see the Miraculous Bed," said the sacristan, a bright
little woman, as she led us through a dark passage by the side of the altar
which led into a small chapel or oratory.   We entered a bare room adjoin-
ing this, with stone walls on one of which was nailed a large crucifix.

The Miraculous Bed of Pistoja.

Facing it was the famous bed which, we were told, was transferred from
the church by the rector in 1636, so as to be near the nun's choir.

It is large and strongly built with four stout posts and is said to have
been made of walnut-wood, now black with age.   The head, which is
higher than the foot, has a cornice along the top and the panel is painted a
dark red.   In the centre is a primitive painting representing the Virgin and
Child, and by them the figure of a saint with a gridiron near him, clad in a
tunic, who is said to be St. Laurence; while a smaller figure in black supposed to be Giovanni da Montecatini is kneeling in the act of adoration.
Above is inscribed in white letters, "Pray for the soul of Condore
Giovanni da Montecatini.   A.D. 1336."

On the panel at the foot of the bed is a painting of the Virgin with a
small figure dressed in white, against a red background, and above them in

black letters, on a white ground, are inscribed the words, "Pray God for the soul of Friar Duccio di Chele Meglioni A.D. 1334."

On the bed itself rests a dilapidated hair mattress and two feather pillows, which are said to be contemporary with it, the whole being covered with a counterpane of old, dark red damask.   On this the sick who are brought to be healed are laid, while the attendant monks recite certain prayers for their recovery.   Although the stories of the "Miracle" differ somewhat as it is recorded by so many chroniclers down to the seventeenth century, there is little doubt there must be some truth in the ancient tradition which has been handed down in the city for generations. It is possible that some patient in the early hospital, suffering from a mild attack of paralysis, made a sudden recovery and found the use of her limbs, owing to the nervous excitement caused by being placed on the bed and the prayers of the attending monks.   This is not infrequently the case at the present time, but in those days the occurrence would no doubt be regarded as a miracle.   In any case, as the monk who told us the story observed, "sufferers are still brought to be laid on the bed and go away apparently healed".

In contrast to this miraculous bed, the famous Celestial Bed which Dr. Graham, the notorious quack-doctor, set up in London in the eighteenth century, forms an interesting study.

James Graham, the son of a sadler, was born in Edinburgh in 1745, and after gaining a smattering of medical knowledge travelled throughout this country and America and eventually returned and settled in London. A man of unbounded effrontery and impudence, he soon attracted a fashionable clientèle who were ready to testify to his skill.

After he had established himself in 1780, he secured the centre house in the Royal Terrace, Adelphi, which the famous brothers Adam had commenced to build in 1768, and here he opened his Temple of Health, which he declared was to be consecrated or devoted to the great purposes of preserving and restoring health.   Over the entrance he had inscribed in letters of gold on a white ground "TEMPLUM AESCULAPIO SACRUM". He spent a large sum of money in decorating and furnishing the building which was said to be "gorgeous in its fittings, impressive in its grandeur and mystical in its electrical and other scientific appurtenances".

The greatest and most intriguing attraction, however, was the "Grand Celestial Bed", by means of which he claimed that children of the most perfect beauty could be begotten.   For the privilege of occupying it couples were charged 500 guineas a night.   The description of this marvellous piece of furniture is best given in his own picturesque style:

The Grand Celestial Bed (he states), whose magical influences are now celebrated from pole to pole and from the rising to the setting of the sun, is twelve feet long by nine feet wide, supported by forty pillars of brilliant glass of the most exquisite workmanship, in richly variegated colours.

The super-Celestial Dome of the bed which contains the odoriferous balmy and etherial spices, odours and essences, which is the grand reservoir

of those reviving and invigorating influences which are exhaled by the breath
of the music and by the accelerating force of electrical fire, is covered on the
other side with brilliant panes of looking glass.

On the upmost summit of the dome are placed two exquisite figures of
Cupid and Psyche, with a figure of Hymen behind, with his torch flaming with
electrical fire in one hand, and with the other, supporting a celestial crown
sparkling over a pair of great living turtle-doves, on a little bed of roses.

The other elegant groups of figures which sport on the top of the dome,
having each of them musical instruments in their hands, which by the most
expensive mechanism, breathe forth sounds corresponding to their instruments, flutes, guitars, violins, clarionets, trumpets, horns, oboes, kettledrums,
etc.

The posts or pillars, too, which support the grand dome are groups of
musical instruments, organ pipes etc, which in sweet concert breathe forth
celestial sounds, lulling with visions of Elysian joys.

At the head of the bed appears sparkling with electrical fire the great
first commandment: "BE FRUITFUL, MULTIPLY AND REPLENISH
THE EARTH"; Under that is an elegant sweet-toned organ in the front of
which is a fine landscape of moving figures, priest, brides and a fine procession
entering the Temple of Hymen.

In the Celestial Bed, no feather bed is employed but sometimes mattresses
filled with sweet new wheat or oat-straw mingled with balm, rose leaves,
lavender flowers and oriental spices.

The sheets are of the richest and softest silk and satin of various colours,
suited to the complexion. Pale green, rose colour, sky blue, white and purple,
and are sweetly perfumed in the oriental manner with the otto of rose, jesa-
mine, tuber rose, or with rich gums and balsams.

The chief principal of my Celestial Bed is produced by artificial loadstones.
About fifteen hundredweight of compound magnets are continually pouring
forth in an ever flowing circle.

The Bed is constructed with a double frame, which moves on an axis or
pivot and can be converted into an inclined plane.

Sometimes the mattresses are filled with the strongest and most springy
hair procured at vast expense from the tails of English stallions, which are
elastic to the highest degree.

Such was Graham's eulogy of his famous bed which, we are informed
later, was built by Denton, a tinsmith who was well known at the time for
his mechanical skill. The bed and the whole of the fittings are said to
have cost Graham £10,000!

Emboldened by the success of the Temple of Health at the Adelphi,
Graham decided to open another establishment in the West End and took
Schomberg House, Pall Mall, which he called the TEMPLE OF HEALTH
AND HYMEN and which he fitted up at considerable expense.

Here, too, was another Celestial Bed and in announcing his new
project in a lecture he gave at the Adelphi, he said:

The Temple of Hymen which is soon to be opened in Pall Mall, is for the
propagating of Beings rational and far stronger and more beautiful in mental

as well as bodily endowments, than the present puny, feeble and nonsensical race of probationary immortals.

Graham provided other attractions at his Temple, including pageants and musical performances, in one of which the beautiful Lady Hamilton who subsequently became the *belle amie* of Lord Nelson, played a part and impersonated the "Rosy Goddess of Health". The final chorus of one of these entertainments was as follows:

To Britain's daughters, To Britain's sons bear the best blessing Health,
Stretch forth thy hand that bears the triple branch
Medicinal, which binds up broken hearts, illumines the Soul,
And fling the Rose of Health o'er the pale cheek of sickness,
Far, far from those who take them and from these sacred walls removing
    pain and death.

Graham became deeply in debt after opening Schomberg House, which did not turn out the success he anticipated, and his property was eventually seized by his creditors and sold in November, 1782. He died in Edinburgh in 1794, but what became of the famous Celestial Beds is not known.

Although there is no mention of magic connected with it, the Great Bed of Ware should be included in the collection of famous beds. This huge bed, twelve feet square, was formerly housed in the Saracen's Head Inn at Ware, in Hertfordshire. Beautifully carved and inlaid, of solid oak, it is said to have been designed for the palace of King Henry VIII, at Nonesuch, and it is mentioned by Shakespeare in *Twelfth Night*. It is now in the Victoria and Albert Museum, London, and was sold by auction for £4,000 in 1931.

Chapter XXV

COLOURS AND NUMBERS AND THEIR INFLUENCE ON HEALING

BOTH colours and numbers have played a part in methods of healing for centuries past, and to them many allusions are made in charms and other means employed to alleviate disease. Red, in particular, was believed to have a curative effect in healing. It was considered to be a sacred and regal colour and one of triumph and victory over all enemies. It was the colour most obnoxious to evil-spirits, who were generally regarded as being the cause of every disease and ailment to which the flesh of man is heir. It also represented heat and therefore, in a manner, that element itself just as white typified the contrary element, cold.

John of Gaddesden, the old English physician who flourished in the fourteenth century, recommended red bed coverings in the treatment of smallpox, with the idea that the colour induced the pustules to come to the surface of the body. "Let scarlet red be taken," he says in his *Rosa Anglica*, "and let him who is suffering small-pox be entirely wrapped in it or in some other red cloth. This I did when the son of the illustrious King of England (Edward II) suffered from smallpox; I took care that all about the bed should be red and that cure succeeded well."

Among the Anglo-Saxon Leechdoms there is one which reads: "Take a clove-wort and wreath it with a red thread about the man's neck when the moon is on the wane, in the month of April and he will soon be healed."

In more recent times, a skein of scarlet silk worn round the neck was said to stop bleeding from the nose and as late as the first half of the last century, scarlet tongues of cloth were sold in a shop in Fleet Street to tie round the necks of sufferers from scarlet fever. In the north of England, great faith is still placed in a flannel belt worn round the waist in cases of rheumatism, but to be effectual, the flannel *must be red*.

Red, too, was the colour most obnoxious to witches and was used to repel witchcraft. Both in the Highlands of Scotland and in Eire, farmers often tie a piece of red worsted or cloth round their cows' tails to prevent them from being ill-wished, and the dairymaids frequently carry a little cross made from rowan twigs bound together with red worsted to prevent witches from injuring their cattle or turning the milk. They have an old saying:

> Rowan ash and red thread
> Keep the devils from their speed.

The bright red berries of the rowan or mountain ash had many superstitions attached to them, particularly as regards witchcraft.

From early times blue has been regarded as a symbol of fidelity, and in the Near East was believed to be the most powerful colour to avert the Evil-eye and bring good luck to the wearer.   As the celestial colour of the heavens, blue charms to bring good fortune were commonly worn in ancient Egypt.

Both black and white were also used in healing and are thus recommended in an Assyrian clay tablet, which dates from about 1500 B.C.:

> Take a white cloth; in it place the marint
> In the sick man's right hand
> And take a black cloth
> Wrap it round his left hand.
> Then all the evil-spirits
> And the sins he has committed
> Shall quit their hold of him.

Apparently, by the black cloth the sufferer repudiated all his former evil deeds, while the white cloth in his right hand symbolized his trust in holiness.

From a very early period certain numerals were believed to have a mystic significance and were regarded as important by magicians, especially in relation to healing.   Both charms and prayers had to be repeated a special number of times, if they were to prove effective.   The peculiar powers attributed to certain numerals have thus been epitomized: *One* was regarded as the Father of numbers and signified harmony.   It was a fortunate and prosperous number.   *Two* was the number of intellect and the Mother of numbers but was generally held to be of ill-repute bringing trouble and unhappiness.   *Three*, on the other hand, was regarded as a Holy number and has always been looked upon with favour in all things.   It was the number of the Trinity, signifying plenty and fruitfulness and the third day was venerated as being one of good fortune. *Four* was regarded by Pythagoras as the root of all other numbers and over it his followers swore their most solemn oaths.   It was the square number and the number of endurance, firmness of purpose and goodwill. *Five* was a magical and important number to magicians as instanced in the form of the pentacle which they regarded as a powerful talisman against the approach of devils, or evil-spirits.   It was also believed to be the number and symbol of justice and faith.   *Six* was considered to be the perfection of numbers.   It was the ideal number of love and was held sacred to Venus.   It was called the "number of man", for in six days the world was made and man was then created, who afterwards multiplied and inhabited it.   *Seven* was the most highly esteemed of all numbers and had a Divine significance.   It was called the "number of an oath" by the Hebrews and was so used by Abraham.   The Pythagoreans called it the "vehicle of human life", for there were seven days, seven planets, seven metals and the seven ages of man.

An ancient writer on witchcraft remarks:

> There are some who cure by observing numbers. Balaam used magian geometriciam. There are some witches who enjoin the sick to dip their shirts seven times in south running water.

Elisha sent Naaman to wash in Jordan seven times; Elijah, on top of Carmel, sent his servant seven times to look for rain and when Jericho was taken, they compassed the city seven times. Seven is frequently mentioned in connection with Jewish ceremonial as instanced in Solomon's Temple and its furnishings. There were the seven lamps in the Temple and seven golden candlesticks. Besides its Divine association, it was said to have a human influence. Thus the seventh son was said to be able to heal ailments and foresee the future. In Yorkshire and some parts of Wales, the seventh son of a seventh son was a born physician, having an intuitive knowledge of the art of healing all disorders.

Eight was regarded as a number of justice and fullness as well as being a number of attraction. *Nine* was a number of power, wisdom, mystery and protection. It was the product of three and was frequently employed in charms and incantations. It was used by the priest-physicians in healing, and from the Assyrian tablets we learn that a threefold cord in which twice seven knots had been tied was a cure for headache when placed round the head. In folk-medicine, for a burn or scald, nine bramble leaves were put into a bowl of water and applied to the part, and for a sprain nine knots were tied in a piece of black wool and placed round the limb. *Ten* was a Holy and Divine number, but *Eleven* had an evil reputation and signified violence and destruction. *Twelve* was especially regarded as a Divine and Holy number, "wherein heavenly things were measured". It is significant that there are twelve signs of the Zodiac, twelve months in the year, and in Jewish history, there were the twelve tribes of Israel, twelve prophets, and twelve stones in Aaron's breast-plate. Later, there were the twelve Apostles.

But of all other numerals, *Thirteen* had the worst reputation and signified death and misfortune. The origin of this widespread superstition is uncertain. The Romans considered it most unlucky and an evil omen for thirteen people to sit down in a room together.

By some the bad repute of the number is attributed to the account given in the New Testament of the Lord's Supper, when thirteen were present including Judas, and Christ said, "He that dippeth his hand with me in the dish, the same shall betray me."

Evidence of the persistent belief in the ancient superstition that certain colours and numbers have the power of bringing good luck to those who wear them, is shown by the fact that up to a few years ago, thousands of small perforated discs of various colours and bearing different numbers which were supposed to bring good fortune to their purchasers, were sold in shops in London.

The mystical symbolism attributed to numbers continued from

the time of Pythagoras throughout the ages. Nothing more simple or conceivable by the human intellect had been taught by the philosophers. Its nomenclature has left visible traces in the literature of Christian theology.

At first, the number "one", the unit or monad, was regarded as the symbol of divinity and a good and pure intellect by Pythagoras and his followers, while "two" was the principle of evil, disunion and strife, and "three" was the number of perfection representing the composition of the primitive Trinity, the human microcosm or body, soul and spirit. The symbolism of numbers thus permeated philosophy, religion and healing.

Number "seven" was regarded as being still more mystical and formed a bond of union between the two threes. It included both body and soul and regulated the generation of mankind—the conception, development, birth, nutriment and, indeed, the whole existence of every individual. Thus the seventh day was critical in all acute diseases; it was then that a reliable judgement could be framed by the physician. The four cardinal points of the horizon, with the zenith, nadir, and the position of the individual observer, formed a number seven. There were seven planets, whose concentric crystalline spheres rotated around our globe as their centre: in order from without towards the earth these were—Saturn, Jupiter, Mars, Sun, Venus, Mercury, Moon. Their revolutions were respectively guided, each, by one of the seven angels which stood in the Divine presence—Zaphiel, Zadkiel, Camael, Raphael, Haniel, Michael, and Gabriel. Each planet presided over a day of the week, respectively, in the same order—Saturday, Thursday, Tuesday, Sunday, Friday, Wednesday, and Monday. Each had confided to its special charge one of the integral members of the human frame, according to the disposition adopted: right foot, head, right hand, heart, organs of generation, left hand, left foot; also one of the seven openings of the head: right ear, left ear, right nostril, right eye, left nostril, mouth, left eye. To each was also sacred one of the birds of the air: lapwing, eagle, vulture, swan, dove, stork, and owl; one of the beasts of the field: mole, hart, wolf, lion, goat, ape, cat; and one of the fishes of the sea: cuttle-fish, dolphin, pike, sea-calf, thymallus, mullet, and sea-cat. The mineral kingdom was also recognized in its more specially estimable representatives. The seven metals were under special planetary protection, in the same order: lead, tin, iron, gold, copper, quicksilver, and silver; so were the seven gems: onyx, sapphire, diamond, carbuncle, emerald, agate, and crystal.

The incalculable influence of the number seven was demonstrated by its governing the movements of the moon, nearest of the planets, and its evolutionary phases—new to first quarter, first quarter to full, full to second quarter, second quarter to evanescence, and return in form of next renewal. By the same ineffable power it regulated the ebb and flow of the ocean tides; and, more mysterious still, its regulating power extended to, and superintended the periodic phenomena of that most incomprehensible of terrestrial entities—the human female. The strange coincidence of periodicity of ocean, moon, and woman was emphasized—in the judgement of those who believed in the mystical influence of numbers—by the fact that the sum of the added digits, up to seven, happens to be twenty-eight ($1 + 2 + 3 + 4 + 5 + 6 + 7 = 28$). In presence of so many associations and influences, it is not a matter of surprise that the seventh day should be regarded as a natural period of rest and recrudescence—even before the general revelation of the Divine will on the subject. The influence of this number (and its associations) with the chosen people is amply testified by the vast number of its repetitions in the Old Testament and the special functions with which it is connected.

Chapter XXVI

TOOTHACHE AND ITS CURE IN ANTIQUITY

THE earliest records inscribed on clay tablets, probably dating from 2,500 years before the Christian era, show that even at that remote period humanity suffered from dental caries and its attendant pain, which we now term toothache.   In further proof of this, prehistoric skulls excavated in different parts of the world clearly show cavities formed by abcesses at the roots of the teeth.

Man's first instinct was apparently to obtain relief from the pain by charms and incantations, or by the application of some substance that he found soothed it.   He probably soon discovered that the application of cold or hot water gave temporary relief and made attempts at extraction.

The Babylonians in ancient times believed that caries was caused by the gnawing of small worms that attacked the teeth and to get rid of these marauders, they recited the following incantation over the sufferer:

> The marshes created the Worm.
> Came the Worm and wept before Shamask
> Before Ea came her tears—
> What wilt thou give me for my food
> What wilt thou give me to devour?
> I will give thee dried bone
> And scented (wood)
> Let me drink among the teeth
> And set me on the gums,
> That I may devour the blood of the teeth
> And of their gums destroy their strength;
> Then I shall hold the bolt of the door.

After chanting this three times, the sufferer was directed to rub the gums with a mixture of beer, a certain herb and a pungent oil, the names of which cannot be identified.

It was probably the belief that dental caries was caused by worms which devoured the teeth that led to the use of crushed henbane seeds to relieve the pain, a custom which was widespread and is still employed in some parts of the country.

In ancient Egypt we know from the *Papyrus Ebers*, which is believed to date from about 1550 B.C., that toothache was rife in that country, for references to dental troubles are numerous and include inflammation of the gums.   One of the remedies recommended was to fill the cavity of the decayed tooth with a mixture of powdered incense and crushed henbane seeds, while for inflamed gums a plaster of goose-grease and honey was advised.

In early Greece more attention appears to have been paid to the teeth and in the Hippocratic period about 400 B.C., we have records of extraction and applications for diseases of the gums. For toothache, a mouth-wash of castoreum and pepper was recommended. In the time of Galen, centuries later, it was recognized that the pulp was the sensitive element of the tooth.

Artificial teeth were known to the Etruscans who introduced gold dentures which have been found in tombs in the Greco-Roman Necropolis at Teano, near Caserta.

That toothache was a common ailment at the time of the Roman Empire is evident from the many recipes for masticatories and narcotics recommended to induce sleep, for use by sufferers. Cornelius Celsus, who wrote an interesting work dealing with medicine and who is supposed to have been born in Rome, or Verona, about 30 B.C., flourished in the first century of our era. "Concerning toothache," he sympathetically observes, "it may be numbered amongst the worst of our tortures."

To obtain relief (he says), the patient should abstain entirely from wine and at first even food; afterwards he may partake of soft food but very sparingly, so as not to irritate the teeth by mastication. Meanwhile, he must by means of a sponge let the steam of hot water reach the affected part and apply externally, on the painful side, a cerate of cypress or of iris, on which must be placed some wool and keep the head well covered up.

For violent pain, Celsus recommends the application of hot poultices to the cheek, or holding in the mouth some hot liquid prepared with a suit-able herb, changing it very often. For this purpose, henbane leaves or mandrake root are advised, or a poppy head boiled in water, which in like cases is employed today.

Celsus also wisely remarks that there should be no haste in having the tooth extracted, but the pain should be relieved if possible, by applications. "Should the swelling be due to abcess, when ripe," he says, "it should be lanced and the pus evacuated, while rinsing the mouth with hot-water." It will be seen that no better advice could be given by a dentist today.

Magic naturally played a part at this period, even in the relief of toothache and many and varied are the charms recommended as infallible cures. Among those most favoured in early Christian times were texts and references in the scriptures, especially in the New Testament, where allusions to the teeth are made, such as that in St. Luke, xiii, 28. "There shall be weeping and gnashing of teeth."

Both St. Peter and St. Paul are mentioned in some of these charms, as instanced in the following:

St. Peter sat at the gates of Jerusalem. Our blessed Lord and Saviour passed by and said, "What aileth thee?" he said. "Lord my teeth ecketh." He

said, "Arise and follow mee and thy teeth shall never eake any more." Fiat †
Fiat † Fiat.

A variation of this charm, used in Lancashire, ran:

I adjure thee toothake, blood, worms and rume, by the virtue of our
Lord Jesus Christ and by the merits of Joseph his foster father and as he was
betrothed to that blessed Virgin Mary, not a husband and a witness of an
undefiled virginite soe by soe much the more suddenly depart thou toothake
from this person now and annoy them noe more nor trouble them, nor vex
them, nor appear in their body by the virtue of the Father, Son and Holy
Ghost, by the virtue of all the Holy Names of God, obey my bidding and avoid
thou toothake from this person, now without anymore delay.
Then say the Lord's Prayer three times and the Creed once.

The following charm written on paper, then rolled up into a ball and
worn round the neck, was used in Cromarty until recent times:

Peter and Paul sat on a marble stone
Jesus came to them alone.
"Peter," said he, "What makes you so quake?"
"Why Lord and Master, it is the toothache."

Whoever shall carry these words for my sake
Shall never be troubled with toothache.

Many other variants of this legend have been found in England and
Scotland, as instanced in this version:

As Peter sat on a stone weeping, our Saviour came to the Mount of Olives
and said, "How is it here, Peter?" Peter answered and said, "My Lord and my
God, grievously torments with the pain of the tooth." Our Saviour said unto
Peter, "Arise Peter and be made whole. Whosoever believeth on me and
keepeth these words in memory or in writing, shall never be troubled with the
pain of the tooth." In the name of the Father, Son and Holy Ghost.

Kerry in his account of the Hundred of Bray, gives another example
of this evidently very general charm which was in use in Bray, Berkshire,
as late as 1860 but the name Berto or Bertnon, a powerful spirit often
conjured in magic, is substituted for Peter.
The *Celestial Telegraph* for 1799 gives publicity to this charm for the
common trouble: "Take a ladybird and having crushed and rubbed it till
warm between the forefinger and thumb, rub it on the affected part of the
gum and the aching tooth. Upon an inflamed gum it is of no avail."
To transfer the pain, it was customary in some places "to go to a young
oak tree and cut a slip in the bark, then cut off a bit of your hair and put
it under the bark, place your hand on the tree and say to it, 'This I
bequeath to the oak-tree in the name of the Father, Son and Holy Ghost'."

In certain districts the parings of nails wrapped in paper were used in place of the hair and an ash tree was visited instead of the oak, the main idea being that, having grafted part of yourself into the tree, the toothache would disappear and you would have no more trouble. A variant of the same idea is evidenced in the practice of cutting the gum with an iron nail until it bled, smearing some of the blood on the nail and driving it up to the head into a wooden beam. So long as the nail remained in that position the toothache would never trouble the patient again.

In some country parishes, especially in East Anglia, portions of human skin are sometimes found nailed to the church door, a custom supposed to have arisen when Danish invaders made raids on our shores. Sufferers from toothache, and also from rheumatism, placed great faith in going to the church and touching the gruesome relics, as a cure for the pain.

In certain villages in Gloucestershire, the custom obtained of washing out the mouth of a newly baptized infant with the remaining sanctified water, as a safeguard against toothache.

There was formerly a significant association between skulls, grave-yards and toothache. Sir Thomas More, the famous English Chancellor, writing in the year 1557, says "for the toothache go thrice about a church-yard and never think on a fox's tail", and Tindal in his *Answer to More* observes "Thousands, while the priest pattereth St. John's gospel in Latin over their heads cross themselves I trow with a legion of crosses".

In the village of Drumcondra which lies to the north of Dublin, a well on the borders of the old churchyard is resorted to by the inhabitants, when suffering from an attack of toothache. On their way thither across the graves, the sufferers looked for an old skull to use as a cup to drink water from the well. Others merely visited the place for the purpose of pulling a tooth from a skull, which they placed on, or over, the decayed tooth in their own heads, affirming that by keeping it there, relief from any pain was ensured. The use of drinking-cups made from skulls in cases of sickness, dates back at least four hundred years, as it is recorded in 1465 that "a certain Leo von Roymital came to Neuss and saw a costly tomb, wherein lay the blessed Saint Quirinus and he drank out of his skull cup", while on the first of May the same year, the *Acta Sanctorus* tells us that the monks of Trier had "enchased in silver, the skull of St. Theowulf, out of which they administered fever drink to the sick". Toothache, in common with many other ailments, had its special patrons among the saints, whose assistance it was customary to invoke in time of necessity.

Apollonia, a Christian maiden who was martyred at the time of the Emperor Philip, was adopted after her canonization as the patron saint of dentistry. While imprisoned, she is said to have suffered terrible tortures and other cruel indignities, including the extraction of her teeth. She is often represented in miniatures of the sixteenth century holding a tooth in a huge pair of forceps and in one of them she is depicted in the act of extracting a tooth from a cripple. In a church at Bonn on the Rhine, a tooth of the Saint is still preserved, which is said to act as an infallible

cure for those seeking relief from the pain.   Besides St. Apollonia, St.
Helena was also associated with the teeth and she is sometimes depicted
on charms carried as a protection against dental trouble.

In England in the thirteenth century, St. Apollonia had a rival in
Bishop William Bytton or Button, the second of that name, who in 1274
preserved the See of Exeter.

St. Blaise, another martyr, who is more especially associated with
throat troubles, was also believed to have a healing influence in toothache,
and candles offered on his altar were supposed to obtain an effectual cure.
He is thus alluded to, in a rhyme of the sixteenth century:

> Then followeth good Sir Blaise, who doth
> A waxen candle give,
> And Holy Water to his men
> Whereby they safely live.

Among the plants and herbs used to relieve toothache were the fruit
of the yellow snake-wort, the root of the herb of the Sun God and the roots
of a thorn "which does not see the face of the Sun when growing".   In the
West of England, to bite the first fern seen in spring, and in Scotland the
root of the yellow iris chewed were said to relieve the pain; while in other
parts of the country there was an ancient belief that the foreleg and one of
the hind legs of a mole, worn suspended round the neck, would avert any
attack.

A curious charm to stop hæmorrhage in the mouth or other parts
found in manuscripts of the eleventh and twelfth centuries, consisted of
the following words, which were to be written on the part affected, or
inscribed on parchment and worn as a charm: "Stomen calcos stomen
meta forfu."   This is a corrupted passage from the Greek liturgy of
St. Chrysostom and means "Let us stand seemly; let us stand in awe".
These words occurring in the most solemn part of the service, came to
be credited with magical power by many people.

Chapter XXVII

THE PSYCHOLOGICAL EFFECT OF MAGIC IN HEALING

IN the healing in which magic was brought in as an aid, its psychological effect on the mind was, no doubt, an important factor. To ordinary people, the workings of magical power meant interference with the regular operations of Nature and were a complete mystery to them. They observed that the magician had first to appeal to some Deity and offer propitiation, by means of prayers or offerings, so as to render the appeal acceptable, before he could call to his aid the supernatural powers, for good or evil. As it was generally believed that disease was caused by the entrance of demons, or evil-spirits, into man's body, it was but natural that the unseen power of magic should enter into the treatment of the sick, as before a cure could be effected the intruders must be expelled.

"He who treats the sick must be expert in magic, learned in the proper incantations and know how to make amulets to control disease," wrote an ancient Egyptian writer. We find, therefore, that the magicians employed physical, together with psychical therapeutics, as well as invocations which, with the solemn and impressive ritual associated with magic, doubtless had their effect in cases of psycho-neurosis. Even the drugs they employed were believed to possess magical powers, as is shown in the following quotation from the *Papyrus Ebers*: "The magic of Horus is victorious in the remedy." An interesting instance of the supposed magical power of the remedy is given in the story of Tobit, recorded in the book of that name in the Apocrypha.

Tobit, a Jew of the tribe of Napthali who was held captive by the Assyrians, became stricken with blindness and "a whiteness over his eyes". He went to the physicians but they could not help him. As it became necessary for him to go into Media, he decided to send his son Tobias and sought someone to guide him. He found a guide in the person of Raphael, who proved to be one of the seven holy angels, and together with a young man called Azarias, they set out on the journey. They camped on the banks of the Tigris and when the young men went down to bathe, a fish leaped out and would have devoured Azarius, but Raphael told him to take the fish and he seized it and brought it to land. He was then instructed to open the fish and take out its heart, liver and gall and put them away safely.

Afterwards, Azarias became curious and asked Raphael what was the purpose of preserving the heart, liver and gall to which the angel replied: "Touching the heart and the liver; if a devil or an evil-spirit trouble any, we must make a smoke before the man, or the woman, and the party shall be no more vexed; as to the gall, it is good to anoint a man that hath whiteness in his eyes and he shall be healed."

Later, when Tobias had returned, his father one day stumbled in his blindness but his son caught him and laid some of the fish-gall on his eyes, which began to smart. "He rubbed them and the whiteness cleared away from the corners of his eyes and he saw his son and fell on his neck."

Before his marriage to Sara, whom he was instructed to take to wife, Tobias remembered the words of the angel as to fumigating the marriage chamber and "he took the heart and liver of the fish which he had preserved and made a smoke therewith. The which smell," continues the narrative, "when the evil-spirit had smelled it, he fled into the utmost parts of Egypt and the angel bound him."

This story is interesting, first on account of the use of gall for the eyes, of which the reputation for ophthalmic troubles goes back over 3,000 years and secondly, in the use of the noxious fumigation, which was a method of driving away demons favoured by magicians throughout the early ages.

Gall, derived from various sources, has been employed for its medicinal properties from a period of great antiquity. As an application to the eyes to make vision clearer, it had a universal reputation and was used by the Egyptians long before the Christian era.

It is mentioned in the *Oxyrhynchus papari*, believed to have been written about the end of the second century of our era. "For deafness," it is recommended "to moisten thoroughly a flock of wool with the gall of an ox, then roll it up and insert in the ear." This, no doubt, acted by dissolving any wax that might have accumulated in the auditory passage.

Celsus (ca. A.D. 30) mentions it as being employed by the Romans as a detergent and when mixed with honey to clear the skin from blemishes. In the Anglo-Saxon book known as *Medicina de Quadrupedibus*, believed to have been written in the eleventh century, it is stated that "a hare's gall, mingled with honey, will brighten the eyes, and the gall of a wild duck will improve dimness of sight, while the gall of the wood-goat is good for the same purpose". The gall of the bull is recommended for "obscurity of vision" and from this source, gall is still included in the British Pharmacopoeia. In the seventeenth century, ox-gall was to be found as a medicinal agent in most of the pharmacopoeias of Europe such as the French, Dutch and German and was given internally as a bitter stomachic and digestive, or when dissolved in water, as an application for the eyes against "specks of the cornea and pterygium". It was also recommended to cleanse the auditory passage and was applied to the face as a cosmetic. Mixed with oil of almonds, it was dropped in the ear to dissolve wax and an ophthalmic ointment for the sight was made by mixing a little gall with walnut oil.

In the *Materia Medica* of Lewis, published in 1768, it is noteworthy that the gall of the eel and pike is mentioned for the first time, together with that from the bull, which is now generally used. Boerhaave, the famous Dutch physician, in 1738, relates that "he cured pale and rickety children by pills made of the galls of the eel and pike".

Pig's gall was strongly recommended by Dioscorides (ca. A.D. 90), for affections of the eyes and was widely used during the Middle Ages for "spots or clouds", or what was commonly called "pin and web", which were really corneal opacities which obscured the vision. The galls of sheep, goats and the ox were further employed as general applications for the ears, whether for deafness or discharge.

A curious use for pig's gall occurs in an early English manuscript on medicine in the British Museum, where it is included in a recipe for making a potion to induce sleep, to be given to a person before undergoing an operation. It reads:

Take iii sponful of the galle of a Carow swine and iii sponful of the wylde neep, (spear-wort) iii sponful of letuce and iii sponful of poppe and iii sponful of hennebane and iii sponful of eysel (vinegar) and medle all them to geder and borle them a lytal and do it in a glasur vessel wel ystopped and to them put iii sponful of good wine and medele it well to gedder and lete hym that schal be ycorven (cut) aytte agens a good fyre, make hym drynke thereof til he falle aslepe and thou mayst savely carve hym and when thou hast done the cure and wilt awake hym take vynrgre and salt and washe well his temples and hys thon wengs and he schal awake anon.

When mixed with camphorated spirit, it was recommended as a useful application for sprains, bruises and rheumatic pains.

From all this it may be gathered that gall, as recommended by the angel Raphael to cure Tobit, came to be regarded as a valuable medicinal agent.

The idea that a foul smell would drive away evil-spirits probably arose from the fact that any smell offensive to human-beings would also be obnoxious to the spirits of evil, as evidenced among barbaric races at the present day. On the other hand, we have the general belief that sweet-smelling odours would attract and propitiate the good spirits, or even the Deity, confirmation of which we find in the use of incense in churches today.

Some of the early manuscripts dealing with magic record formulae for making evil fumigations, of which the following are examples: "To drive off evil demons, take sulphur, black myrrh, red sandal wood, putrid apples, vinegar, galls and arsenic. Mix with dregs of wine." Another was composed of "asafoetida, sulphur, salt, olive and laurel leaves, galbanum, St. John's wort and rue. Mixed together they are capable of creating a fume which would drive out the devils however powerful they be."

Grotius observes that the Hebrews attributed all diseases arising from natural causes to the influence of demons and therefore exorcism was the most powerful method employed to cure them.

Probably the most general means used to expel the demons of

disease from the body were exorcisms and magic, in one form or
another, in order to subject the intruders to command and obedience.
This practice naturally lent itself to the impostures and impositions which
were carried on by practitioners of magic. In the Acts of the Apostles,
xix, 13, we read of certain "vagabond Jews, exorcists, who travelled the
country and like the Apostles, took upon them that had evil spirits, to
call over them the name of the Lord Jesus". It would appear from the
context that many of these men were "magicians", or "sorcerers", as we
are told "they used curious arts and brought their books together and
burned them". These were probably the books on magic, which on
account of their value "were counted at fifty thousand pieces of silver".
But the failures of such impostors proved their false pretensions and only
served to establish the claims of the Apostles to the power bestowed on
them by their Divine Master.

Josephus, in referring to the exorcisms of demons, states:

God enabled Solomon to learn the skill which expels demons. He composed such incantations also by which distempers are alleviated and he left
behind him the manner of using exorcisms, by which they drive away demons
so that they never return. And this method of cure is of great force unto this
day. (*Ant.* viii, 2.)

About the close of the third century, a particular ecclesiastical order
of exorcists was established in the Christian Church, which has been
attributed to the ideas prevalent at that time among the Gnostics.
According to the tenth Canon of the Council of Antioch, held in the year
341, exorcists are expressly mentioned in conjunction with sub-deacons
and readers, and their ordination is described by the fourth Council of
Carthage. In it, it is mentioned that "the bishop delivered a book
containing forms of exorcism and the direction that they should exercise
the office upon energumens, whether baptised or only catechumens".
The last named were exorcised for twenty days previous to the administration of the Sacrament.

These exorcisms were prayers collected out of the scriptures to break
the power of the devil and expel the spirit of wickedness and were not
directed against any supposed demoniacal possession.

In the Greek Church it was customary at one time for the priest to
blow three times upon the child before baptism, to free it from any evil-
spirit that might threaten it, just as in the Anglican Church, the priest
makes the sign of the Cross with Holy Water on the face of the infant
during the baptismal service, which is symbolic of the power of the
Church of Christ over Evil.

The exorcists formed one of the minor orders of the Romish Church and
at their ordination, the bishop addressing them concluded with the words:
"Take now the power of laying hands upon the energumens and by the
imposition of your hands, by the grace of the Holy Spirit and the words
of exorcism, the unclean spirits are driven from obsessed bodies."

In one of the most complete manuals for use by exorcists of the Roman Catholic Church, published in 1608, there are detailed instructions for exorcizing as well as formulae for making noxious-smelling substances for fumigations to be employed, when found necessary. In one section there is a form of service for "ridding a house haunted by evil-spirits" in which the service varies during every day of the week. In relation to this, the account of a service held a few years ago by the rector of an East Anglian village is not without interest in showing that belief in evil-spirits still exists in some country districts. It appears that from the sixteenth century, a curse was supposed to have been put on an old Hall in the village, now a farmhouse surrounded by a few cottages. The rector was asked to rid the place of the evil spell. He consented and held a public service in the ruined churchyard, using an old altar tombstone as a lectern. The villagers and others from places round about, flocked to the service. After it concluded, it was generally believed that the wicked curse had been removed and the evil-spirits that had haunted the place had fled.

In another manual, *Fustus Daemonum*, the exorcist is instructed, should the evil-spirits remain obdurate, to use "vituperative addresses" and if they still refuse to tell their names, as usual in the magical ceremonies, "fumigations must be employed". Holy Oil is to be used on the body of the person and a draught of Holy Water swallowed on an empty stomach. Recipes for making emetics and perfumes are given, and a list of some of "the devils that commonly come, to vex man's body".

Material aid in the form of drugs was sometimes administered by the exorcists and no doubt stimulated the psychological effect on the sufferer. Thus, in the *Medicinale Anglicum*, which dates from the tenth century, we find a recipe for "A drink to be given to a man possessed of devils". The text reads:

For a fiend-sick man or demoniac; when a devil possesses a man or controls him from within with a disease, a spew-drink of lupin, bishopwort, henbane, and crop-leek, pounded together, adding ale for a liquid. Let it stand for a night; add 50 lib corns or cathartic grains and Holy Water.

Another curious recipe, in which the influence of the Church is exhibited, is headed: "For a fiend-sick man."

It consisted of cynoglossum, yarrow, lupin, betony, attorlothe, flower-de-luce, fennel, church lichen, and lichen of Christ's mark or cross, together with lovage. "Work up the drink with clear ale. Sing seven masses over the worts (herbs), add garlic and Holy Water. Then let him sing the Psalm *Beati immaculati* and *Exurgat and Salvum me fac deus* and then let him drink the drink out of a *church bell* and let the mass-priest after the drink sing over him, *Domine, sancte pater, omnipotens*."

The last occasion on which the Form of Expelling Evil-spirits was included in the prayers ordained after the Reformation, was in the first

Liturgy of Edward VI (Ann 2) and occurs in the Form of Baptism. It reads, "Then let the priest looking upon the children say, I command thee unclean spirits, in the name of the Holy Ghost, that thou come out and depart from these infants, whom our Lord Jesus Christ has vouchsafed to call to his Holy Baptism. Therefor thou cursed spirit, remember thy sentence, remember thy judgement, remember the day to be at hand wherein thou shalt burn in fire everlasting, prepared for thee and thy angels."

Bucer, in censuring this prayer, declared that exorcism was not originally used on any but demoniacs and it was uncharitable to imagine that all were demoniacs who were brought to baptism; and so later, in the reign of Edward VI, it was omitted altogether from the Prayer Book.

Owing to the advance of science and research during the past century, we now know that the dreaded disease demons of former times were but the germs and micro-organisms we fight today, in constant combat waged against the scourges that still afflict humanity.